# Parents
## Cry Too

# Parents
## Cry Too

Lillian Sparks

**FIRST EDITION**
**1990**

Library of Congress Catalog Number: 90-61177
ISBN: 0-89221-182-2
2nd printing February 1992
3rd printing August 1999

Unless otherwise indicated, all Scripture references are taken from the New American Standard Bible, copyright 1960, 1962, 1963, 1968, 1971, 1972, 1973, 1975, 1977 by The Lockman Foundation. Used by permission.

Quotes marked TLB are taken from The Living Bible, copyright 1971 by Tyndale House Publishers, Inc., Wheaton, Illinois. All rights reserved.

Quotes indicated Scofield are from the New Scofield Reference Bible, copyright 1967 by Oxford University Press, Inc.

Quotes marked OB are taken from the Open Bible, Expanded Edition, copyright 1985 by Thomas Nelson, Inc., used by permission of the publisher.

Names and identities of some of the persons and places in this book have been changed to protect their privacy or to prevent embarrassment to them or their families.

Back cover photo: Olan Mills

Cover art: James Gerhold

Lovingly dedicated to my parents, who taught me, by their sterling example, the meaning of "gold tried by fire."

## THANKS TO:

My honey — for loving me and always being there when I needed him the most.

My children — for sharing their mother with the ministry and the call of God.

Dr. Alvear — for his continued support and friendship and the "giving" of himself for sick children.

My mom — for the hours of correcting and revising this manuscript.

Our friends and family — who by their prayers and financial support have made the "Tough Cookie Ministry" possible.

Lillian Sparks

# CONTENTS

# INTRODUCTION

(EXCERPT FROM THE BOOK, *TOUGH COOKIE*)

This moving story will intimately acquaint you with our son, Bryon, who has been called "tough cookie." You have to watch out for this blue-eyed seven-year-old youngster, for he has been known to eat his way into people's hearts. Bubbly and cheerful Bryon Todd Sparks has known what it is to live in a world of constant pain and torture since the day he was born.

Medically, it's known as "Epidermylosis Bullosa Dystraphica Recessive," but we simply called it "Bryon's disease." His complete outer skin and every internal organ and mucous membrane — with the exception of his colon — are infected with the rare (1 in 600,000) and incurable disease which is characterized by unexplained extreme vulnerability to minor trauma.

Bryon's skin blisters and peels at the slightest touch, so it means twice a day — every day — he must be covered with a special Silvadene Cream and wrapped with yards of Vaseline gauze and bandages to protect the open and bloody sores that cover his thirty-one-pound body.

At birth, doctors said he would never survive past six months. Other experts reported that if by some miracle he did, he would be little more than a vegetable. They offered very little hope, saying he probably would never be right mentally because of the large amounts of drugs which he had to take.

But despite our tears, we defiantly refused to accept the grim advice of the experts. Somehow we knew that God would intervene in this course of events and change Bryon's life. Eventually He would change all of our lives.

Today, Bryon is a happy, bright and determined little boy — he is no vegetable! His cheerful disposition is a tremendous contrast to the severity of his condition. Everyone who meets this little fellow immediately falls in love with his face of sunshine. He has learned to cope with the constant bandages and blisters, the stares and questions of strangers, and even the teasing of his neighborhood playmates.

His pediatric surgeon, Dr. Domingo Alvear, was the first to nickname Bryon a "tough cookie" after he survived a tragic accident during which he lost all the skin from his right hand and arm. Knowing that he might lose the use of his arm and fingers still did not dampen Bryon's boisterous spirit, as he rode through the hospital corridors in a little red wagon, singing "Jesus loves me, this I know" with all the gusto a two-year-old can muster.

Bryon was deprived of so many of the normal experiences of a child. He was never hugged or bounced on someone's knee. He was never allowed to crawl or climb on the stairs. He couldn't because his skin would peel off. Even though the disease has fused his fingers (and toes) together with scar tissue, he can do all normal schoolwork by holding a pencil or crayon between his two wrists. He also feeds himself using the same method.

Bryon is so determined that he has made a way for himself. Even though he cannot dress himself, bathe, take care of his toilet habits, or open a door without assistance, he has found a way to ride a bicycle around the block, shoot basketball, swing outdoors, and play with his puppy. He loves to sing solos in church, and one of his ambitions is to be a preacher like his daddy when he grows up.

Bryon realizes he has a handicap and is different from other children. At times when he is bleeding and fevered from infection, he has asked, "Why did God make me like this? Why is my body so ugly?" or "Why does my little sister have fingers and I don't?"

We have always assured him that what a person is on the inside is more important than the outside and that God has a special place in His heart for him.

Each night when Bryon prays to God, it becomes more difficult for us to fight back the tears. In his sweet earnest voice he pleads, "Dear Jesus, I love You. I know someday You will give me all new skin and new fingers. I know You can take away this terrible pain. But please, God, hurry up!"

Through Bryon, our small bundle of joyous energy — a gift from God — we have discovered that in the midst of sorrow God alone can draw the sting out of every trouble and take the bitterness from every affliction. You will soon realize that it is impossible to read about this "tough cookie" without wiping tears from your eyes and experiencing a change in your life.

*"For whatever is born of God overcomes the world; and this is the victory that has overcome the world — our faith" (1 John 5:4).*

Stephen and Lillian Sparks

---

# 1

# THE IMPOSSIBLE DREAM

The blinding glare from the studio lights and television cameras caused me to blink for just a second. The tearful voice of PTL's Television Network President, Jim Bakker, brought me quickly back to reality. He was asking Bryon, our seven-year-old son, if he would sing for the program audience. Bryon quickly nodded his head with his "John-boy" hairstyle and with a twinkle in his blue eyes, responded, "Sure, Mr. Bakker. I would love to sing."

Before I realized it, I was seated at the most beautiful grand, Steinway piano I had ever seen. My fingers trembled as I placed them on the ivory keys. Just moments before, Dino Karsinakas had enthralled his listeners with a magnificent performance of "How Great Thou Art." Mechanically, I began to plunk out the introduction to the "Bullfrogs and Butterflies" Production of *My Hands Belong to You, Lord.* All my anxiety melted away as Bryon's angelic voice filled the building. A sweet presence embraced all those who listened.

Who was this "tough cookie," handsomely dressed in a light-blue pin-striped suit, white shirt, and matching tie? His parents spoke of his nightmarish birth when his skin peeled away from his body and left him covered with blisters and open sores. They cried and then laughed with joy in recalling many incidents when God miraculously intervened. The doctors predicted that he would never walk...yet he stood before the microphone like a soldier. Other experts warned that he would be mentally damaged...but his clear tenor tones rang out with no hesitation. His bright blue eyes and bubbly personality showed definite wit and intelligence. It seemed that the past trauma and suffering were hidden from the viewer's eye.

"My heart belongs to You, Lord. My heart belongs to You," the young lad sang with gusto. As the music slowed its pace, Bryon continued, "My hands belong to You, Lord. My hands belong to You." The audience audibly drew in a breath. "I lift them up to You, Lord, and sing allelujah." His scarred, fingerless clubs were lifted in surrender to the Lord. The left hand was covered with a heavy white bandage; the other was contracted into a rough mitten of skin with a small protruding bulge, where his thumb used to be. Unashamed and with transparent child-like faith, he raised them in an offering of praise.

The deafening sound of a thunderous applause jolted my senses. In disbelief, I caught a glimpse of the entire studio audience, who were standing, cheering, and wiping tears from their eyes.

Mr. Bakker kept saying, "Bryon, they love you! Do you hear that? These people believe in you, Son! Oh my...oh my!" For ten minutes or more the crowd refused to be seated, but continued to respond to Bryon's song of praise. The miracle of his birth and struggle to survive this dreadful skin disease — Epidermylosis Bullosa Dystraphica — had touched their hearts. From that moment on, Bryon belonged to the PTL family and partners. They loved him.

This special day was March 9, 1982. The producers from the PTL Television Network had arranged to fly Bryon, my husband, Steve, and me to Charlotte, North Carolina, where we made our first national television appearance. Presently, Steve and I were on the teaching faculty of Zion Bible Institute, in East Providence, Rhode Island — a "faith" school that did not charge its students for room, board, or tuition. Our family was not receiving any regular source of income, but trusted God to supply our needs. Staying in the PTL Mansion, and now sitting on the program set chatting with the Bakkers about Bryon's traumatic beginning and consequent struggles were all highlights in our lives. Only God knew that this event was to be the catalyst for a greater miracle in Bryon's life: bringing to reality an impossible dream.

* * *

At the age of six, Bryon crept into our room early one morning and awakened us. Tears were streaming down his cheeks. Thinking that perhaps he was hurt or in pain, we cried out, "Honey, what's the matter? Tell Mommy and Daddy what is wrong! Did you have a bad dream?"

"Oh no!" Bryon exclaimed. "I had a dream...but it was wonderful. I woke up and climbed out of bed and for the first time in my life I didn't hurt anymore. I looked down at my pajamas, which are usually stuck to my body and covered with blood, and they fell on the floor with my dirty bandages. I felt so different...then I looked at my skin...it was brand new...just like a baby's."

Snuggled together on our bed, we hugged each other, laughed and cried all at once.

"But, Mom, wait!" Bryon interrupted. "I haven't told you the best part yet. When I looked at my hands, God gave me ten beautiful new fingers. New hands to praise Him with!"

With growing excitement, Bryon continued. "Do you think God can really do it? Can He make it happen for me? That would be the best gift anyone could ever give me...a new body...and new hands."

Overcome with emotion, Steve answered, "Bryon, if God gave you this dream, don't let anyone take it from you. He is a great God and He can do a miracle in your life. Keep trusting Him! Okay, Buddy?"

No one knew better than Stephen and I just how impossible this dream appeared. More than sixteen years has passed by since this fragile child came into our world. Now, looking back, we can see the providential design in every traumatic occurrence. Knowing that "all things work together for good to them that love God" (Rom. 8:28) helps to give purpose for the hospitalizations, surgeries, devastating accidents, and the overwhelming daily care of a child with an incurable skin disease.

Memories, like stored video tapes, play back mental images from earlier days. I can still hear Dr. McLinn's voice as he entered the recovery room, four hours after Bryon's birth, and said those tragic words... "Your son has been born with a very rare, incurable skin disease, called 'Epidermylosis Bullosa Dystraphica Recessive.' We have no hope for his life. If he lives through the first night it will be a miracle!"

The following day, my honey and I stood peering into a sterile incubator at a piece of raw flesh that was our little son. He had lost about 80% of his skin. Large blisters filled with blood and water hung in clusters over his body. He screamed relentlessly in pain as each movement against the sterile sheets tore new flesh away from his body. We clung to each other in desperation, as the nurses wheeled Bryon down the hall, farther away from us, to transport him to another building for intensive care treatment.

The painful thought pounded in my brain, "Will I ever see my son alive again?"

Gastronomy tubes, intravenous blood transfusions, pneumonia, Silvadene, Vaseline gauze, sterile gloves, bandages, and placenta-transplants...were vital words within my vocabulary. Without the prayers of God's people and the loving support of my husband, there was no way I would have survived this initial nightmare.

There were victories too. He was almost two months old the day we brought him home from the hospital. Our hearts were filled with thanksgiving to God for allowing our firstborn to live thus far. How can we forget the moment he took his first steps and began to walk? At two years of age we had almost given up hope. Doctors had predicted that he would spend his life in a wheelchair. But God saw the future differently. When Steve came home for supper that evening, Bryon ran to the front door to greet him. Steve shouted with joy, "You're walking, Buddy! Praise God!" Our meal was forgotten as we paraded through our small house trailer in a march of victory, Bryon leading the way.

Shortly after Bryon learned to walk he had the most debilitating accident of his life. Strolling along with his dad, he tripped over an uneven piece of cement and started to fall face forward. Quickly, without thinking, Steve grabbed his coat sleeve and firmly held on. My honey felt a sickening sensation in his stomach as he realized that Bryon continued to slip away from him. He had grasped the skin from Bryon's arm. Like a playtex glove, the entire outer layer of skin came off from the elbow down. We rushed him to the Polyclinic Hospital's Emergency Room. After working on his damaged arm for an hour, the doctors felt that new skin formation would be doubtful, and he might never regain full use of the arm. Yet, much to their surprise, within ten days, new skin covered his entire arm and hand. The physicians openly admitted that God was doing a miraculous healing in accelerating the new skin formation.

By the time Bryon was three, he had great difficulty in swallowing. His esophagus had developed a stricture that allowed only a liquid diet and caused hemorrhaging, choking, and vomiting of blood with saliva. He steadily lost weight and energy. It was our close friend and pediatric surgeon, Dr. Domingo Alvear, from Harrisburg, Pennsylvania, who became an instrument of God in saving Bryon's life. He replaced our son's damaged esophagus with eighteen inches of his lower intestine — a colon transplant. After eight hours of intensive surgery and eighteen days of recuperation in the Harrisburg Hospital, Bryon was ready to eat "big people's food" for the first time in his life. Thirteen years later, he is still able to eat normally without major complications.

Because of the several "degloving" accidents, Bryon's fingers began to grow together into fused mittens of skin. It was a fight of frustration to prevent this from happening. The book, *Tough Cookie*, tells about the painful surgeries involving skin transplants, pig skin, tractions, steel pins, and rubber bands. Not to mention the months we spent away from home at St. Christopher's Hospital for Children in Philadelphia, Pennsylvania. Yet, despite this handicap, Bryon learned how to write by holding a pen or pencil between his wrists and feed himself the same way. He also managed to ride a two-wheel bike, shoot basketball, play soccer, do all normal schoolwork, and help around the house by emptying the garbage or setting the table.

To look at Bryon today, no one could possibly imagine the suffering he has survived. His small stature and bandaged hands give a hint that there is something different about this child. If you happen to look into his grey-blue eyes, you will see a depth of painful experiences that reach beyond his sixteen years. When he speaks or sings there is a ring of maturity that comes from life-changing struggles. The quiet joy he radiates to all those he meets reflects his personal faith and commitment to the Lord Jesus.

Well-meaning people have said to us, "God certainly chose the right parents for Bryon when He picked out the Sparkses!" There have been many times when I have asked God if perhaps, just this one time, He might have made a mistake. In ourselves, we felt inadequate, frustrated by a lack of medical training and overwhelmed by the pressure of constant care. I knew that God's Word says, "There hath no temptation taken you but such as is common to man; but God is faithful, who will not permit you to be tempted above that ye are able, but will, with the temptation, also make the way to escape, that ye may be able to bear it" (1 Cor. 10:13; Scofield). Over and over again, I found myself telling the Lord, "I think You have given us too much to bear; please show us the way to escape."

God was patient with me. At times when I felt like giving up, He would speak to me, "Not that we are adequate in ourselves to consider anything as coming from ourselves, but our adequacy is from God" (2 Cor. 3:5). When we are weak, He becomes our strength!

No one could have sufficiently prepared us for being the

parents of a handicapped, chronically-ill child. Both of us had been raised in strong Christian homes. In fact, our fathers were old-fashioned Pentecostal preachers, born in Aroostook County, Maine. Stephen and I attended our parents' alma mater, Zion Bible Institute, in East Providence, Rhode Island for a three-year ministerial diploma. Then we continued our education at Northwest College in Kirkland, Washington and received our Bachelor of Arts degrees. Yet, I do not ever remember taking a course on parenting...and needless to say...nothing even hinted towards the role of parenting handicapped children.

After facing the initial shock of our son's possible premature death, we realized that if he did live, we would encounter the dilemma of coping with severe disabilities and intensive medical treatment. The task was enormous. If we had the choice of selecting our destiny, certainly we would not have chosen ourselves to be the parents of an EB (abbreviation for Epidermylosis Bullosa) child. But God tells us, "You did not choose Me, but I chose you, and appointed you..." (John 15:16). He was absolutely right! We did not choose His ways, but in His great master plan for our lives, He selected us to be the parents of a special gift from heaven. This thought is aptly expressed in the article someone sent to me:

### HEAVEN'S VERY SPECIAL CHILD

*A meeting was held quite far from earth!*
*It's time again for another birth.*
*Said the Angels to the Lord above,*
*This Special Child will need much love.*

*His progress may be very slow,*
*Accomplishment he may not show.*
*And he'll require extra care*
*From the folks he meets down there.*

*He may not run or laugh or play;*
*His thoughts may seem quite far away.*

---

19

*In many ways he won't adapt,*
*And he'll be known as handicapped.*

*So let's be careful where he's sent.*
*We want his life to be content.*
*Please, Lord, find the parents who*
*Will do a special job for You.*

*They will not realize right away*
*The leading role they're asked to play.*
*But with this child sent from above*
*Comes stronger faith and richer love.*

*And soon they'll know the privilege given*
*In caring for their gift from Heaven.*
*Their precious charge, so meek and mild,*
*Is Heaven's Very Special Child.*

— *Edna Massimilla*

Can you imagine what it would be like to wake up one morning and discover that you had Epidermylosis Bullosa? Your first thoughts would be: "I wonder what bandages are stuck...if my pajamas are soaked with blood...and my bed is soiled? I feel so guilty because I know my disease makes lots more work for Mom."

Bryon is never in a hurry to come down for breakfast, since he knows it will be the same diet of semolina with milk, eggs, or toast with natural apple butter. He has many restrictions to help his skin. He watches his sisters, Leann and Jenell, and his younger brother, Brent, gobble up pancakes, French toast, bacon, or Bob Evans' sausage, while he is content to sip a cup of chammomile tea with a little sugar.

Following breakfast is "treatment time," which he must face every morning and evening. The dining room table is transformed into a medical center, covered with rolled gauze, cotton squares, needles, scissors, creams, antibiotics, alcohol, and tape. After his clothes and old bandages are removed, blisters must be popped and drained of fluid, dead skin removed, and all the open sores covered with cream and wrapped. This whole procedure takes about thirty to forty-five minutes, depending on how many new blisters and sores there are. Meanwhile, Mom helps to direct the other children in getting dressed for school. Everyone works together to get teeth and hair brushed, lunches packed, book bags ready, and "Docker," our playful puppy, fed and walked.

The genuine miracle is getting everyone to school on time, without forgetting something at home. More than once, Mom has had to run a sack lunch, pair of gym shoes, or class project to a crying child — still dressed in her bathrobe!

The real pressure of being "different" starts as soon as Bryon walks through his homeroom door. He is grateful that he can attend the Christian School at our church and for the great friends he has, but nothing can erase the fact that he is not like the other kids. He is totally dependent upon others to help him open doors, remember his locker combination and open it, take him to the bathroom, help with zippers and buttons on his clothes, and prepare his special lunch.

At times Bryon has stood in front of a closed door for ten or fifteen minutes waiting for someone to open it, fearing he would be late for the next class. One afternoon his buddy, who helps him open his locker and take out his books for the next class, went to the doctor without telling Bryon. No one else knew his combination and he had to go to class without his textbook. The teacher did not accept this explanation and he received a detention.

Gym class is out of the question — not because Bryon is unable to participate, but for fear of injury. Most of the sports are very physical and he would come home pretty "beatup."

Bryon excels the most where he can use his mind. His favorite subjects are language, Bible, music, English, social studies, and of course, study hall! He was chosen "Student of the Month" and was treated to a lovely lunch by the principal. His picture and biography were displayed on the school bulletin board.

He prefers to eat his lunch alone. It is very difficult to watch his classmates chow down candy bars, ice cream, and pizza, while he sips carrot soup with feta cheese and munches on homemade applesauce and butter cookies. Yet, he seldom complains.

Coming home from school is a favorite time for Bryon. There is security there. He enjoys riding his bike, swinging on the gym set, playing Ping-Pong or table pool, and sometimes sacking-out on the living room couch for a "siesta." Meal times and family altar are special also. Often we sit on the floor as Dad reads from the Bible, and we sing songs and share important things from our hearts. Jenell calls this the time when "we can cry out all our sins." For some it takes longer than others.

Special moments with Dad are the best. Together, going for a bike ride, working in the yard, watching the Celtics in the NBA playoffs, or battling in a two-hour chess game — is what makes life worthwhile.

Bryon's condition has affected the whole family. His sisters and brother have compensated in many ways for Bryon's handicaps. They have learned to give unselfishly of their mother's time for Bryon to be properly attended to. Throughout numerous hospitalizations, months of separation, and overwhelming loneliness, their one response has always been, "If this will make Bryon better...we don't mind!"

Perhaps now you may understand a little better why Bryon's dream to have new skin and ten fingers seemed like a far-fetched miracle. The struggles, hopes, and tears are all part of this heartwarming story. It is Bryon's story...but also his parents'...who dreamed that one day the "Tough Cookie" miracle would touch the hearts of thousands of people and encourage their faith in God. It is a family story too...as each member has learned to give, make personal sacrifices, help carry another's burden, and wipe each other's tears.

As parents, we try to protect our children from hurtful experiences. When pain comes, we attempt to soothe the trouble by saying... "Now, don't cry. Mommy and Daddy will make it all better." But there are times when you look into the face of an impossibility, and your own helplessness pierces your soul...you discover...PARENTS CRY TOO.

*"With men it is impossible, but not with God; for all things are possible with God" (Mark 10:27).*

# 2

# THE TOUGH COOKIE MIRACLE

I wiped the beads of cold perspiration from my forehead, as I pulled another piece of correrasable bond from my electric typewriter. I glanced at my watch...it was 2:30 a.m. I had buried myself in this musty cubbyhole in my parents' basement for a sum total of sixteen hours already. My bloodshot eyes begged to close in sleep and my aching back muscles longed to stretch out on a good firm mattress. But my mind, alive with inspiration, caused my brain to send the proper nerve messages to my fingers — and once again the sound of keys in rapid succession could be heard.

It was the tepid summer of 1979. The days melted into one long continuous day as I endeavored to put together my first book manuscript. My husband, Steve, had helped to move our small family to my parents' home in Clark, New Jersey. Then, he returned to our busy pastorate in Middletown, Pennsylvania. My mother had agreed to watch Bryon, then five years old, and Leann, six months, while I went through the long labor pains of birthing a book.

I breathed a disgruntled sigh as I realized that I had

mistyped another word. Searching for my lost eraser, I began to paw through the piles of notes, medical records, diaries, dictionaries, and concordances I had stacked around my desk.

"Where could it be?" I mused, a little disgusted with myself at misplacing something so simple. But then again I shouldn't be too upset. It was three o'clock in the morning.

"Ah ha, here it is!" I exclaimed right out loud. My eraser had rolled underneath my typewriter.

Two years before, Dr. Domingo Alvear, Bryon's pediatric surgeon, had purposely teased me, "Why don't you write a book?"

I had laughed in disbelief and replied, "Who, me? You're kidding of course, aren't you?"

With a more serious tone, he continued, "No, I really mean it. I think you have a terrific story. Who else could tell about the heartaches and moving experiences Bryon has endured better than his own mother?"

I tried to dismiss the idea from my consciousness. But every few weeks the phone would ring and a soft, gentle voice on the other end would question, "Well, how are you doing on the book?"

Trying to evade Dr. Alvear's kind prodding, I would invent some reasonable excuse about how busy I was being a mother, a pastor's wife, and a leader in our church's denomination. Yet my answers never seemed to discourage him, and he continued to persuade me to become an author.

Perhaps this was the reason I found myself in a damp basement hide-away, glued with fanatical fascination to my portable typewriter. Or was it possible after months of verbal nudging, I finally believed that deep inside I really did have a story? A tender story about a courageous little boy, who would inspire thousands of people to put their trust in a loving God.

This was the beginning of months of writing, rewriting, editing, and tedious correcting. There were moments of intense excitement as I read parts of the manuscript aloud and found myself laughing or crying at my own words. Then there were hours when I sat in front of the typewriter staring at a blank piece of paper and praying that the words would start flowing. But there was nothing. No thoughts. No inspiration.

It didn't seem possible, but after seven months of "blood, sweat, and tears," I placed the treasured manuscript into an empty stationery box, wrapped it in brown postal paper, and addressed it to a leading Christian publisher in the Midwest. Accompanying the parcel were also letters of reference from our doctors and the district superintendent of our denomination — and various photographs of our family and Bryon.

The night before we delivered it to the post office, we brought the package to bed with us, and, by laying our hands on it and saying a prayer, we committed it to God. Now everything depended on whether or not a certain publisher would reject or accept my work.

December 31, 1979 marked the date it was mailed. Nothing to do but wait. January flew by. February passed with no word. Then towards the end of March, I happened to peer outside our front bay window and saw a United Parcel Service truck pull up to the curb. A blond-haired young man jumped out of the driver's seat and bounded up our driveway. A lump in my throat temporarily shut off my oxygen and my heart stopped beating...under his arm he was carrying the package I had sent three months before...it was my manuscript! It had been rejected!

He rang the doorbell and I fumbled down the stairs. I felt the hot tears coming and I furiously batted my eyelashes. Somehow I managed to sign my name on his clipboard, mumbled an insincere "thank you," and then shut the door. I held the package tightly in my arms, leaned against the closed door, and then slid down onto the soft green carpet. I sat at the foot of the stairs motionless for what seemed like an eternity. I didn't even feel like breathing. The waves of disappointment were drowning me. I ripped open the box and found a letter of cold acknowledgement inside. My eyes scanned over the words:

> *"Thank you for submitting your work* A Spark of Faith *for our consideration. We have doubts about the marketability of this work and we feel it is not*

*distinguished enough from other books on illness and suffering...to warrant our publishing it..."*

I couldn't believe what I was reading... "No marketability?" In other words, they didn't think Bryon's book would sell. Perhaps they were right. Maybe no one would buy a book and we would be stuck with thousands of useless copies. This could be God's way of sparing us from financial disaster. My heart was broken. I had put so much time and effort — and so much of myself — into this manuscript. Now it seemed a tragic waste of energy. I was convinced that I would never become an author.

A few days later the phone rang again. It was Dr. Alvear. His cheerful voice inquired, "Well, how is the book coming along? Did you hear from the publisher?"

I cringed inside, but offered reluctantly, "Yes, I did. They...I mean the publishers...well, it was rejected."

With confidence, he replied, "I guess they don't know a good story when they read one. Where do we go from here?"

"Oh, I don't know what to do," I whined. "I feel like throwing in the towel and calling it quits. I don't think I will ever be the author of a book."

"Hey, you can't give up now, just when the going gets a little rough," he asserted, half-jokingly. "Give yourself a little time, read the manuscript over, and get some fresh ideas. Then submit it to another publisher. You must believe in yourself!"

A month passed by and the packaged manuscript sat on my desk untouched. Towards the end of April, Steve offered to watch the children for a day if I wanted to review my story. Without much enthusiasm, I agreed.

I stretched out on the couch in the family room, kicked off my shoes, propped my head with a pillow, and began to read. First with indifference, then with mild interest, and finally totally absorbed in every detail and happening of Bryon's life. Even though I knew all the experiences personally, I went through the varied emotions of a first-time reader. I cried...I laughed...I felt the frustration...I was moved.

I finished the last page, leaped off the couch, and headed

upstairs towards the kitchen to put on a pot of coffee. "It is a good story!" my mind argued. "It just needs a little revision and some fresh beginnings."

As I sipped some of the steaming "Taster's Choice," I organized my new plan of strategy. First of all, I needed a new title for the book. *A Spark of Faith* just didn't portray the spunk and determination of a bubbly little fellow like Bryon. It sounded like an exegesis on the doctrine of faith. I tossed a few concoctions around in my mind, and then a brainstorm hit me like a ton of bricks... "How about Bryon's nickname...the one Dr. Alvear tagged him with during his hospital stays? Yes, it would be perfect...and eye-catching too. 'Tough Cookie.' It was brilliant!" I squeezed myself with delightful satisfaction. *Tough Cookie* would be the new title for Bryon's biography.

In the next three months I made a lot of changes. I divided up the chapters to make them shorter and rewrote the preface to sound like a newspaper reporter doing a special human interest article. I also tried to include more of Bryon's contagious personality — which made him one really "tough cookie."

Just before I resubmitted my revised manuscript to another publisher, the *Harrisburg Patriot News* did a splendid full-page article on Bryon for the life-style section. On June 29, 1980 the headline read: "Middletown Boy Has Rare Courage." Constance Bramson, the staff writer, was tremendously moved after interviewing Bryon at our home. She mentioned to us, "Your son certainly has all the necessary ingredients to be a winner!"

When the article was printed in the Sunday paper, we made an announcement in our morning worship service. Within a few hours every newspaper in the Middletown area had been purchased. Some of the members of our congregation bought ten to fifteen papers and gave them out to their family and neighbors. They were quite excited about their pastor's son becoming an overnight celebrity.

The local response from the story was encouraging. In the following weeks we received numerous kind phone calls, heartwarming letters, and even home visits. Many parents conveyed their own trying experiences with handicapped children. The most enlightening correspondence were the shared stories of other children with EB (Epidermylosis Bullosa).

It was time to take the big plunge again — to submit my book to another publisher. Steve and I had really prayed about the right one to send it to and felt a definite leading towards Logos International in Plainfield, New Jersey. On July 15, 1980 we mailed the manuscript with a prayer for God's direction.

During the dreadful waiting period we received some unexpected, but delightful news. Another little Sparks baby was on the way! Bryon and Leann would have a new brother or sister by January 1981. This additional event in our lives helped to alleviate some of the anxiety about the "tough cookie" story.

* * *

Once again we were settled into the busy routine of family life and pastoring our growing congregation. Yet, I found myself watching for the postman every morning about eleven o'clock. After the mail arrived, I scurried down the stairs, shuffled through the bills, form letters, and correspondence, looking for the return address of Logos International. Finding nothing, I would toss the unopened mail on the dining room table.

On September 15, 1980, I was going through the same routine, when my eyes lighted on the blue lettering of the publishing company in the upper left corner. I dropped all the other letters, screamed, and ran up the stairs. My hands were shaking and my heart pounded dangerously, as I tore open the envelope. The words leaped off the page and confirmed my joyous expectation...*Tough Cookie* was accepted for publication!

I dialed the church's office number. When Steve answered, I began to scream into the receiver, "It's been accepted... they're going to do it...I can't believe it...we made it, Honey!" All in one big breath.

---

Slightly exasperated, Steve interrupted, "Whoa!, calm down, Sweetheart. Tell me what happened."

With a forced calmness, I read him the letter from Logos.

"Only forty manuscripts out of a thousand are accepted!" Steve exclaimed. "What a beautiful miracle. Praise the Lord! This is the open door we needed for Bryon's story."

I didn't wait for the usual phone call from my friend, Dr. Alvear. I immediately called his office and left a message with his answering service. In ten minutes he returned the call.

"Well, what's happening? Good news?" he inquired.

"*Tough Cookie* was accepted for publication, projected for Spring '81. Isn't that great?" I replied with enthusiasm.

"What did I tell you!" he radiated, "I knew you had a story inside you!"

Enclosed with the letter of acceptance was also a special contract for first-time authors, designed especially for *Tough Cookie*. There were so many legalities concerning payments, copyrights, royalties, reprints, and deadlines that we sought the advice of a Christian lawyer in Harrisburg. He carefully explained every detail of the contract and then suggested that we make a visit to Logos' offices so that the editors could meet Bryon.

On September 25, we drove the four hours to Plainfield, New Jersey. We were warmly greeted by Lloyd Hildebrand, one of the editorial assistants. He was a gracious host and treated us with extreme kindness. We received the red carpet...which included a grand tour through the administrative offices, the art layout department, the typesetting room, and the ordering center for all publications.

Lloyd discussed the various aspects of the contract with us. Then we shared how important it was to keep the copyright in my name so that we could make a financial investment for Bryon. We wanted to set up a special trust fund to help with the costs of bandages, medications, and foods. Bryon's unique needs had been staggering over the past seven years. It was our hope that *Tough Cookie* would alleviate some of the tremendous financial pressure our family had been under.

During our conversation, Lloyd shared a beautiful note of encouragement concerning the manuscript. He explained that his wife worked part-time for Logos by reviewing and evaluating unsolicited manuscripts. When *Tough Cookie* arrived it was assigned to her. This happened at a time when the Hildebrand family was going through a period of discouragement and anxiety concerning their son, Timmy, who had been born with a serious heart problem. The possibility of surgery loomed ahead and many unanswered questions. As Timmy's mom read each page of Bryon's story, her faith in God was strengthened and her spirit uplifted. She gave the manuscript a very high rating and recommendation for publication.

We returned home and waited to hear the final results. The publisher phoned and offered us a contract with Personal Book Publishing. I would be able to have the copyright in my name, sell the books on my speaking tours, and eventually make an investment for Bryon. But there was one problem ...and it was a BIG one...we needed over $13,000 for the first printing!

I pondered, "Where in the world would a small-town pastor and his wife come up with $13,000? Especially when we lived from check to check to make ends meet and take care of Bryon's medical needs."

"Dear Jesus," we prayed. "This book belongs to You. We know there are thousands of people who will be inspired to greater faith after reading Bryon's testimony. Nothing is impossible with You. Thirteen thousand dollars is but a small thing to You. We know that You can open the windows of heaven and provide this immediate need."

And the windows of heaven were opened! We shared our situation with our family and friends. Their response was overwhelming. Through relatives, friends in the congregation, and colleagues in the ministry, interest-free finances were lent to us for an indefinite period of time. It was exactly what we needed to make the first deadline. Praise God...we were shouting!

On November 9, 1980 our church, Glad Tidings Assembly, held a special program called the Tough Cookie

Story. It was publicized in the local newspapers and by members of the congregation throughout the community. An overflowing Sunday morning crowd was moved to tears as Bryon stood and sang in crystal clear tones, "God is so good, God is so good, God is so good to me."

After I shared Bryon's experiences, from birth through early childhood..the tears, the tragedies, and the triumphs...a gracious love offering was taken. Over $500 was given towards the publication of *Tough Cookie*. The ladies' organization of the Assemblies of God denomination, known as "Women's Ministries," helped to advertise and promote the book without charge. Other surprises included the hundred dollar checks for just one copy.

One of the most outstanding contributions given towards the publication of the book was donated by the women's group of the Assembly of God in Greencastle, Pennsylvania. These dedicated ladies raised finances by sponsoring a "walk-a-thon" in their city. Many of them walked numerous miles to help our son. One lady, who could not walk very far, found someone to push her in a wheel chair. The sum total of their gift was the amazing amount of $1,400.00!

When Pastor Holt and his lovely wife, Kathy, handed us a card and check for this amount, we were speechless. What a beautiful expression of sacrificial love given by a group of people who had never even met Bryon. Our eyes were moist with emotion as we embraced this sweet couple.

In a few short months the remaining monies were raised by the advance sale of books and the gifts from friends. By January 1981 the balance was paid and *Tough Cookie* was on the way! Looking back, I wondered why I had ever doubted God's ability to hear and answer earnest prayer. Our minds have a difficult job of grasping the magnitude of God's omnipotent resources. Isaiah put it this way:

*"For My thoughts are not your thoughts, neither are your ways My ways, declares the Lord. For as the heavens are higher than the earth, So are My ways higher than your ways, and My thoughts than your thoughts" (Isa. 55:8,9).*

---

The supplying of the $13,000 was a splendid cause for rejoicing. But the Lord was preparing us for a greater storehouse of blessing just around the corner.

# 3

# TEARS GOD UNDERSTANDS

The frilly brown and white curtains blew gently in the early morning breeze. I gazed out the kitchen window at the acres of empty corn fields and the white-washed barns of the Pennsylvania Dutch farms. I placed my elbows on the window-sill and relished the peacefulness of a new sunrise. The cold gray November skies cast shadows on the tidy rows of subur-ban houses. This small rural community, known as "Shope Gardens," really felt like home.

The sizzling smell of melted butter quickly drew me back from my daydreaming, and I returned my attention to the stove. I sprinkled seasoned bread crumbs over the hot butter to make a topping for my family's favorite vegetable dish — "broccoli puff." I set the oven at a moderate 350 degrees and placed the beef roast with mushroom gravy, baked potatoes, and broccoli casserole on the second shelf. Then I whisked a leafy green salad together and stowed it in the refrigerator to keep fresh. Finally I rolled out the prepared pastry to form two crusts for my first autumn apple pie. I sealed the edges with a fork, brushed the top with some whipped egg, and licked the sweet apple-cinnamon filling from my fingers.

Pleased with my busywork, I thought, "This will make a perfect Sunday dinner! Especially since we are having guests come home with us following our morning service."

I gathered all the dirty bowls and cooking utensils and plunged them in the warm sudsy water. I glanced upward at the clock and groaned...it was already eight o'clock. Only an hour remained before we left for church. I wondered anxiously, "How will I get everything done in this short time?"

I breathed in the last few moments of quietness before I flew down the hall to coax the children out of bed. Peeking through the door at my angelic-faced two-year-old, I began to whisper, "Get up..get up...you sleepy head. It's time...it's time to get out of bed!"

Leann rubbed her droopy eyes, shook her blond curls and stretched her arms out to Mommy. I reached over the side of her crib to hoist her to the floor. Just then I felt a sharp pain in my lower back and across my expanded abdomen. I remembered the doctor's advice not to lift anything heavy in my last tri-semester of pregnancy. But I reasoned that the distress was probably just another "braxton hicks," known as false labor pains.

I squeezed Leann's hand and we crept across the hall to Bryon's room. This little bear was a lot harder to wake up. We teased and cajoled, but he only pulled the covers higher over his head. We turned to leave and I yelled over my shoulder, "Okay, no breakfast for Bryon. We'll have to eat his share."

There was only enough time for cold cereal, so the choice was Raisin Bran or Wheaties. I put Leann in the highchair and she started slurping in her bowl. Bryon appeared around the corner, his hair sticking straight up like "Alfalpha," eyes swollen with infection, and pajamas soaked with blood from a restless night.

"Where's my cereal?" he piped.

"Right here, Buddy. Sit down." I tried to sound like an enthusiastic mother.

While the kids were eating, I jumped into the shower for five minutes of deserved relaxation. I held my face under the jet spray in an attempt to revitalize myself for the busy day ahead. Sundays were always filled with added pressure and hectic schedules. It is no picnic living in a parsonage and being actively engaged in the church. I knew what was ahead...get the kids dressed...finish dressing myself...put coats on...drive to church... greet twenty people at the door...answer another fifteen questions...get the kids to their Sunday school classes ...help with opening exercises...organize the parade for the closing day of kid's crusade...take attendance...add up points ...award the prizes...count the offering...sing...worship... smile...shake more hands...come home...entertain guests...do dishes...and on and on. I wanted to collapse just thinking about it.

"Dear Jesus," I cried. "Please help me get through this day. I have no strength left. And this new life within me, kicking and moving, was trying to get my attention and say, 'Mom slow down. Take time for me too. I need to grow strong and healthy and you need to rest.' " I bit my lip and dried the tears with a soft white towel.

"Come on, girl...this is no time to feel sorry for yourself ...there is too much to be done," I scolded.

I heard screaming coming from the kitchen and ran down the hall half-dressed to investigate. Bryon was yelling at his sister, who had turned her bowl of Raisin Bran and milk upside-down on the carpet.

"Enough is enough!" I asserted and then grabbed Leann out of the highchair, spanked her bottom, and put her in the tub for a bath. Bryon had eaten only two bites, so I wistfully reminded him to "get a move on" and finish his breakfast. We had to leave in forty-five minutes.

I cleaned up the spilled cereal, finished dressing, and then bathed and dressed Leann. She sat down in the middle of her room and began to play with her baby dolls.

Now to get big brother dressed. As soon as I took off his pajamas, Bryon began to whine and fuss. All his bandages were stuck to his flesh, and soon he was standing in a pool of blood. I tried to stop the bleeding with gauze pads, but it continued to soak through the compresses and cloths. His eyes were also crusted with infection, and I had to wet them with cotton balls so that he could see. After an agonizing hour of wrapping, crying, and frustration — Bryon was done. Not to my satisfaction, but it would have to do until we got home from church. We were already running late.

I located Leann's winter coat and looked into her bedroom. She was gone. "Where did she go?" I questioned, peeking into each room. "Oh, no!" I shouted out loud. She was sitting in the middle of the living room floor surrounded by records and tapes from the stereo cabinet. She gleefully held up two cassette tapes that she had successfully unwound — the brown ribbons hung like confetti from her arms.

I thought to myself, "This will really make Daddy's day!"

Five minutes later we were in the car racing up Spring Garden Drive to route 441, and then on to Glad Tidings Assembly. Today was the last big meeting of a weekend Kid's Crusade with Tony and Janet DeRosa. The parking lot was full and the vestibule was jammed with activity. Everyone was in readiness for a grand march from the classrooms to the main sanctuary for a fun-filled program. Apparently, the teachers were waiting for me to answer some questions on the point system and attendance. My tardiness was holding up all the events.

I could tell by the strained look on Steve's face, as I walked through the side glass doors, that he was upset with me for being late. Bryon refused to hurry, so he dragged his feet and whimpered behind me. I pulled Leann down the flight of stairs to her classroom, opened the door, and tried gently to push her inside. She didn't budge. She had made up her mind that she was not going to class today. Her feet were firmly planted into the carpet and she hung onto my hand for dear life.

I pleaded with her, "Leann, please be a good girl and go to your class. Your teachers love you. They want to tell you a story and show you pretty pictures."

She shook her head "no." "All right, I guess I will have to pull you in the room," I whispered in exasperation. I took her arm and yanked her towards the door. She began to cry and clutch her tummy. Then I noticed that she was standing in a puddle on the floor. She had wet herself. This time it was my turn to cry.

In front of fifteen little pairs of eyes, two nursery teachers, and others in the hall, I sat down on the floor with Leann and began to sob. A whole church bulging with people were waiting for the crusade to begin and I couldn't do one thing about it. The daily pressure of the ministry and my family had finally crumbled me into pieces.

Marie, one of the workers, took Leann into her arms, and someone ran to tell Pastor Sparks. I tried to stand, but the weight of the world was on my shoulders. My mind screamed, "Doesn't anyone know that I'm human too? I bleed, I hurt, I cry! Why does everyone think that I can take pressure, heartache, and disappointment...one thing after another...and never be affected...just keep on going? Well, I can't do it! Please, let somebody understand what I'm going through."

I stumbled down the hall and into an empty classroom. I stood in the corner, my face buried in the wall. Muffled sobs enveloped me. Without turning around, I heard Steve open the door and then he tenderly took me in his arms. The dam of frustration broke loose and the tears of healing began to flow. It felt so good to cry without someone telling me to stop.

For a long time Steve held me quietly. Then he whispered in my hair, "What's the matter, Honey?" All I could get out was, "I can't take it anymore. Please help me!"

He gave me a reassuring squeeze that said, "I love you...I understand."

I dried my tears and we walked hand in hand upstairs to the front pew in the church. For the first time in months we sat together in a service and enjoyed the Lord's presence in a fresh way. Like a child, I listened intently to each Bible story and laughed at the crazy puppets. When the awards were presented, I swelled with pride for each youngster who went forward. During the closing prayer, Steve squeezed by hand tightly between his.

Very few members of the congregation realized what happened to their pastor's wife that day — it was the closest point in my life to a nervous breakdown. Some of the ladies did recognize the pressure I was under and tried to relieve part of the load. It was the first time in six-and-a-half years of pastoring that a number of people asked what they could do to help. The healing was gradual...but it had begun.

Throughout this time a beautiful Scripture kept running through my mind — "There remaineth, therefore, a rest to the people of God" (Heb. 4:9; Scofield). Also, the words of Jesus:

*"Come to Me, all who are weary and heavy-laden, and I will give you rest. Take my yoke upon you, and learn from Me, for I am gentle and humble in heart; and you shall find rest for your souls" (Matt. 11:28,29).*

My soul definitely needed a rest. I was so busy doing God's work, ministering to others, counseling and encouraging, that I had forgotten to feed my own soul. I longed to sit at the feet of Jesus and allow Him to heal the hurts, bind up the bruises, and strengthen my inner man. Jesus said to Martha, when she was anxious about the cares of life, "But one thing is needful..." (Luke 10:42a; Scofield). Mary, Martha's sister, had chosen that part — to sit at the feet of Jesus. Jesus would not take this away from her.

A chorus we learned while attending Bible school reflects the desire of my heart:

> "Jesus I am resting, resting
> In the joy of what Thou art;
> I am finding out the greatness,
> Of Thy loving heart."

In the midst of my own inner turmoil, our ministry within our fine congregation and the community was at an exciting peak. The Sunday school had tripled in the six years we had been there, and the finances had quadrupled. God was certainly blessing His people. Our Sunday morning crowds were packed out, and our evangelistic and prayer meetings were growing. There was an air of expectancy, warmth, and Christian love between families. After many of the services, we attempted to shut off the lights and chase people out of the building by ten or eleven at night. Many families had an active ministry of hospitality and opened their homes to newcomers.

Steve was maturing in his pastoral leadership — he truly had a shepherd's heart. His preaching developed into messages that burned in his heart and were delivered with a divine anointing. The congregation was fed and grew through the inspired preaching of the Word. They responded to his enthusiastic direction in praise and worship. It was sheer joy to bask in God's holy presence as we stood on Sunday morning and raised the notes of "Like a River Glorious" to the heavens.

Pastoring provided us with a wealth of memorable experiences — some humorous, others heartbreaking, and many rewarding. Our phone rang incessantly day and night. Whenever I picked up the receiver, I asked myself, "Who has lost a loved one? Is someone in the hospital? Who needs counseling? Who has run away from home? What young person has been arrested? Who has overdosed on drugs? Who has attempted suicide?" The list of needs was endless.

I still chuckle when I recall the request that came one morning about five o'clock. An elderly woman, who attended our church occasionally, called to say she needed assistance immediately. Steve threw on a shirt and trousers, then drove straight to her home. The woman appeared at her door in a negligee, frantic with worry and in tears. After several minutes, Steve was able to calm her down and piece together the details.

The distraught woman had apparently awakened early and discovered that her false teeth were missing. She was determined that this was a serious spiritual matter. In fact, she believed that either God or the devil had stolen them! Struggling to gain his composure, Steve answered, "Well, dear, according to my knowledge of the Word of God, neither the devil nor God wear false teeth! So I sincerely doubt they would steal yours!"

But to ease the woman's fears, Steve spent an hour rummaging through her house looking for the set of false teeth. They were ultimately discovered in a pile of dirty laundry beneath her bed! The life of a minister is certainly not without its amusing anecdotes.

There were also tragic experiences. One young man my husband had counseled for a year suffered from substance abuse. He was caught and arrested for selling and distributing drugs. Steve did everything humanly possible to salvage this fellow. He went to court for him, helped him get accepted by the Teen Challenge rehabilitation center in Harrisburg, and counseled him and his family for hours.

One night about one o'clock, his father called to inform us that his son had overdosed on drugs and intended to take his own life. Steve jumped in his car and raced the twenty minutes to boy's trailer. The doors and windows were locked. The young pastor pried open the front door with a tire jack. He walked down the narrow hall towards the living room. Sitting on the floor in a pool of blood, the twenty-one-year-old held a shotgun to his head in a death grip. Although he was still gasping for breath, part of his face and brain had been blown away.

Overcome with grief, Steve sat down beside the dying youth and held his bloody form in his arms. Within a few minutes, he ceased to breathe and the warm life flowed out of his body.

This young man's funeral was perhaps the most difficult for Steve to conduct. The shortness and tragedy of a wasted life weighed heavily upon his heart. Only twenty-three-years old himself, Steve shared with the family and friends the challenge from Matthew 16:25,26 (Scofield):

> *"For whosoever will save his life shall lose it, and whosoever will lose his life for my sake shall find it. For what is a man profited, if he shall gain the whole world, and lose his own soul? Or what shall a man give in exchange for his soul?"*

We have no promise for tomorrow. Life is full of uncertainties. James said, "How do you know what is going to happen tomorrow? For the length of your lives is as uncertain as the morning fog; now you see it, soon it is gone" (James 4:14; TLB).

Without Christ in our life, there is no purpose or reason for living. Acknowledging Jesus Christ as our Lord and Saviour gives life new purpose, perspective, and a fresh beginning. Paul puts it this way, "Therefore if any man is in Christ, he is a new creature; the old things passed away; behold, new things have come" (2 Cor. 5:17).

Thank God, even in the face of certain death, Christ can bring hope and encouragement. We saw this evident in the life of our neighbor's son. Bob and Dottie were a great couple who lived next door to us. We shared many hours together working on our yards or playing basketball on the court. In the summer of 1980, Ron, their youngest son, came home seriously ill with carcinoma of the lungs and internal organs. He lost most of his hair due to the radiation treatments and his skin hung on his frame. He sat for hours in a rocking chair covered with an Afghan, watching television or trying to read.

One warm autumn evening I took Bryon over to meet Ron. When Bryon held out his contracted club to shake hands, Ron immediately identified with Bryon's suffering. A sparkle came into the young man's eyes and a bond of friendship was formed.

Ron stayed alone in the house most of the day because both of his parents worked. Steve mentioned to Bob that he would be glad to visit with Ron and perhaps play some chess. So the next day on his way to work, Bob left the house keys with Steve. That afternoon, Steve spent three hours talking with Ron. When he returned home, his face was alive with excitement.

I asked, "What happened, Honey?"

Thrilled with the news, Steve announced, "Ron committed his life to Christ this afternoon! He talked to me about his failures, his life of sin, his pain and suffering...and his desire to live a full life. I explained to him that our life here on earth is only temporary, and each one of us is appointed a time to die. But the life that we live after death is forever...and we can have eternal life through Christ."

At this point Steve was weeping with joy. He continued, "I asked Ron if he wanted Christ to give him a new life and to forgive him of his past sins. He was so eager to make the commitment. We prayed the sinner's prayer together. A beautiful peace came over him when we were finished. Praise God! He is ready to meet the Lord!"

It was only a few weeks later that Ron was relieved of his pain-racked body. He was with Christ! Steve had the honor of sharing Ron's confession of faith at his funeral. What a tremendous witness to his family and friends who did not know the Lord.

The ministry comprises a wide spectrum of experiences ...from the lighthearted moments to even the valley of death. But in all of our giving and caring for the multitudes of needs, Christ has always been the focal point of our lives. This saying summarizes our life's philosophy:

> *"Only one life, will soon be past,*
> *Only what's done for Christ will last."*

> *"For to me, to live is Christ, and to die is gain"*
> *(Phil. 1:21).*

# 4

# CHRISTMAS
# IN A WHEELCHAIR

The crisp November air stung our faces as we stepped outside the front door. Leann's cheeks were like two small red apples and her breath like puffs of white smoke. She cuddled next to me in the car and held her baby doll in her arms. She chattered aimlessly about turkeys, trees, her Sunday school teacher, and her new brother or sister. I maneuvered the car along the familiar route 283 towards the obstetrician's office.

Today was my monthly check-up. My mind was cluttered with projects, decisions, holiday cooking, and Christmas shopping. Yet a gnawing fear continued to haunt me.

I pondered the thought, "Was I leaking amniotic fluid from the sac surrounding the unborn baby? Could it be the same sequence of events which occurred when Leann was born?" I shuddered at the prospect of delivering another baby two months prematurely. I was still only six-and-a-half months pregnant!

Dr. Paul Fairbrother listened to the baby's heartbeat, measured the circumference of my enlarged abdomen, and then asked, "Well, Mrs. Sparks, how are you feeling?"

I hesitated, bit my lip, and then blurted out, "Doctor, I think there is a possibility that I am losing amniotic fluid again."

A worried frown creased his forehead. He paused for a moment and then suggested, "Well, girl, I think we should have a look."

Meanwhile, Leann had climbed onto the examining table with me and was beginning to read from her storybooks. She was having a great visit with "Mommy's doctor" and enjoyed making herself right at home. Dr. Fairbrother picked up a very surprised little girl and carried her to the waiting room. The nurses kept her busy with cookies and toys.

The doctor proceeded with an internal examination and then tested the fluid with a special paper. The color of the paper indicated that the normal vaginal fluids were mixed with secretions from the amniotic sac also. He then pushed the baby away from my cervix to see if the leakage was near the birth canal. No more fluid escaped, so he concluded that the membranes had ruptured in a higher position. Finally, he did a sonogram to determine the approximate size and age of the fetus. The test showed that this little life was about twenty-eight weeks developed. Not a very convenient time for a baby to be born.

Slowly and deliberately, he proceeded to explain the alternatives. It sounded like a replay of a record from two years ago.

"Mrs. Sparks, we need to use extreme caution in protecting the life of your unborn child. You could go home and resume your everyday activities and responsibilities, but I think that in a very short time you will go into labor and have a premature baby. At twenty-eight weeks the child has only a 10% chance of surviving. In considering your past history and previous pregnancy with Leann, I feel the best choice is to admit you to the hospital immediately."

I felt numb with unbelief. I wanted to cry, but I couldn't. My mind was barraged with countless questions: "What will I do with Leann? Who will care for Bryon? Will I have to spend the holidays in the hospital away from my family? How will Steve manage the kids and his responsibilities at the church? Who will take charge of the children's Christmas program?''

Without feeling, I muttered, ''Can I drive home and get my clothes?''

''No, I don't think that would be wise,'' he answered gently. Then sensing my dilemma, he suggested, ''Why don't you call your husband and have him bring your clothes? Then he can take Leann home. I want you to stay here in the office until someone can drive you over to the hospital.''

I nodded my head in quiet agreement.

In the receptionist's area Leann sat on a nurse's lap and jabbered steadily about her new baby sister who was on the way. She stuffed another cookie in her mouth and then noticed that I was standing in the doorway.

''Hi, Mommy!'' she yelled. Crumbs fell all over the clean carpet. ''Can we go home now?''

''No, Sweetheart, Mommy must stay in the hospital to help the new baby. We will call Daddy and let him know.''

Oblivious to the seriousness of the situation, the curly blond-haired two-year-old scooted into the waiting room to investigate the toy box in the corner.

I dialed the church office. Ring...ring...ring...no answer. I tried our home number. No answer there either. Sighing to myself, I resigned to wait a few minutes and attempt another call. I leafed through a *Parents'* magazine and glanced at the other ladies dressed in tent-like attire. I dialed the numbers over and over, but always the same response — no answer.

''Where was Steve? Perhaps out on visitation or at a special committee meeting.'' The muscles in my lower abdomen became tense and anxiety gripped me. ''He could be away for the entire day and it would be impossible to reach him!'' My mind raced.

Suddenly, I felt a sharp pain across my stomach for about fifteen seconds. My face contorted in agony and I drew in my breath. The receptionist looked my way with concern, ''Mrs. Sparks, are you all right? Are you in pain?''

''Well, I hope it's not what I think it is — a contraction!''

---

I blurted out. But before I gained composure...there was another severe cramp. I grabbed my stomach and cried, "Oh Lord, not labor! Please help me!"

Brenda, a tall, brown-haired nurse, helped me to a small adjoining room where I could relax alone. I spied a phone and tried to dial again. No answer. I decided to call our youth pastor, Brother Bill, to see if by chance he was at home. A gruff, low voice answered.

"Oh Bill, thank God you're there!" It was a welcome relief to talk to someone I knew. Bill was glad to drive me to the hospital and then take Leann to one of her "nannies" from the church.

Meanwhile, Steve had phoned to see if my appointment was finished. He wanted to meet me for lunch. The nurse who answered the phone didn't see me in the waiting room, so she told him I had left. Unknown to me, Steve was only a few miles away. But when he discovered I had gone home, he continued with his errands, assuming everything was fine.

When I returned to the waiting room from the lavatory, the nurse gasped, "Oh, Mrs. Sparks, I thought you had gone home! Your husband just called and I told him you had left. I'm so sorry. I didn't realize you were still trying to get in touch with him."

Discouraged, frustrated, and on the verge of tears, I collapsed into a chair to wait for Bill. The dark, athletic youth minister arrived in half-an-hour. Leann shouted, "Yeah! Brother Bill is here!"

I climbed out of the blue sports van and placed a seat belt around my daughter. She looked so tiny in the big black leather seat. I gave her a tight hug and kissed her sweet rosy lips. Then with motherly concern, I said, "Leann, I want you to be a good girl for Gramma Burkett. Daddy will pick you up later and bring you home. Okay?"

She nodded yes. Then she began to cry, "Mommy, I don't want you to leave me...please come home now."

"Honey, Mommy must go to the hospital right now. But as soon as I get better I will be home. I promise."

Bill waved good-bye as the van pulled away from the front

steps of the hospital. Leann's usual sparkly blue eyes were clouded with tears. I tried to ignore the slight contractions, which were reoccurring every ten minutes. In a very short time, I was admitted, undressed, and lying in a labor room, attached to a fetal monitor. Technicians took blood and urine samples to the lab. Nurses examined the graphs from the monitor to chart the length and intensity of the contractions.

The warm room and the comfortable bed lured my exhausted body into a sound sleep. I awakened two hours later, feeling rested and more conscious of my plight. I asked the head nurse for permission to phone my husband. She unstrapped me from the machines and took me to the father's waiting room. I was able to contact a neighbor to look for Bryon's school bus and take care of him until Steve picked him up later.

It was at 4:30 in the afternoon when I finally contacted Steve. I had been trying to reach him since 10:30 that morning. He was so dismayed to learn that the nurse had given him the wrong information. When he arrived home and found no one there, he was very perplexed. Calmly, I explained the unplanned sequences of the day and the whereabouts of the children.

A friendly nurse's aid wheeled me into room 309 and stopped alongside the further bed. She placed my maternity clothes on the nightstand and switched on the overhead light.

"Okay, dearie. This is the end of the line...hop in bed," she said jokingly.

I tried to smile, as I held on to the back of my open "johnnie" and maneuvered to the bed. Linda, my sixteen-year-old roommate, was engrossed in a discotheque program that featured wild dancing. At eight-and-a-half months pregnant, she was suffering with severe toxemia. She acknowledged my presence with a simple "hello" and then turned back to the television.

I gazed out the window at the darkening autumn sky. The colorful leaves had fallen to the ground in picturesque piles. The trees stood naked, cold and bare. It was November 21, 1980, only one week before Thanksgiving. We had planned to

49

spend the holidays with my family in New Jersey. Now I would eat a microwave turkey dinner in the Polyclinic Medical Center. Sarcastically, I thought, "This will be sheer joy, I'm sure!"

True to form, Steve did his best to cheer me up and help brighten my outlook. In his arms, along with my suitcase, bathrobe, toiletries, and busywork, he held an adorable red glass booty filled with candy canes, mistletoe, and pine cones. I loved it! He whispered something about "an early Christmas present" and I squeezed him so hard I almost broke his neck.

We had been through this trial before and we knew what to expect...days of patient waiting...staying in bed...off my feet...blood tests two or three times a day...frequent sonagrams...and hopefully, buying the baby some extra needed time to grow and develop.

The greatest fear was infection. If bacteria entered the womb through the tear in the amniotic sac, the baby would be in serious danger and labor would be induced. The presence of infection was determined through the blood tests (the white count), fetal stress, and activity. Also the mother's general condition (fever, uterine tenderness) were monitored.

"Well, Honey, you asked the Lord to give you a rest and He finally answered your prayer," Steve chided me. "You told me just a week ago that you couldn't handle any more pressure."

He looked at me squarely, "I knew you were at the end of your rope last Sunday when you broke down uncontrollably at church. God answers our prayers in many different ways. In your case, He knew you wouldn't slow down on your own." Steve was smiling, "So He decided to put you in a place where you had no choice in the matter. Right here in bed!" He chuckled and then embraced me.

His words hit me like a ton of bricks. He was absolutely correct! The Scripture from Hebrews 4:9 (Scofield) became a reality. "There remaineth, therefore, a rest to the people of God." Although it was difficult to be separated from my family, I had hours to spend in God's presence and in His Word.

We decided to send Leann to my parents, who lived in

Clark, New Jersey. (Even if I did come home in a few days, I wouldn't be able to care for her.) Bryon stayed with his daddy. They were good company for each other. Steve took special care in bathing, bandaging, and dressing Bryon each morning. On the way to work, Steve dropped Bryon off at the Middletown Christian School. Some of the ladies from our congregation offered to babysit while Steve visited with me in the evenings.

I quickly settled into the antiseptic routine and contrived various methods of keeping myself occupied. I addressed our Christmas cards and inserted the sweet picture of our two darlings into the centerfold. Our family and friends would be delighted to receive them. I worked on the new "tough cookie account" and organized letters to key people, asking them to assist us in pre-selling the book. I wrote a newsy Christmas letter to all the women's groups in the Harrisburg-York area, of which I was the sectional representative. And in my spare time, I learned how to sew some creative stitchery for gifts.

Vases filled with thriving greenery, flowers, cards, and gifts arrived. Soon my room looked like the hospitality shop on the first floor. My first roommate, Linda, went home only one day following my admission. So, for the next four days I was alone. This opportunity provided hours of serenity and choice moments of waiting in God's presence. His Word was life, truth, and strength, at a time when I searched for reality. God loved me enough to set me aside from the cares of life, so we could have time together. That was a comforting awareness.

Often I basked in the quietness of the afternoon sunshine as it filtered through the blinds and drifted across my bed. The warm presence of the Lord surrounded me and I spoke to Him in heavenly sounds of praise. This experience seemed to lift my spirit directly into the courts of heaven. It was then I felt refreshed; the pressures of life took their proper places.

Throughout the weekend, I heard a shrill female voice yell out complaints and, at times, curses. She sounded confused and hurt. I was curious who this woman might be. So, one day I asked the nurse, "Do you know the girl who is making so much racket a few doors away? Why is she in the hospital?"

"Well, believe it or not," she chippered, "Nancy is here for the same reason you are. She has ruptured membranes and is in danger of losing her baby. The biggest difference is that she is only five months pregnant."

Immediately, I felt compassion for Nancy and wished that I could talk with her. But being marooned to my bed gave me little opportunity to sneak down the hall. Besides, my room was directly across from the nurses' station — no chance!

On Tuesday afternoon two nurses came into my room and yanked the empty bed into the hall. I puzzled, "What in the world are they doing?" Five minutes later, I heard the screech of rubber wheels against the shiny linoleum floor and sat up to see what was coming. In through the door rolled a bed, suitcases, flowers, a bedpan, and Nancy!! My new roommate.

We jabbered like two old women catching up on all the news. I liked her instantly. Nancy was brutally honest, at times loud-spoken, but a caring and loving person. She wanted her unborn child to live and was willing to stay in bed through Christmas if it would give the baby a chance.

Her husband, Jim, was a speech writer for the senators from the Pennsylvania House of Representatives. Their three-year-old daughter, Brooke, was a beautiful, sensitive child with big brown eyes and long dark hair.

I was embarrassed when Nancy's mother arrived with a bag of Arthur Treacher's Fish 'n Chips and Nancy shouted, "Ugh! I don't even want to see that fish. It will make me sick! Here, Lil, do you want some?" Then she threw the bag on my bed.

"No thanks. I'm still full from supper," I apologized.

The atmosphere was a little tense as my roommate continued to complain about the food, the nurses, and the doctor. I soon discovered that we had the same doctor — Dr. Paul Fairbrother, a friendly chap, who spoke with an English brogue and a twinkle in his eye!

Nancy didn't touch her food trays for days. She called Jim on the phone and asked him to bring her pizza, sub-sandwiches, or MacDonald's hamburgers. One evening, while

Jim was visiting, our supper was served. Nancy peeked under the warmer cover at her selection, curled up her nose, and yelled, "This is disgusting!" I had already started eating my dinner. She looked over at my tray and said, "Yours looks disgusting too!"

I swallowed a piece of chicken and replied, "Oh, it's not that bad." I continued eating.

Every morning at eight o'clock the hemoglobist arrived from the lab to get blood samples. Of course, after a week of being pricked three times a day, we both felt like pin cushions. When Nancy recognized who was coming, she said nervously, "Oh no, it's them again. They're going to kill me. It feels like the needle is going straight through my arm. I sure hope they know what they're doing. Oh Lord, help me...here it goes...Ouch!!"

Steve brought Bryon with him to the hospital to see me every other night. It was a real uplift to see my buddy and get some hugs and kisses. Jim and Nancy were more than kindly interested in Bryon's story. They listened intently as we shared six-and-a-half years of heartache. We spoke of our faith in God and the many opportunities we had to prove that God is faithful. They were openly touched. The seeds of faith were planted within their hearts — now they needed time to grow.

Nancy's attitude and outlook on life drastically changed. She thought more positively about herself and her unborn child and committed the baby's future to the Lord. It was so beautiful to hear Nancy talk to her family or a friend on the phone and say, "Well, Jim and I are trusting God to take care of us and the new baby. Whatever happens we know it will be for the best."

She even started eating the hospital food..and liking it! One nurse came in our room and discovered that Nancy had eaten her first hot meal in a week. In utter amazement, she replied, "Mrs. Hertzler, are you sure you aren't sick? I can't believe you're eating institutional food!"

Nancy and I gave each other a knowing grin.

Thanksgiving Day, November 27, was unlike the traditional family gatherings around a table filled with scrumptious fixings and trimmings. But we managed. Steve and Bryon were invited out for dinner by a church family. Leann was visiting with Nanny and Pop-Pop. Mommy watched Macy's Thanksgiving Parade, wrote letters, did some sewing, and then concentrated on enjoying our prefabricated turkey dinner.

Steve popped in the door about eight p.m. carrying his goody bag of homemade treats. I savored every morsel of the cold turkey sandwiches, cranberry fruit salad, pumpkin and mincemeat pies. Nancy and I amused ourselves by tasting each other's treats from the holiday table. Ummm, good!

After I'd spent eight days of confined bed rest, Dr. Fairbrother felt it was safe enough for me to go home. He added a few stipulations — continued bed rest, no housework or heavy lifting, and return visits to the doctor three times a week. He also instructed me to phone him if there was the slightest change in my condition.

Steve was an absolute sweetheart! When I came through the front door of 114 Nissley Street, the first thing I noticed was the vacuumed carpets and dusted furniture. Further inspection revealed that the laundry was done, beds were changed, the kitchen was spotless, and supper was ready. He arranged the living room couch with pillows and blankets and placed a desk nearby for my work. He even moved the television from its usual spot so that I could watch the programs.

My first night home we had onion burgers, potato chips, and coke. It was great! I was so grateful to be with my family.

Our days revolved around our numerous trips to the obstetrician. Each visit marked more time for our baby. Steve made his plans to go with me in case something changed and I was put in the hospital. Several times we stopped to see how Nancy was progressing. In an attempt to brighten her day, I brought her homebaked cookies or goodies. But Nancy was still losing a lot of fluid from the ruptured membranes. I was concerned about her.

On a bleak December morning we made the familiar trip for my check-up. One glance at Dr. Fairbrother's face told me something was seriously wrong. His eyes were dark and puffy from lack of sleep and his voice trembled with emotion.

---

"Dr. Fairbrother," I inquired, "what has happened?"

He proceeded painfully, "Your friend, Nancy, suffered from a violent infection during the night, which caused her to go through hours of labor and the delivery of a one-and-a-half- pound baby girl. The child lived for one hour — at six months there was almost no hope of survival. Needless to say, the Hertzlers are heartbroken."

We left the professional building and drove over to the hospital. Our friends were hurting deeply, and we wanted to reach out in love and comfort during this time of disappointment. We peeked into room 309 — no one was there. As we looked down the hall, we saw Jim staggering towards us...his hair unkept, face unshaved, shoulders stooped...succumbing to exhaustion. His clouded eyes responded with a flicker of light when he recognized us. We embraced him and whispered, "Jim, we are praying for you." And we meant it.

The head nurse in labor and delivery gave special permission for Steve and me to visit Nancy in one of the labor rooms. Only two hours earlier, she had delivered her tiny girl. Nancy wept when she saw us. She hugged us tightly and then held our hands.

"I'm so glad you guys stopped by. The Lord must have heard my prayers," Nancy cried.

The bereaved couple took turns telling us the details of the nightmare they had been through. Their pain was vivid. Our hearts reached out to them. They were Roman Catholic and would soon call their priest, but we still took time to minister the grace of God. We spoke of putting our trust in a faithful God, knowing that He "doeth all things well." Before we left, the four of us joined hearts and hands in prayer. A wonderful peace filled the room like a sweet fragrance. God was there.

During the following weeks, Nancy and I kept in touch almost daily with a phone call. Sometimes just a word of encouragement, a listening ear, or time to laugh together was enough. We became close friends.

The wintry days and weeks passed slowly. The soft powdered snow covered the rolling Pennsylvania hills in the Susquehanna Valley. Brightly colored lights, angels, tinsel, and manger stalls decorated homes and retail stores. The strains of Christmas carols filled the air with expectancy. The King's birthday was drawing near.

I awoke on December 10 feeling unusually warm and uncomfortable. My uterus was extremely tender. After Dr. Fairbrother examined me, took my temperature, and had the blood work done, he decided to admit me to the hospital again. He stated very matter-of-factly, "Mrs. Sparks, I want to take all the necessary precautions. I can't be positive, but you show all the signs of an infection. If this is true, I will have to induce labor and take the baby by force."

We were ready for anything. Ten minutes elapsed and I was lying in a labor room, attached to a fetal monitor. I was having some mild contractions and the heart rate indicated fetal distress. The most important factor was the results from the blood tests, which showed the "white cell count," or level of infection. The doctor ordered a series of three tests taken at different intervals throughout the day to make his final decision about inducing labor.

The first two tests revealed a progressive rate of infection. At 6:00 p.m., Dr. Fairbrother whisked into the room and informed me that there would be one more test at eight o'clock. If the "white count" was still high — then a delivery by Caesarean would be necessary.

My heart stopped beating for a few seconds. I whispered, "Lord, I belong to You. If this is Your will and perfect timing for this little one, then I accept it without fear. Your will be done, O Lord."

I quickly dialed the church's office number. Steve was putting the final touches on his Wednesday evening Bible study. I anxiously filled him in on the details. He immediately responded, "Honey, I will come right to the hospital. I want to be with you."

"Sweetheart, you don't have to come this minute. The blood test is scheduled for eight and the results will take an hour or so. Let me call you about nine o'clock when I know the outcome...then you won't miss the service."

He hesitated, "If you will be all right, then I will wait to

---

hear from you. But I plan to have the congregation spend time in intercessory prayer for you and the baby!"

The minutes ticked by. Time for the test...then it was 8:30 ...8:45...8:55. Dr. Fairbrother appeared in the doorway wearing a green surgical shirt and pants; a mask hung from his neck. I held my breath. I was resigned to the will of God.

"Mrs. Sparks!" he exclaimed, "You fascinate me. I never know what to expect from you. The white count was a high fourteen only a few hours ago, and now it has dropped down to one! I don't know what to say...apparently the infection has subsided, or perhaps it was a false alarm."

"Our entire congregation is praying for me right now! I believe God hears and answers prayer. It wasn't time for the baby to be born." I winked at him and smiled.

"Well, I guess someone was praying. But anyway, you can go home tomorrow, providing you follow the same routine and restrictions. Okay?"

I nodded in agreement. He patted my leg, then turned to leave, still shaking his head.

The next month was filled with Christmas preparations. I struggled with feelings of inactivity and helplessness. The ladies of our church had completely taken over my responsibilities with a genuine spirit of love and unity. There was a beautiful sense of working together and the challenge of supporting the pastor and his family. Some were directing the Christmas program, others leading the children's church, playing the piano, assisting the choir, and even cleaning my house!

My biggest frustration was the inability to participate in the holiday festivities of shopping, gift wrapping, picking out the tree, decorating, and baking. Steve recognized my depression and sought to find a solution. The statement "Where there is a will, there is a way" certainly applies to my man.

One afternoon he burst through the front door pushing a wheelchair and gleefully announced, "Who said you couldn't go Christmas shopping? Jump in, Honey, and we'll take a spin. I'll push and you can shop!"

It certainly sounded like loads of fun. Christmas in a wheelchair! Well, it *was* making the best of the situation. We had a grand time together. While Bryon was in kindergarten, we rolled through the crowded malls, buying our holiday treasures. Steve piled the gift boxes on my lap and did "wheelies" around the corners. We delighted in the puzzled looks from the other shoppers. When they first noticed me in the wheelchair, they expressed sympathy. But when they realized I was eight months pregnant, they glared at Steve. It was a riot! Steve wanted to pin a sign on me that read: "Yes, I am pregnant. No I am NOT crippled!"

On the way home from a shopping spree, Steve pulled into a lighted parking lot filled with Christmas trees for sale. He ran around the car and held up several trees for my approval. After a few selections, I shook my head "yes" and Steve loaded the tree in our trunk. We had an enjoyable evening decorating it with crocheted candy canes and bells, hand-painted figures, sea shells from Martha's Vineyard, knitted stockings, and shiny red apples. The brightly trimmed evergreen proudly stood in our front window and cast colorful shadows on the fresh snow. Christmas carols played on the stereo; holly draped the fireplace; and candles burned fragrantly in every room.

We made delicious butter cookies in the shapes of stars, bells, trees, camels, santas, angels, and snowmen. Red and green sprinkles added the right finish. Steve mixed the dough; I cut out the shapes while sitting at the table; and Bryon threw on the sprinkles. (Sometimes more on the table than on the cookies!)

Leann came home the day before Christmas. My parents had kept her for five weeks, and she was really homesick. One of her big surprises was waiting in her bedroom — a new dark pine bunk bed that matched Bryon's. The crib was moved into another room for the new baby. Leann was no longer the baby, but a grown-up little girl.

Christmas 1980 was a warm, close family time. We enjoyed being together. We all seemed to give extra of ourselves, and in return we received so much more. I thought of another mother who lived almost two thousand years ago. I, like her, was anxiously awaiting for the birth of my child. Yet, I had a warm cozy bed, good meals, a roof over my head, and a modern hospital only fifteen minutes away. Mary didn't know where she would eat or sleep. She gave birth to the Saviour in a stable filled with hay and animals, and no one assisted her but Joseph. Her song of praise, known as the "Magnificat" inspires my faith:

*"My soul doth magnify the Lord, And my spirit hath rejoiced in God my Saviour" (Luke 1:46, 47).*

Contrary to Steve's prediction, he didn't get to claim the third Sparks' baby on our 1980 income tax return. The new year, 1981, dawned as a promise of God's love. A time for new beginnings, resolutions, and a new child.

On the morning of January 13, 1981, I awoke in a state of sheer exhaustion. I had just recovered from the flu, when I was attacked with a severe case of diarrhea. To top it off, I suffered with a terrible congestion and was awake all night coughing. Every muscle in my body ached, and my abdomen was extremely sore. I was miserable.

I called the doctor and described my symptoms. He told me to pack my suitcase and meet him in labor and delivery. He sounded dead serious. Steve took Bryon to school and dropped off Leann at Gramma Burkett's with an overnight bag.

When I arrived at the hospital the nurses performed all the routine tests. Dr. Fairbrother walked in about 10:30 a.m., gave me an internal examination, reviewed the test results, and announced, "Today is the day! I have decided to induce you this afternoon. You are thirty-eight weeks pregnant and I suspect from your various symptoms that you are fighting an infection. So...I will finish my office visits and I will be back about one o'clock to start your labor."

He smiled confidently and left the room.

In a way I was relieved that soon the waiting would be all over. It had been a real strain on me emotionally...wondering ...praying. Steve went down to the cafeteria to grab a bite of lunch before the doctor returned. I dozed off for a nap. I awoke to the sounds of the fetal heartbeat coming from the monitor. My love for the unborn child was incredible. I rubbed my stomach gently, as if giving the baby love pats.

Except for the beep...beep...of the monitor, the room was surrounded with quietness. I savored these few, rare moments and talked with the Lord. "I know this might be a selfish request, Lord. If it is, please forgive me. But I am afraid of being induced by drugs. You made my body, and You created this child within me. I believe that You can begin my labor naturally. It is a small request...but it means so much to me, Lord. Thank you for listening to me...I trust You."

A few minutes later I noticed that the needle on the graph, recording contractions, began to move. I wondered...could it be true? I waited. Sure enough the needle moved again in a small arch, sketching the height of the contraction. Within an hour I was having thirty-second pains every five minutes. When Steve and the doctor arrived simultaneously, I was beaming from ear to ear.

"Guess what?" I shouted. "I am in labor!"

Dr. Fairbrother chuckled, "Mrs. Sparks, you never let me win. Just when I decide to induce you...you begin labor all by yourself. This isn't good for my ego, you know!" He enjoyed teasing me with his dry English humor.

The afternoon passed quickly as Steve and I talked. We walked up and down the halls, watched television, and did some breathing exercises. Steve ran down to the cafeteria for a brief supper and when he returned found me in a great deal of distress. The labor pains were sixty seconds long, with only forty-five seconds in between. I was having difficulty breathing due to my congestion. The flu had left me in a weakened condition.

In agony, I pleaded, "Honey, tell the nurse to call the doctor right away. I don't know what's wrong, but I can't take any more pain."

Within a short time, Dr. Fairbrother bustled into the room. He checked me internally and then expressed concern, "You are in transition, but the baby's head is coming the wrong way. I will have to put my hand on the baby's head and turn very slowly during each of your contractions. Now do your best to work with me."

Steve held my right leg in the air, while the doctor maneuvered the head into birth position. There were a few anxious moments when I lost control of myself. I couldn't breathe or bear down. The doctor ordered a sedative and oxygen. It was then they lost the baby's heartbeat and had to attach an electrode to the baby's crown.

When I thought I was going to pass out from the intense pain, the nursing team began to wheel me into the delivery room. My body was shivering uncontrollably. I glanced at the clock — it was 10:00 p.m. I had been in transition for almost four hours! The nurse beside me became my coach.

"Come on, Lil, you can do it! When the pain starts, breathe in and out two times, and then take a deep breath and hold it and PUSH!! Ready? Now breathe...in and out...take a big one...now hold it...and PUSH!"

After several attempts to push the baby down, I collapsed on the table. I moaned, "I can't do it; I don't have any more strength."

The nurse coaxed, "Please, Lil, just one more big push and the baby will be born."

I know it was God's strength that helped me take a final deep breath and push until my face turned blue..but a moment later a wriggly warm piece of life came into the world. It was a seven-pound-one-ounce baby girl! I started to crawl off the delivery table to get a closer peek at her.

Dr. Fairbrother yelled, "Whoa, come back here, Mrs. Sparks. My work isn't finished yet."

Unknown to me, the doctor was having trouble delivering the placenta and I had started hemorrhaging.

The nurses brought the sweet chubby-cheeked girl over to my side — she was absolutely adorable. The neonatal specialist gave us a word of encouragement, "Your little girl looks fine. Her vital signs are excellent and I see no immediate problem with her skin. We will keep her in isolation for twenty-four hours, just as a precaution. Then she can go into the regular nursery."

I was elated beyond words. And so glad the delivery was

over! Dr. Fairbrother put in the last stitch and then congratulated me. I gave him a big hug and a kiss of appreciation. He had fought with us all the way. His skillful confidence had aided in the safe birth of our beautiful child.

Steve kissed me good-night in the recovery room and hurried to call our parents. In spite of the physical ordeal I had been through, I felt wonderful. It was 10:30 p.m. and I was ready to stay up all night. I gave myself a sponge bath, splashed on perfume and powder, and snuggled into a pretty pink nightgown.

At three in the morning, the nurse transported me to a room on the maternity floor. As we passed by the newborn nursery, I queried, "Do you think I could see my little girl?"

She disappeared for a few moments and returned with a tiny bundle in a pink blanket. She placed the baby in my arms. I was awed at how fragile she was. Carefully, I opened her blanket and touched her downy soft skin. I tickled her toes and rubbed the light brown hair around her face. She stretched her arms and yawned. I tried to suppress my emotions, but the tears of joy streamed down my cheeks. I held this precious gift from God close to my breast. I felt her warm skin against mine. I whispered, "I love you, Jenell Lynn Sparks. Jenell means 'a precious gift from God,' and that's exactly what you are."

*"Delight thyself also in the Lord, and he shall give thee the desires of thine heart. Commit thy way unto the Lord; trust also in him, and he shall bring it to pass" (Ps. 37:4, 5).*

# 5

# NIGHTSONG

*"I will remember my song in the night; I will meditate with my heart; And my spirit ponders...Weeping may last for the night, But a shout of joy comes in the morning" (Ps. 77:6; 30:5b).*

"A tear in the eye, a lump in the throat, but a song in the heart" was the title of a sermon I will never forget. As a Bible school student I heard hundreds of sermons, sat in countless class sessions and seminars, but this masterpiece, delivered by Dr. Leonard W. Heroo, president of our school, struck a tender chord in my heart. Little did I realize how often I would experience the reality of this message.

The "night" experiences occurred frequently for our family. Each one was another opportunity for God to prove His faithfulness to us. I thought of different Bible personalities who endured tribulation and yet the Lord gave them a "song of deliverance." The psalmist David cried, "He brought me up out of the pit of destruction, out of the miry clay; And He set my feet upon a rock making my footsteps firm. And He put a new song in my mouth, a song of praise to our God" (Ps. 40:2,3).

During the Lord's Last Supper with His followers, they sung a hymn together. A song even in the hour of betrayal.

Imprisoned deep within a Philippine dungeon, Paul and Silas learned how to sing in the night. In spite of the open cuts in their backs, the uncomfortable stocks around their feet, and the damp darkness of their inner cell, they began to sing a nightsong. "...about midnight Paul and Silas were praying and singing hymns of praise to God, and the prisoners were listening to them" (Acts 16:25). Their songs shook heaven and caused a tremendous earthquake, so that the foundations of the prison were shaken, the doors were opened, and the chains were loosed from all the inmates!

Even in the darkest night God can put a song of victory within our hearts. It isn't easy to sing praises when life hands you a raw deal and trials come knocking at your door..but when we learn the secret of singing in the "nighttime," God always brings sweet deliverance. "Joy comes in the morning" to those who sing songs of praise in the night.

Bryon was ready to celebrate his seventh birthday, when a literal nighttime clouded his life. He awoke one morning with an excruciating pain in his left eye. I kept him home from school, thinking he probably had an infection or a cold in his eye. He slept restlessly throughout the day. The area surrounding the eye continued to swell and turn a dark blue. I placed cold compresses on the left side of his face to reduce the swelling and administered Tylenol for the pain. During the night he whimpered like a hurt puppy and begged to be held. Nothing seemed to relieve the distress.

By the next morning fluid was dripping from his sore eye, causing crust to form on his face. I gingerly lifted the swollen lid to peer inside — I was shocked to see a gray film covering the pupil. His eye looked like one of someone who was blind. It was cold and glassy, like a marble.

Without trying to sound anxious, I mentioned to Steve

that we should call an eye specialist and have Bryon examined. It was only a few weeks before that we had visited Dr. Chotiner, a pediatric eye specialist, for a routine check-up to see if Bryon needed glasses. Patients suffering from EB often have difficulty swallowing, eliminating, and seeing — due to the involvement of all the mucous membranes. Bryon had a colon replacement due to an esophageal stricture when he was three-and-a-half years old — now we feared his eyesight would be damaged.

I scheduled an appointment for 11:00 a.m. with Dr. Chotiner. Bryon could not stand to have a light on in the room. So going out into the sunlight was sheer torture. Wearing a pair of Mickey Mouse sunglasses while clinging to my arm, Bryon stumbled into the professional medical building and down the hall. My little "blindman" could not see two feet in front of him.

When I lifted Bryon into the optical examination chair, I cautioned the doctor to be very gentle with his eye. Not only was it extremely painful, but the surrounding skin was vulnerable to trauma and might slough off. Dr. Chotiner attempted to use care, but when he pulled up the eyelid to determine the problem, the skin peeled away leaving a large denuded area.

Bryon screamed out in terror, "Please don't touch my eye, it hurts so bad...I can't stand the pain any more!"

"Bryon, honey," I whispered gently. "The doctor needs to look in your eye to help you. We really need your cooperation."

Bryon took his small contracted clubs and pulled the eyelid open by himself. He knew exactly how to manage the skin without causing any more damage.

Dr. Chotiner was able to do a thorough examination. When he laid his instruments on the tray, the look on his face told me something was wrong. He stood up and beckoned me to move out of Bryon's hearing range.

Hesitatingly, I inquired, "What is it, doctor?"

"Mrs. Sparks, Bryon has a very serious eye problem. I hope we can help him. He has an ulcer on the cornea of his eye...this is a very devastating and deteriorating condition.

There is a 90% chance he could lose the vision in this eye. We need to begin treating him immediately. I need to do cultures on the ulcer, start him on antibiotics, and put medicated drops in his eye every hour round the clock.''

I found myself at a loss for words. I gulped, "Do you think the hospital is the best place for the treatment?''

"Yes, of course!'' he acknowledged. "In fact, let me call the pediatric floor of the Polyclinic Medical Center right now and set up the admission. I want you to take him right over.''

Somehow I managed to thank the doctor, smile at the nurses, and help Bryon back to the car. In his sweet innocent way, he queried, "Mom, will my eye be okay? When will I be able to see again?''

I was relieved to see that Bryon held his eyes tightly squeezed together to avoid the sunlight...for the salty tears ran down my cheeks and dripped off my chin. The road seemed to be a blur in front of me. My brain was exploding!

"Who was going to take care of Leann and Jenell? How would I nurse Jenell and spend all day in the hospital with Bryon? Three days from now I was in charge of a district women's convention for a hundred churches...how could I go? Who would stay with Bryon?'' There were no easy decisions...I was sure.

Besides all the mundane details of organizing Bryon's hospitalization, there lodged one fear in my mind..."Would Bryon lose the sight in his left eye?''

I raced home and stayed long enough to grab a bit of lunch, fill Steve in on the details, pack a few of Bryon's clothes, and take off again for the hospital. Soon after Bryon was admitted to the pediatric unit, Dr. Chotiner and Dr. Alvear arrived to perform surgical cultures on the delicate corneal tissue of his eye. Hopefully, these tests would reveal the type of bacteria causing the ulcer and rapid deterioration.

Due to the extreme caution used in performing this procedure, Bryon was anesthetized with an injection of ketamine directly into his leg muscle. Within fifteen seconds, he was frozen into a catatonic state...his eyes remained wide open, tears still flowed down his cheeks, and his mouth formed the words of his final cries. _____

With a razor's edge, Dr. Chotiner gently scraped the surface of the cornea and deposited the tissue into a culture dish. Bryon's face was still grotesquely swollen and discolored. His eye had changed from a bright blue to a deathly gray, and the eyelid was raw and exposed where the skin had peeled away.

Following the procedure, I lifted Bryon's stiffened form and carried him back to his room. The sedation caused him to drift into a much needed sleep. I phoned Steve to see how he was managing with the girls. Of all days for this to happen — it had to be a Wednesday! Steve had Bible study and prayer meeting on his mind. He had already missed a whole day of preparation, due to emergency babysitting. Gratefully, one of the young girls from the church volunteered to stay with Leann and Jenell for the evening. This allowed Steve to attend the service, and I was able to stay at the hospital.

As soon as Bryon awoke, the nurses administered his eye medication. Antibiotic drops were given every hour, along with a special salve. Very bravely, my buddy used his clubs to open his sore eye for the medicine. Each time he said, "I wonder when I will be able to see again? I know if I pray real hard, Jesus will heal my eye...He really loves me, doesn't He?"

I always assured him that Jesus did love him, and he had a special place in God's heart. I knew many people were praying for Bryon, as the urgent need was shared.

Secretly, my soul cried out, "Lord, this little fellow, whom You love, has been through a tremendous amount of suffering in his short lifetime...certainly more than his share. Please perform a miracle and touch his eye. Restore his sight and heal this ulcer. Allow this healing to be a genuine witness to our Jewish doctor and the many others who care for Bryon. Even though this dark experience has tested our faith, we place our complete trust in You, and look for the dawning of a new day in our lives. Jesus, we love You...You are more precious to us than life itself."

Somehow we arranged a schedule where Steve was able to work at the church, the girls were taken care of, and I was free to visit Bryon. The hardest part was leaving him alone at the hospital each night. He hated to see me leave and bravely fought the tears when I walked down the hall towards the elevator.

He received stacks of get well cards, phone calls, and visits from church friends, his school teacher, and relatives. Several grades from the Middletown Christian School, where Bryon attended, compiled colorful scrapbooks for him to read. We displayed the cards all over the walls and lined up the flowers and gifts in the window.

Dr. Chotiner had to leave town for the weekend so he asked an associate eye specialist to checkup on Bryon. He planned to return Sunday evening.

By Friday, the swelling around Bryon's eye had decreased considerably and the bluish color was fading. He was tolerating the twenty-four-hour treatments extremely well, without complaints. He gobbled down the hospital entrees, like he had never seen food before. He looked forward to being propped up in bed, having his meals served to him by a pretty nurse, and watching remote-controlled television. He was able to watch a few programs, but only with his right eye. He still couldn't see because of the ulceration. He also enjoyed the craft activities, brought to his room by the play therapist. This helped to make the long hours away from home more bearable.

At suppertime, I went down to the cafeteria for a sandwich. I briefly munched on a hot ham and cheese and then rushed back to the fourth floor. As I walked down the hall, sweet music filled the corridor. When I got closer to Bryon's room, I recognized the tune. I stood quietly outside his door and listened.

"Wherever I am, I'll praise Him. Whenever I can, I'll praise Him...for His love surrounds me like a sea..." He hit a high note and his voice cracked..."I'll praise the name of Jesus, lift up the name of Jesus, for the name of Jesus lifted me." Heartily, he sang it again.

The raindrops steadily coursed down my cheeks. My little soldier melted my heart. I was so tired and discouraged, wondering if Bryon would regain his sight. I was very busy worrying and fretting, forgetting to praise the Lord. But Bryon was singing a song in the night. He lay on his bed, eyes closed, and offered the sweetest music to heaven. God's presence filled the room and drifted out into the hallway.

When he finally finished the last note, I soundly applauded and cheered, "Bryon, that was beautiful! Sing some more songs!"

He teased, "Hey, Mom, that's no fair! You were hiding on me. I didn't know you were there."

I leaned over and gave him a big hug and ruffled his soft blond hair. His little face glowed with God's love. Truly, Bryon was a priceless gift from God. Through his life we have learned more about the faithfulness of God than any other way.

The next two days were sheer torture for me — I had to be away from Bryon to keep previous commitments. Saturday was an all-day annual convention for the Women's Ministries of our churches. About five hundred women gathered at the First Assembly of God in Harrisburg to participate in a display of floats and a "dime march" to raise finances for two new churches. I was the appointed coordinator for the day's activities. My mother was the invited guest speaker for both the morning and afternoon sessions. I arranged for Lori, Bryon's favorite babysitter, to spend the day with him in the hospital.

Somehow I made it through the day. I smiled at everyone, even though I felt like crying inside. In the closing service, Jayne Grove, our district president, tearfully shared about Bryon's condition and asked the ladies to pray for a miracle. I knew churches across Pennsylvania would begin to intercede.

When the convention concluded, Mom and I headed for Polyclinic Hospital. We were anxious to see how our buddy was doing. Bryon shouted to us as we walked into his room, "Hey, Mom, guess what! I can open my sore eye! Look, it doesn't hurt as bad."

I peeked at his ulcerated eye — it seemed that the color had changed — it appeared a more normal blue. The white part surrounding the pupil was streaked with red, but he was able to follow objects in the room and focus on different things. In one way it didn't surprise me, though, because people from churches across the district had started prayer chains for Bryon's healing. We knew God was answering our prayer.

On Sunday, my mother stayed with Bryon while Lori and I drove to a church in Gettysburg where I was scheduled to speak. I shared in the Sunday school hour and the morning service. The people were moved to tears after hearing Bryon's story from birth. The congregation united in prayer for the healing of his eye.

After a lovely dinner with the pastor and his wife, we returned home. I dropped Lori off at church and drove directly to the hospital. Mom gave me an excellent report of Bryon's progress. He was able to see everything clearly and had very little pain in his eye. I was thrilled.

I encouraged Mom to go to our evangelistic service and I spent the evening with Bryon. It felt so good to relax after running around for two days. Bryon and I played checkers, word match, and candyland. About eight o'clock Dr. Chotiner popped in.

"Hi, Bryon! How are you doing?" he asked cheerfully.

Bryon answered, "Great, doctor! My eye feels much better."

Dr. Chotiner took out his instruments and examined Bryon's eye with a small flashlight. He got up and left for a few minutes and returned with a nurse and more instruments. He reexamined Bryon's eye, then squirted some orange liquid onto the pupil. A puzzled expression came over his face. Finally, he announced, "Let's make a trip to the hospital's optical department. I want to use more professional equipment in checking Bryon's eye."

We positioned Bryon in a wheelchair and whisked along corridors and underground tunnels before arriving at our destination. Bryon was perched high in the optician's chair, while Dr. Chotiner performed various tests. After peering through high intensity lenses for several minutes, he made a big sigh, folded his arms, and leaned back in his chair.

"Well, Son, you must have someone praying for you!" he exclaimed.

_____

Instantly Bryon responded, "Dr. Chotiner, everyone prays for me!"

The doctor chuckled and shook his head, "I'm serious, Bryon. I can't understand it...the chances were so slim for recovery...but your eye is completely healed! There isn't a trace of the ulcer, or even scar tissue! It's unbelievable!"

My heart was filled with praise. Gratefully, I said, "Yes, Doctor, people all over Pennsylvania are praying for Bryon. We put our faith in God and were believing for a miracle. I can't express how thankful we are at this moment. God is so good!"

The Jewish physician stared in open amazement. He was profoundly moved by the evidence he had witnessed to the power of God. With controlled emotion, he asked, "Bryon, would you like to go home with your mom tonight?"

"Yipeeeee!" Bryon screamed. "Let's go pack!"

When we arrived home, we called Daddy at the church. The Sunday evening evangelistic service had just finished. Unable to contain my excitement, I exclaimed, "Guess where Bryon is?"

Cautiously, Steve replied, "Did he come home from the hospital?"

"Yes. Dr. Chotiner released him tonight. He gave him a thorough examination and the results showed that Bryon's eye has completely recovered. It is a divine miracle...God really touched him."

Steve shared the great news with our church people and there was a joint time of rejoicing. God had answered our prayer. We learned to sing in the night and to praise Him when it was easy to complain. There is a sweetness that grows out of righteous suffering that cannot be experienced in any other way. When you walk with the Lord through life's dark valleys, His presence becomes a reality. The songwriter has adequately penned:

> Some thro' the waters, some thro' the flood,
> Some thro' the fire, but all thro' the blood;
> Some thro' great sorrow, but God gives a song;
> In the night season and all the day long.
> —G.A. Young

During the past year I had collected and organized a scrapbook with medical information and newspaper clippings on Bryon's disease — Epidermylosis Bullosa Dystraphica Recessive. There had been no medical research or government-funded projects to discover a cause, treatment, or cure, so I undertook accumulating as much material on the subject as possible. Dr. Domingo Alvear sent me copies of articles that appeared in pediatric journals. Other interested persons continued to send me newspaper articles about children who suffered with this dreaded disease.

It was through these articles that I discovered a national non-profit organization, called D.E.B.R.A., which was founded to help those who suffered with EB and also to promote research. The Dystraphic Epidermylosis Bullosa Research Association was founded by Arlene Pessar, a registered nurse from Brooklyn, New York. Her ten-year-old son, Eric, was also born with EB.

I became a member of DEBRA and eagerly looked forward to the quarterly newsletters, which contained happenings about local DEBRA chapters being formed, helpful hints from medical authorities, and letters from EB victims or their parents. It made me gratefully aware that our family wasn't the only family going through this struggle. Other parents faced the similar frustrations and medical problems of caring for a child with EB. DEBRA helped tremendously in educating doctors and nurses about the need for specialized training in the nursing care of EB children.

Whenever I felt discouraged and complained that my "burden" was too heavy to bear, the Lord always allowed me to meet individuals who suffered more than we had. One such fellow, affectionately nicknamed "the crisco kid," was Michael Hammond. I first learned about Michael through an article from the *National Inquirer*. Michael also suffered from Epidermylosis Bullosa Recessive and had spent most of the ten years of his life in the Sunland Center (a mental institution) of Gainsville, Florida. When he was only two years old, his mother placed him in this hospital, so that she could go to work and support Michael's other brothers and sisters.

Michael was nicknamed "the crisco kid" because he received a treatment twice a day with Crisco vegetable shortening. The nurses scraped his tender skin to remove the previous ointment and bandages, placed him in a whirlpool tub, and then completely wrapped him in Crisco and gauze.

Michael never attended school, and he couldn't feed himself or even sit up without assistance. He had never gone for a ride in the car, played with friends, or received a hug. My heart was moved with compassion. I typed a letter to the director of the institution and related Bryon's condition, treatment, and previous surgeries. I felt that Crisco was not the best choice for treatment and suggested Silvadene, Vaseline gauze, and rolled bandages. I provided the doctor with information on Bryon's colon bypass operation, since Michael was having great difficulty swallowing his food. I received a kind, but formal reply, saying that the doctors were already doing their best for Michael.

A few months later Steve picked up the *Harrisburg Patriot News* and shouted, "Can you believe it? Hey, everybody... here is another story about the 'crisco kid!'" Bryon and I ran from different parts of the house. By the time we reached the living room, a cloud of despair had descended. In big black letters, the headline spelled out — "Crisco Kid Dies!"

With a tremor in his voice, Bryon asked, "Daddy, what happened to Michael?"

"Well, Honey, the paper says that he had trouble with his heart and aspirated during the night. This means he couldn't breathe anymore."

Bryon uttered a pathetic "Oh."

Silence.

"I know it's sad because Michael died...but just think, Dad...he doesn't hurt anymore. No more pain, or bandages, or sores. Michael has all new skin now...right?" Bryon was trying to sound very brave.

"Yes, Bryon. Michael will never hurt again," Steve answered softly.

I was filled with mixed emotions. Realizing the terrible fatality of this disease brought a fresh awareness of the brevity of life. We were grateful for the seven years Bryon had blessed our home. It had not been an easy road. There were many times of intense struggle against infections and repeated damage to his skin — not to mention the constant attempt to achieve a normal way of life. I knew in my heart that Bryon envied Michael just a little — now he didn't hurt anymore!

Several months passed by before Bryon brought up the subject of death again. In June 1981 Bryon was hospitalized for a fever of unknown origin. For two weeks he experienced a high temperature every afternoon. He came home from school, dragged himself through the front door, and collapsed on the couch until supper. He didn't have any energy to play or do homework.

One afternoon I peeked into the living room and found Bryon lying on the couch. I was frightened by what I saw. Bryon had vomited all over the couch, carpet, and his face. His head was tilted back in an awkward position and his eyes were tiny slits. I panicked and ran over to his side.

"Bryon!" I screamed. "Answer Mommy! Are you all right?"

No response.

"Please, Buddy, look at me." I wiped the mucous from his eyes, nose, and mouth and blew gently down his throat. He started to choke and blink his eyes. I blew another puff of air into his mouth...he looked at me and said, "Mom, I am so sick; please help me."

Later that day Dr. Daly admitted Bryon to the Polyclinic Medical Center to do some tests. Bryon stayed fourteen days and kept the doctors puzzled as to the origin of the fever. They finally concluded that he had a viral infection in his lymphatic system, which flared up at certain times during the day. This made Bryon very lethargic and weak. The only cure was bed rest, proper food, and time.

I was forced to leave him alone at night to care for Leann and Jenell, but every morning I was there by nine o'clock to help with breakfast and his skin treatments. While I read, studied, or wrote letters, Bryon played games and worked on his school lessons. We spent valuable time talking about life,

God's plan for our lives, and heaven.

After lunch one day, Bryon bombarded me with questions about heaven. What will heaven look like? What will we eat? Will kids have toys and play games? Will we have to do homework in heaven? Does everybody go there? Will anyone be sick?

Bryon paused for a few moments, thinking about our conversation. Then very seriously he asked, "Mom, do only old people die, or do kids die too?"

I explained, "Death is no respecter of persons. In other words you may die at any age — as an infant, child, teenager, or older person. Age is not a factor. Death may come as a disease, long illness, an accident, or tragedy. The most important thing is to know that we are ready to meet Jesus and spend forever with Him."

"Ummmmmmm," mused Bryon, pondering more deeply these heavy subjects. "Mom, can you answer just one more question? Does it hurt to die?"

I paused and weighed each word, "Well, Sweetheart...sometimes people just fall asleep in the arms of Jesus and they don't feel any pain. But other times people hurt very much when they die; especially if they are sick for a long time. For those who know the Lord it is just passing from one life to another...going through an open door into heaven... where there is no pain!"

Bryon stared at me with intense concentration. He lay back on his bed and folded his arms across his chest. I could almost hear the wheels turning inside his little brain.

With an air of subtle finality, he looked into my eyes and declared, "Going to heaven sounds great...but it's the dying part that gets me!"

I suppressed a grin and allowed the truth of this statement to strike home. Bryon was right — dying is the part that gets most of us. Dying to self and selfish desires. Paul expressed it so beautifully in Galatians:

*"I have been crucified with Christ; and it is no longer I who live, but Christ lives in me; and the life*

---

*which I now live in the flesh I live by the faith in the Son of God, who loved me and delivered Himself up for me" (Gal. 2:20; NAS).*

# 6

# THE WHITE TORNADO

The hot beads of water massaged my shoulders and ran down my spine. I worked up a foamy lather between my hands and rubbed it into my wet hair. An early morning shower always gave me new incentive to begin each day. Bristling with energy, I began to hum the tune of the praise chorus, "This is the day/this is the day that the Lord hath made/I will be glad and rejoice in it…"

I heard my two-year-old daughter, Leann, slam the bathroom door several times. She was busy muttering to herself in monotonous chatter. Each time she opened the door, a gust of cold air blew into the room. Slightly annoyed, I yelled above the spray, "Leann, what are you up to?"

Very innocently, she replied, "Nuttin', Mom!"

"Well, I hope it's nothing!" Somehow I knew Leann was into something mischievous, but I wasn't too anxious to find out her preoccupation.

I turned off the water and slid open the glass door. My lower jaw dropped to the floor — I could not believe my eyes! There were clothes in the sink, on the toilet, all over the floor, and bulging out of the hamper. They were all Leann's clothes. Apparently, she had emptied her entire dresser drawers and closet. Standing in the middle of the heap was a bare-bottomed little girl. She was scrutinizing one piece of clothing at a time...first a blouse, then a pair of pants, next a dress, and then some underwear...all the while vigorously shaking her blond curls. I felt my blood pressure slowly rise. I placed my hands on my hips and whispered through clamped teeth, "Leann Joy Sparks, what do you think you are doing?"

Leann quickly imitated me by putting her hands on her hips and replied matter-of-factly, "Mom, I don't know what to wear."

She was so serious and calm about the whole situation and looked so comical standing there stark naked that I burst out laughing. On the other hand, I felt like crying because of the time it would take to sort, fold, and put away all her clothes. My mind jutted back to a few minutes earlier when I was enthusiastically humming, "This is the day that the Lord hath made." Thoughtfully, I questioned, "Lord is *this* really the day that You have made? Or perhaps I should go back to bed and start over again?"

Our family has experienced a wide spectrum of living — ranging from unexpected humor to heartbreaking trials. Each child the Lord has entrusted us with has taught us valuable lessons in character building. We have learned how to laugh together and even laugh at ourselves. Most important — to have more patience. When I tease my honey by saying, "Steve, you don't have any patience," his immediate response is, "I do have patience, Dear, but just not enough!"

A verse I often heard as a child sums it up: "Patience is a virtue, possess it if you can, seldom found in women, but never found in men!"

I don't know how true this statement is, but I do know that children have a way of stretching our patience. The Bible says — "tribulation worketh patience" (Rom. 5:3; Scofield), and kids certainly provide the tribulation.

Our second child, Leann Joy, was nicknamed various things like "hurricane," "disaster area," and "white tornado." Perhaps these expressions will give you a faint idea of some of Leann's early escapades. Someone once commented after meeting Leann, "Your little girl must wake up looking for something to happen!" And believe me, wherever Leann was — it happened!

Reflecting on the contribution Leann has made to our family, I can truthfully say that she has been God's special instrument in teaching me the meaning of 1 Thessalonians 5:16-18: "Rejoice always; pray without ceasing; in everything give thanks, for this is God's will for you in Christ Jesus."

Rejoicing, praying, and giving thanks is a full-time effort. There are many times I don't feel like rejoicing or praying, and I especially don't feel like giving thanks for everything! But the Word of God doesn't give us much choice; in fact, it really sounds like a command in these verses. God expects the best from His followers.

One evening as we prepared to go out for dinner, I had an opportunity to test my spiritual growth in these areas. I had given the children an early supper, stacked the dirty dishes in the dishwasher, and then left Leann in the kitchen to play with our six-week-old cocker spaniel. I scurried into the bedroom to put on some make-up and slip on a pretty dress. Only five minutes had passed when Bryon started screaming for help.

"Mommy, you better come quick. I think this could be dangerous...I can't believe it — there is soap everywhere!"

The serious tone of Bryon's voice caused me to drop my lipstick on the dresser and dart down the hall. I stopped in front of the gate in the kitchen doorway — my eyes widened in amazement at the scene before me. Mountains of white soap-suds were bubbling out of the dishwasher and onto the kitchen floor.

Leann and "Buffy," our cocker spaniel, were delighted at this strange occurence and were gleefully sliding from one end of the room to the other. The dog was barking and wagging his tail. Leann was laughing and throwing the bubbles into the air. Poor Buffy wasn't trained yet and began doing messes all over the floor.

In a slightly elevated tone, I commanded, "Leann, stop

sliding in that water right now! What is this? A circus? I can't believe my eyes. What a horrible time for the babysitter to arrive."

Leann stopped dead in her tracks. She looked terribly guilty. Sheepishly she offered, "I'll help you clean up, Mommy...I'm sorry." Without waiting for me to answer, she reached down and picked up a doggie "poop" in each hand. She wanted to throw them away.

I gasped a big breath, made an ugly face, and shouted, "Leann, put them down right now...they are dirty and will make you sick. Yuk! Yuk!" I shuddered thinking about it.

Leann looked down at her soiled hands, crinkled up her nose, and then wiped her hands on her clean yellow dress.

I was horrified, "Leann, not on your dress, Honey!"

Then absolutely mortified, I watched as she wiped the waste in her hair. "What is this, a soap opera? Or the little rascals? I must be dreaming." But to my dismay it was very real.

Before I could climb over the gate and rescue my daughter, the doorbell rang. It was the babysitter. I grinned as I opened the door, "Come in, Lori. You have arrived just in time to help me clean up a colossal catastrophe!"

Lori peeked into the kitchen, took one glance at the suds, "poopy" Leann, and scared Buffy, and began to double over with laughter. Before long I was giggling so hard that the tears were running down my cheeks. Leann was the only one not overjoyed. She kept repeating, "I don't think this is very funny!"

Thank the Lord for Lori. In a few minutes we had the kitchen cleaned up, Leann too, and Steve and I left for our dinner engagement.

Leann was born with an unusual dose of vivacious energy. Even though she was a seven-month premature baby, she quickly made up for lost time in weight gain and activity. The first week she was home from the hospital she gained over a pound. In three months she had doubled her birth weight, and in six months she had tripled it. Her Norwegian ancestry was evident by her fair curls, milky skin, bright blue eyes, and round chubby cheeks.

_____

At five o'clock in the morning my bouncing daughter was ready to begin the day. As soon as the sun peeked over the horizon, she was out of bed, tugging on my nightgown, asking for bacon and eggs. One morning she awoke at 3 a.m. and wanted me to take her to the pottie. I sat her on the training chair and knelt beside her. She rubbed her eyes, yawned, and then inquired, "Mommy, what are we going to have for breakfast?"

"For breakfast!" I exclaimed. "Leann, do you know what time it is? It is three o'clock in the morning! The sun isn't even up yet!"

"Oh, yes it is!" she announced defiantly. "I just saw it out the window."

I chuckled to myself and then corrected her, "Honey, that's not the sun — it is the moon! Now back to bed for a few more hours of sleep."

Leann certainly added the spice to life in our family. There was never a chance for boredom or time to wonder what was next — Leann's imagination worked overtime in that department.

One escapade, which I will call "the flour caper," is an experience never to be forgotten. Some day Leann will be able to describe all the details herself. She had just celebrated her second birthday — it was November 1980.

Our church was hosting a weekend seminar on Bible prophecy with teacher/evangelist Rev. Robert Lundstrom. Our former Bible college professor was a guest in our home and I wanted to be the perfect hostess and pastor's wife. In the back of my mind I desired to show him that his hours of instruction were not in vain — I was living proof!

The house was nearly spotless, the meals were gourmet specialties, and the children had been tutored in their behavior. Each evening I planned an early supper so that we had time to enjoy fellowship, wash dishes, dress the children, and get myself ready for the service.

Saturday night everything was completed except to throw on a dress and brush my teeth. Steve had left early to get the church ready for the meetings. He warned me not to be late, as

I was playing the piano and escorting the evangelist. When I buttoned Leann's red velvet dress and combed her pretty locks, I sternly advised her to "sit down and be a good girl until we leave for church."

Two minutes later I heard Mr. Lundstrom anxiously calling my name. I ran to the top of the stairs to discover the problem. The astonished minister reported, "Sister Lillian, you better come down here and see what your daughter has gotten into. I can't figure out what it is — but everything is white — from one end of the basement to the other."

I silently groaned and raced down the stairs and into our guest's room. White "stuff" covered his bed, dresser, and floor. Little footprints led into the adjoining laundry/furnace room. I pushed open the door to behold the all-time disaster area. Leann stood behind the furnace in a mountain of white powder. My heart stopped beating and I put my hand over my mouth to stifle a scream. Her hair was white, her red velvet dress was plastered, and the entire room was dusted with white stuff...like an indoor snow storm!

"Where in the world did all this white stuff come from?" I wondered.

Then I spied an empty bag near Buffy, our cocker spaniel ...it was a ten-pound bag of FLOUR! Leann had thought to herself, "Wouldn't this be great fun to dump a bag of flour on Buffy's head." She proceeded to do just that. Poor Buffy was covered from head to toe with flour. He was sneezing and shaking causing the flour to rise like billows of smoke into the air. His eyes were so caked that they began to tear — making paste between his lashes. Leann had made little white footprints all through the laundry, family, and guest rooms.

I glanced at my watch...it was 6:50 p.m. Only ten more minutes until church started. I was inches away from losing my cool — I felt like a boiling tea kettle ready to blow off steam. Leann looked like she could cry any second and Buffy's tail was between his hind legs. I was still debating mentally on exactly how to respond, when I heard a soft voice over my shoulder — it was Bro. Lundstrom! In my exasperation, I had forgotten he even existed.

"Well, Sister Sparks, what are you going to do?" he quizzed.

Inside I wanted to say, "Oh bug-off, Buddy!" But I didn't. Instead I took a deep breath to gain control and unexpectedly began to double with laughter. In fact, I laughed so hard the tears ran down my cheeks. The distraught evangelist didn't know I was laughing — he thought I was having an emotional breakdown! So he put his hand on my back and began to pray out loud for God to help me. The louder he prayed, the harder I chuckled.

I thought to myself, "We're going to be here all night if I don't do something!" So I finally replied, "Dear Brother, I'm really all right. In fact I think this is the funniest thing I've ever seen. I am going to dust Leann off and get everyone ready for church. I know the devil would be pleased if I used this mess for an excuse to stay home. I have a suspicion that the flour will be here when we return from church. I will clean it up then."

I was absolutely right! The flour was there after the service, and even though I swept and vacuumed, I still found flour in our basement months later.

I learned an important lesson through this childish mishap. It would have been very easy for me to respond in anger, lose my self-control and a spiritual victory. This would have only added to the confusion and stress. For it is not enough to have spiritual will power and courage in the face of tragedy, but we need the constraining power of Christ even in the daily interruptions and inconveniences.

It isn't pleasant to start to work on a winter Monday morning and discover that your car has a flat tire, and you must change it in your business suit. We don't feel like shouting when we burn our supper, run our pantyhose, ruin our husband's shirt in the wash, or get the telephone bill in the mail. But Paul tells us to "rejoice always." It is a difficult command, but one that makes the difference between the Christ-controlled character and the unbeliever. Our neighbors, people at work, and our family members want to see the evidence of "down-to-earth" Christianity in our lives. Not just a "do as I say, but not as I do" religion.

Christ changes us from the inside out when He comes into our lives. Second Corinthians 5:17 tells us, "Therefore if any man is in Christ, he is a new creature; the old things passed away; behold, new things have come." The "old things" include grumbling, complaining, losing one's temper, doubting, and gossiping. The "new things" are praising, giving thanks, praying, and saying kind, encouraging words.

I love the words to the chorus recorded by the Brooklyn Tabernacle Choir on their live album — "Jesus on the inside/working on the outside/Oh, what a change in my life!"

Someone has said, "Your walk talks, and your talk talks, but your walk talks louder than your talk talks." (There is a lot of meaning in this tongue-twister.)

When I felt confident that I had mastered one more lesson towards Christian maturity, the Lord tested me in another area. If I ever complained about Leann's endless energy and continuous mischief, I was cured when she became violently ill.

The warm spring weather of May 1981 had lured the children outside to play on the swings or in the sandbox. Leann mentioned at lunchtime that she didn't feel well and had a stomach ache. I laid her down for a nap and she slept for three hours. When she came out to the kitchen and fell down on the floor by my feet, I guessed something was wrong. I felt her forehead — she was burning with a fever.

During the evening I tried to force liquids and give her some Tylenol, but she couldn't keep anything on her stomach. She vomited every half-hour all night and then started with diarrhea about three o'clock in the morning. She was so pathetic, sitting on the commode, holding a bucket in her lap. I was so exhausted from getting up every fifteen or twenty minutes, that sometimes I didn't even hear her weak cries for help as she lay in her bed or on the floor covered with body fluids.

At 6 a.m. I rolled over in bed and realized that Leann hadn't called me for quite a while. I threw back the covers and darted into her room. She lay on the floor, stained with vomit, her eyes closed. I noticed that her skin had turned a pale blue color, and small red spots had formed on her arms and legs. I called her name, but she didn't respond. I tried to sit her up and shake her shoulders — her head dangled precariously backwards. Her skin felt scorching hot, so I decided to take her temperature.

When the thermometer registered 106 degrees and then went higher, I was shocked. I took it again to make sure...the red mercury rose to the highest point on the instrument. I gently slapped Leann's cheeks and called her name again, but she was unresponsive.

Very calmly, I shook Steve and whispered, "Honey, Leann is delirious. Her temp is 106 and she is not answering me. I am going to call the doctor." Steve opened his eyes and tried to comprehend what I was saying, but like most fathers he had slept through the nightmarish hours and was unaware of the severity of his daughter's condition.

The pediatric nurse stated very matter-of-factly to place Leann in a tub of cold water to bring her temperature down. I kept repeating that her fever was over 106 and she was incoherent, but apparently she thought I was over-reacting. I hung up the phone and attempted to follow her instructions.

I undressed my limp babydoll and laid her in the bathtub filled with cool water. Her skin turned a deeper blue and she began to tremble violently, I could hardly hold onto her.

Fear gripped my heart. I shouted, "Stephen, please come and help me. Leann is very sick." Together we wrapped her in a large towel and carried her back to bed. I took her temperature one more time...it was 105.8.

This time when I called the doctor's office, I asked to speak directly to Dr. Daly. I briefly related some of Leann's symptoms...continuous vomiting and diarrhea...high fever of 106 ...blue skin covered with red dots...delirious and incoherent.

Dr. Daly immediately urged, "Bring her to the office right away. We want to see her."

In twenty minutes she was lying on the examining table in

---

the pediatric treatment room. Dr. Daly and Dr. Jones discussed the various possible causes for her high fever. They considered food poisoning, meningitis, a viral infection, and internal complications. They finally decided to admit her to the hospital for blood tests and x-rays. Due to the fact that she hadn't kept anything on her stomach for twenty-four hours, they were concerned about dehydration.

I carried my thirty-pound baby across the parking lot and up to the fourth floor pediatric unit. The resident intern immediately took her vital signs and started intravenous fluids. They drew blood and tested her urine and stool samples for infection. She was still very groggy, but more aware of my presence. I held her gently in my arms and helped her to sip on a ginger ale. As I rocked her to sleep, her sweaty forehead nestled against my breast. I stroked her soft curls and whispered a prayer: "Lord, forgive me for ever complaining about my little girl's joyous energy and wild imagination...she is a precious gift from You. You have filled her with love, excitement, wonder, and creativity. Help me to never take her for granted again. Lord...You only lend us our children for such a short time...to nurture...love...and guide their footsteps. I want to make every moment count for eternity. Touch her weakened body by Your great power and make her well. I want to praise You and thank You...Amen."

The five days Leann spent in the hospital were traumatic. It tore me apart to leave her alone at night. She clung to the sides of her crib, shaking the metal bars, and calling "Mommy" down the hall. The pain grew more intense with each step I took. Five-month-old Jenell and seven-year-old Bryon were depending on me to care for them also.

The tests showed that Leann had a respiratory infection and also a rare form of dysentery, called "salmonella." The only treatment was to starve the bacteria in her intestines for four or five days, by giving her only fluids and intravenous medication. She was kept in protective isolation and every member of the family had to have tests for evidence of the bacteria.

We were puzzled as to how Leann contracted the germs. I

racked my brain trying to think of the places we had been, what she had eaten or had come in contact with. Then one morning, looking out the kitchen window, it hit me...the sandbox! The day before Leann got sick, she had spent the morning playing with her neighbor friend, Adam, in the sandbox. It was the first time this spring. The doctor had asked if we had visited a foreign country, or entertained missionaries, or come in contact with the waste from animals. Now I put the two together — the stray cats defecated in the sandbox at night and then the kids played in the sand during the day. Besides, Leann had a runny nose, so she probably wiped her face with her hands. Thus she picked up the germs and became infected. What an unbelievable set of circumstances!

On Mother's Day we were able to bring our little sweetheart home. For the next few weeks she clung to me and always wanted to hold my hand. It took a long time for her to be toilet-trained after this traumatic experience. She had previously been trained, but after being catheterized, she refused to go "pottie" or move her bowels and became very constipated. Bushels of love, patience, and time were the ultimate cure for Leann.

The healing process was slow, but it was complete. In a month our little girl was back to her normal self, getting into everything possible. When I discovered one day that she had unrolled the toilet paper into the commode, I remembered my prayer...not to complain about her abundant energy. I scolded her, patted her bottom, and then took her with me to the kitchen to make cookies.

Paul said, "In everything give thanks." This is definitely a tall order! Many times we are tempted to complain and we don't feel like thanking or praising. Perhaps this is the praise that pleases God's heart the most — when it is a real sacrifice of praise. Hebrews 13:15,16b tells us "Through Him then, let us continually offer up a sacrifice of praise to God, that is, the fruit of lips that give thanks to His name...for with such sacrifices God is pleased."

The well-known songwriter Lanny Wolfe has expressed it this way:

*In everything give Him thanks, give Him thanks,*
*In everything give Him thanks, give Him thanks,*
*In the good times praise His name,*
*In the bad times do the same,*
*In everything give the King of Kings all the praise.* [1]

[1]"In Everything Give Him Thanks," Words and Music by Lanny Wolfe, Copyright 1978 Lanny Wolfe Music/ASCP. "Reprinted by special permission of Pathway Press, Cleveland, Tennessee."

# 7

# A STILL SMALL VOICE

"How can I know God's will for my life?" is perhaps one of the most perplexing questions a young Christian faces. As a recent high school graduate and at the tender age of eighteen, I was convinced that I had my future precisely planned. In my mind I envisioned myself as the perfect housewife, neatly dressed, every hair in place, make-up on, and a frilly apron tied around my waist. I greeted my family each morning with a cheery "hello" and seated them at a breakfast table decorated with scrambled eggs and bacon, orange juice, toast and jam, and steaming cups of freshly-perked coffee. I spent hours a day reading to my three children, going for leisure walks in the park, and playing the baby grand piano in the living room. My husband, a well-known recording artist, traveled from coast to coast to appear in concert.

In all of my dreams I had forgotten the most important factor — "Where does God fit into my plans?" Being raised in a Pentecostal minister's home, I had always been very sensitive to the presence of God. Even at the young age of two, my mother discovered me kneeling at our church altar, tearfully expressing my love for Jesus. When I was five, I accepted Christ as my personal Saviour during our family devotions. Dad read a beautiful Bible story about heaven and stressed the importance of being ready for Christ's second return. I quietly raised my hand and announced to the family — "I need Jesus in my heart...I know I am not ready to go to heaven!" With heads bowed, Dad led me in the sinner's prayer of repentance. What a blessed peace filled my young heart. From that moment, I had the joyful assurance of being a child of God.

My teenage years were the usual times of struggle, confusion and indecision. Many influences caused my commitment to Christ to take a second place. I felt the pressure from school peers, church friends, and the fellows I dated. My only ambition in life was to marry the young man I was "madly" in love with and have a family. But God had other plans for my life.

One Sunday morning during our worship service, God began to deal with my heart. I felt the tender conviction of the Holy Spirit pricking at my conscience — yet I ignored God's presence. Even though God was ministering to many people in the congregation, I refused to soften my stubborn will. I clamped my teeth shut, squinted my eyes into tiny slits, and gripped the edge of the pew with my fists.

The Lord gently nudged, "Lillian, you have left Me out of your life. I love you and I want to use you for My glory. Commit yourself to Me...give Me your all...you will be amazed at what I have in store for your life!"

I batted my eyelashes furiously, but it was in vain. The hot prideful tears streamed down my cheeks and onto my flowery print dress. Futilely, I dabbed my hanky at the green and blue mascara dripping from each eyelid. In this moment of brokenness, I surrendered my life to Christ once again. The cleansing process at work in my heart was exhilarating! My unyielding pride and selfish will melted away. In its place came the peaceful resignation to do the will of God.

During this experience God called me into full-time ministry and gave me the desire to attend Bible school for training. I attended Zion Bible Institute for three years and it was there I met my husband, Stephen Sparks. The Lord blessed my life with a precious man of God — someone whose dedication and love for Christ is now the stronghold of our family. His joyful optimism, uncanny wit, and romantic mannerisms are the reasons for my loving adoration.

The Lord has always given us direction for each new step in our lives. After we were married, we knew He was leading us to finish our education at Northwest College in Kirkland, Washington. Then the opportunity opened to pastor a small rural church in Middletown, Pennsylvania. During the seven-and-a-half years we ministered to this lovely congregation, God blessed our home with three precious children: Bryon Todd, Leann Joy, and Jenell Lynn. The church family was growing, the finances had multiplied, and we enjoyed living in our new split-level home. We were happy and contented. We desired nothing else but to spend the rest of our days in this comfortable setting.

Yet we kept our minds and hearts open to the voice of God. We were willing to stay in this place of ministry as long as God kept us there, and we were also willing to follow God's direction.

For about a year God had been speaking to us about going back to our alma mater, Zion Bible Institute, as teachers. But there seemed to be no opening. Naturally thinking, it was not the most rational decision, due to the fact that teachers and staff members were paid no stipulated salary. The administration provided housing and some food staples, but remuneration only occurred after all the school's expenses were taken care of. To uproot a family of five from a comfortable living and trust God to provide all of their needs would be a tremendous step of faith. Whenever we discussed the possibility of moving to Zion, Stephen usually expressed his reluctance.

In May 1980 we attended the Spring Convention and Graduation exercises held in East Providence, Rhode Island. We delighted in renewing old acquaintances and meeting former classmates. On a Friday evening following our annual alumni banquet, we returned to Sinclair Hall (the main men's dormitory), to find our children sound asleep. We tip-toed into the room and crept into the large walk-in closet. We started to prepare for bed. All of a sudden, Steve took me into his arms and began to cry softly.

Surprised, I whispered, "Honey, what is the matter?"

"I have struggled in my heart for a long time about coming to Zion and living by faith. For the first time since we graduated, I can say that I have made the commitment and I am willing to do whatever God wants me to." Steve was genuinely broken.

We lingered in each other's embrace and relished the quietness of our secret closet of prayer...we determined to follow God's will...no matter the cost. We felt the sweet presence of the Holy Spirit.

We expressed our desire by writing to the principal of the school. Rev. Mary Campbell wrote us a beautiful letter telling us that there were no openings at the present time. We received this reply as a closed door and felt that perhaps God was testing our consecration.

Nine months later a letter arrived from the president of the school, Dr. Leonard W. Heroo. My hands trembled as I tore open the envelope. My eyes filled with tears as I read..."if you are still interested in belonging to Zion's family of faith, please notify me immediately."

My heart pounded for joy. I couldn't wait until Stephen came home, so I called him at the church office. "Honey, come right home. I have something here for you to read!" He was home in five minutes.

When he picked up the letter and started to scan its contents, I saw a light in his eyes. His face softened into a relaxed smile. We looked at each other. No one had to tell us. We knew deep in our hearts — this was God!

We made a special trip to Zion's campus for an interview with Dr. Heroo. This outstanding world Pentecostal leader was kind, honest, and yet challenging. We felt the Holy Spirit tugging on our hearts to move in this direction.

As we drove the four hundred miles back to our cherished congregation, we were torn with mixed emotions. Each time I thought about saying good-bye to our flock and some of our dear friends, it was difficult to control the tears. This would be a tremendous transition indeed, but we knew the call of God was greater than our earthly feelings.

I thought of the Old Testament prophet, Elijah, who had camped in a cave at Mount Horeb. He was feeling very alone and was looking for a word from the Lord. He was in despair because the children of Israel had forsaken God's covenant, destroyed their altar, and killed off the prophets. He said, "And I alone am left; and they seek my life, to take it away" (1 Kings 19:10b).

God was faithful and He revealed Himself to Elijah. The Lord showed Elijah "a great and strong wind," an earthquake, and a fire. But God was not in any of these things. Finally Elijah heard "a still, small voice" (1 Kings 19:12b; Scofield), and God spoke words of comfort and reassurance. Elijah was not the only one left, but seven thousand others in Israel had not bowed down to Baal.

Often when individuals are seeking for God's will in their lives, they are looking for the wind, the fire, and the earthquake. They seem to expect lightning to strike from the sky and thunder to roar in their ears. They are too busy finding the solution themselves to hear the "still, small voice" of God. As we wait quietly in God's presence, we will feel the gentle tugging at our hearts and the soft whisper in our ears, saying, "this is the way, walk ye in it."

Sunday, May 31, 1981, was a very difficult day in our lives. It was our resignation service from Glad Tidings Assembly of God, in Middletown, Pennsylvania. We had faithfully served this closely knit family of believers for seven-and-a-half years. The separation was painful. When we arrived in these rolling Dutch farmlands, we were twenty-two years old, expecting our firstborn, and everything we possessed fit into a small U-haul van. The church provided a minimum óf living expenses, and we had to spend our first week house-hunting in the bitter February cold, as there was no parsonage. But now we were saying good-bye to a vibrant body of Christians, lifetime friends, neighbors, and a beautiful bi-level home. The future was uncertain in many ways, but we knew God would supply.

Stephen conducted himself admirably throughout the service. His exuberant spirit encouraged the congregation to worship in a spontaneous volume of praise...it was as the sound of "many waters." As I hit the keys of the upright Chickering, I don't even remember what hymns we sang...I was bracing myself for the dreaded speech. After an anointed sermon, Stephen cautiously pulled a single sheet of paper from the back of his Bible. He cleared his throat and began to read the carefully thought out words. The tone of their finality filled the air.

The congregation sat in stunned silence. I saw their confusion, and then a sorrowful realization at the sound of their pastor's words. I tried not to gaze into their eyes...the hurt was too much to bear. We were so happy and contented in our ministry, the people felt we would stay forever.

Near the end of Stephen's letter, his voice wavered with emotion and for a moment I thought he might cry. But he pulled himself together with great courage and led the people in singing the doxology. "Praise God from whom all blessings flow..." the voices lifted the strains toward heaven. Many were openly weeping, handkerchiefs covering their faces. I felt the tears flow freely down my cheeks, and I didn't try to stop them. I needed to cry...it was a hurting time.

Our church family was saddened by our leaving, but they graciously accepted God's will for our lives. They would not stand in the way of the call of God. Most them were consoled by the fact that "just another church" didn't steal us away, but that we were going to teach in a Bible college. It made them feel like they were sending us out as home missionaries.

In the remaining six weeks of pastoring, we spent every night in a different home for dinner. We received about forty invitations for fellowship. Besides having a wonderful time of sharing, we also gained about ten pounds! We ate a variety of delectable dishes — ranging from southern fried chicken to lobster and shrimp scampi!

In the midst of the packing and running to engagements we had time to reminisce over many meaningful experiences. Like the elderly woman who lovingly gave us the finances each month to send Bryon to the Middletown Christian School. Another white-haired saint diligently upheld our family with prayer and kept me supplied with dainty crocheted hankies. My mind breezed over the delightful times we had at church picnics and suppers, special birthday parties for the pastor, children's crusades, teachers' seminars, ladies' night out, Christmas programs, kids' musicals, and choir productions ...the list was unending. Stephen reminded me of the young people he had counseled, baptized in water, and dedicated children of couples he had married. And perhaps the most precious times..the hours spent around the altars rejoicing over one who had found Christ or received the fullness of the Holy Spirit.

The Church people were always loving and giving. They remembered us with love offerings at Christmas and on birthdays. They gave a harvest food shower each year, baby showers when I was expecting, and special treats for the children. How could I ever forget the ladies who helped clean my house, provided babysitting, and remembered me with special gifts? They would always be our cherished friends.

God's timing is always perfect. It was no exception in the life of one of our young girls from the church — Lori Ann. When Lori was fifteen her family started attending our assembly. They were a tremendous blessing to our church family. Her father became our Sunday school superintendent, and her mom was a leader for the Women's Ministries. Lori was a timely God-send for our family. Because of her sensitivity and devotion for children, she fit right in our home. Bryon fell in love with her. She spent long hours learning how to care for his needs, mastering his bandages and blisters. Her patience with our kids was amazing. They would climb all over her, play tricks, and even try to disobey...but Lori was always firm and loving.

Lori had a difficult struggle during her junior and senior years of high school to find God's will for her life. We spent many evenings together going for a drive or sitting in Dempsey's restaurant eating cheese steak sandwiches and drinking diet coke. We discussed her interests of child care, music, and sports. Most of the time I tried to be a good friend and listener. I knew she had the qualities to make an excellent ministry student, but I didn't want to push my feelings — it had to be her decision.

When Lori told us she was applying to Zion Bible Institute as a freshman, I could hardly contain my excitement. Unknown to Lori, we had already been approached by the president, Dr. Heroo, to join the faculty. We kept our secret as long as possible until we knew Lori had confirmed her acceptance to the school. The one drawback for Lori was that she knew she would be separated from the church and our family. She was such an asset in caring for Bryon.

When we confided in her about our invitation to go to Zion, she was ecstatic! What a timely confirmation of God's will for her life. Her desires to learn God's Word, gain musical ability, and care for children were all fulfilled.

The month of June was filled with packing, sorting through accumulated junk, having a neighborhood yard sale, and saying good-bye to many friends. Our last day as pastor and wife of Glad Tidings was Sunday, July 12, 1981. Stephen preached a heartfelt sermon taken from 2 Corinthians 13:11 — "Finally, brethren, farewell."

In the afternoon, following the service, we had a lovely picnic lunch for the entire church in a nearby park. The ladies presented me with a farewell card and generous gift. I hugged each one tightly and expressed my gratitude. One woman whispered in my ear, "Sister Sparks, I hope the next pastor's wife is as warm and loving as you. I don't know what the ladies will do without all your hugs and kisses."

I quickly responded, "I'm sure the Lord will give you the best."

For our final worship together, Stephen decided to have a "bread-breaking service." It was a tender moment in our lives. First we shared the cup of communion individually, and then we turned to a close member of our family (spouse or children) and shared a piece of bread with them. Afterwards we endeavored to commune with as many church members as possible. There was such a melting of spirits, a union of mind and soul...words were really inadequate. We wept...embraced ...and prayed. The Holy Spirit hovered over our small assembly until almost midnight.

It was difficult to send the people home...some lingered until Stephen turned out the last light. We locked the doors and stood side by side in the moonlight. Steve held me around the waist and I felt the warm summer breeze blow through my hair. The church was peaceful and quiet now, bathed in the evening light. There was a part of me that wanted to stay there forever, nothing changed, maintaining our routine of ministry and life in this small town. But another part of me yearned to soar with the eagles and meet the challenge of the future. A still, small voice seemed to say, "Your work is done here. I have another harvest field waiting for you...obey My voice."

The call of God was stronger than the desire to stay. Stephen grasped my hand and led me to our car. As we pulled out of the parking lot, I looked over my shoulder at a memory which represented seven-and-a-half years of our lives. I lifted my hand and gently waved..."Good-bye, Glad Tidings, we love you!"

> *"Then I heard the voice of the Lord saying, 'Whom shall I send, and who will go for Us?' Then I said, 'Here am I. Send me!' " (Isa. 6:8).*

# 8

# MISSIONARY MANSION

We followed Libby, the school librarian and head matron, across Zion's neatly laid out campus. In the heart of East Providence, this New England cloister of seventeen red and white painted buildings and Cape-Cod style houses comprised one of the most unique Bible schools in America. The July heat beat down upon us as we rounded a corner and entered the bottom floor of one of the duplex dormitories. The matron's keys jangled as she tried different ones to unlock the apartment door.

Apologetically, Libby explained, "We really don't have room for a family of five. There are only two apartments available and they are quite small. Nothing has been done to get them ready for your coming...they need lots of WORK! As in WORK!"

We peered into the three small rooms and knew imme-diately the kind of work she meant. Wallpaper hung down in strips from the ceiling. Broken windows were propped open with sticks or whatever could be found. The linoleum was cracked and worn away to show the base wooden floor. All the faucets leaked. The bathroom mirror was broken, and the grayish-green rug was heavily soiled. One room would have to serve as a kitchen and eating area, another as a living room, and the third...well, could five people sleep together in one room?

Steve sensed my perplexity and knowingly squeezed my hand. For a quick moment, his deep blue eyes met mine, and I understood the meaning, "We're in this together, Honey. Don't worry. Everything will be okay."

With his usual gentle calmness, he asked, "Is it possible for us to look at the other apartment, Sister Libby?"

"Sure, if you're interested. But I'm warning you, the other one is in worse shape than this. You folks will be all summer fixing it up...and classes start the end of August, you know!"

She shuffled her small frame out the door, passed two more red-and-white houses and through the parking lot of the large brick Zion Gospel Temple, the Bible school's center of worship. We crossed Leonard Avenue and climbed the stairs to a similar two-story cottage, which housed senior men students on the second floor. A white sign on the right side of the entry read "Missionary Manor." Down the hall and beyond the sagging steps that led upstairs, I spied a door with brown chipped paint. As the wispy, yet energetic woman pushed open the door, I held my breath. Steve took my arm and lead me into our "possible" new home.

Libby was right. It was a mess! Someone had fallen through the kitchen wall and left a large hole in the plaster in the shape of a body. There was a deep crevice in the floor about six inches wide, where a wall used to be. The shower door was broken and wouldn't slide along the tub. Windows were held up with more sticks, and there were no closets or cabinets for dishes. But there were five tiny rooms, separated by walls and doors. It would do. It would *have* to do!

Steve said confidently, "Tell Dr. Heroo, we'll take it. I'm sure we will be just fine." I had my doubts, but knew in my heart that God was leading us into a new ministry. I fought the quick tears as I thought of the beautiful bi-level parsonage with wall-to-wall carpeting, in Shope Gardens, an upper-middle class suburb of Harrisburg, Pennsylvania. It was a part of our lives that we had left behind. Seven-and-a-half years of memories — were now a long way from here. The faces of our loving congregation mentally appeared and brought fresh pain. The small rural community of Middletown, where we began our ministry following our graduation from Bible college, tried our first "wings of faith," and where all three of our children were born — would not be easily forgotten. The comfortable living and moderate financial security were now gone. We were learning to live a "life of faith."

During the sultry months of July and August, 1981, we discovered new meaning for the cliche — "blood, sweat, and tears!" We rolled up our sleeves and attempted to transform "Missionary Manor" into "Missionary Mansion." Improbable? Yes. Impossible? No.

We emptied the twenty-four foot U-haul rental truck of all our furniture, boxes, and belongings. Everything was stored in the upstairs dormitory while the reconstruction crew was at work below. At night we slept on the students' metal bunkbeds or rolled-out mattresses on the floor. My parents helped by taking care of our two-and-a-half-year-old, Leann, for two weeks. I still had to care for Bryon, with all his medical needs, and nurse a seven-month-old baby in the middle of all this confusion. Jenell never seemed to mind. She crawled from room to room observing people paint, install cabinets, light fixtures, a new shower door and bathroom mirror, build closets, plaster and sand ceilings and walls, and actually enjoyed the commotion.

As she watched one black deacon from the church go into a room and then appear several minutes later completely white with dust, her eyes widened in amazement.

Zion's "live-on" family came to our aid. The next morning, Libby showed up at the front door with a box of donuts and a promise to find us a stove and refrigerator as soon as possible. Two girl students, who were in the summer work program, came by to help put up wallpaper. Doug, the campus handyman, completed the electrical wiring and installed light fixtures. Our brother-in-law John, the "painter," came for five days to plaster, sand, and paint. My cousin, Steve, a self-employed construction worker from Cape Cod, lent his carpentry skills in building bookcases, closets, and cabinets. Many others stopped by just to say hello or give an encouraging word.

We were so thankful that Dr. Heroo, the school's president and pastor, authorized the financial assistance for all the remodeling. We would never have been able to afford such a task.

We were deeply honored that Dr. Heroo had considered us for the positions, as many others had applied. Ten years earlier, we had learned to appreciate his ministry as students. He was considered one of the world's greatest Pentecostal orators. In his prime, he was asked to speak at The World Pentecostal Conference held in Canada. His life, ministry, and sermons made an impact on thousands of people. He instructed my parents and Steve's parents in Homeletics (the art of preaching) while they were students. Now we had the opportunity to teach and minister under his leadership.

Dr. Heroo called Steve the "Cliff Barrows of Pentecost!" His enthusiastic songleading became a favorite time of worship for the Temple congregation and students. We worked together as a team. Steve led the singing; I played the piano. I also helped to organize the special music for all the worship services and begin a twenty-voice choir from the church. Because the three hundred and fifty students made up a sizable part of the congregation, they tended to receive the spotlight. The eighty-voice sanctuary choir was comprised totally of students. Many of the other ministries were under the direction of the young people also: nursing homes, Pawtucket and Chad Brown story hours, children's church, Sunday school, etc. It was important for us to build up the body ministry among the church members. We felt very loved and accepted.

Besides ministering in the Temple, our consuming commitment was to be instructors in the Bible school. Steve taught the History of Christian Education, Comparative Religions, and Church History (where they had more "church" than history!). His real interest was in Pastoral Studies and Church Administration, but during the four years we taught, these subjects were never available. The young people could sense our pastoral hearts, and many affectionately called Steve "Pastor Sparks."

For eight years the music department had been at a minimum. It was a real excitement and challenge for me, after training for four years in this field, to be allowed to organize a music minor course. The subjects offered were Music Fundamentals, Music Appreciation, Hymnology, Conducting, Songleading, Church Music History, and some Arranging. This was close to my heart and I enjoyed every class.

Steve and I were also asked to take on the directorship of the school's traveling choir. This was a sixteen-voice ensemble, with five accompanists, and a sound manager. The "Zion Collegians" ministered throughout the United States, Canada, and on a mission's trip to Sicily, Italy. A tremendous amount of time and effort were needed to put together a team like this.

Our week involved hours of practice, Friday night "prayer and share" times, sectionals, and a commitment to the Sanctuary Choir as well. We were allowed to minister several weekends a month and take a spring break tour in March and a summer tour in June. The Collegians who were selected had musical ability, but beyond that they had key leadership and ministry qualities.

The "Collegians" were a close-knit family. Through the many hours of practice, prayer, and traveling together, we experienced a special bond of God's love. At the end of each year, as we said good-bye to the seniors, our last service on summer tour was more like a "funeral." I always felt bad for that particular church. While they thought we were receiving a special blessing, in reality we were crying over the imminent separation.

To this special group of kids, we became affectionately known as "Mom" and "Dad," even though some of the students were about our age. Our lives were so transparent that a very special kind of discipling took place in their lives. They felt the frustrations we experienced in caring for Bryon, always saying farewell to our children as we left for another tour, and trying to show a proper balance between the "real" and the "spiritual" in ministry. They cried with us over disappointments, misunderstandings, and the loneliness that results when you are committed to God's will.

Through the years we have kept in touch with some of these students. Many of them "fell in love" while they were in Collegians. Now they are married and have children of their own. A large percentage of the group are in active full-time ministry as educators, pastors, or musicians. In fact, our present youth pastor and wife, Peter and Lily Conforti, were some of the first Collegians we ministered with.

Missionary Manor was situated in the middle of Zion's campus. Both our front and back doors were constantly knocked upon by students in need. One night, about 11:00 p.m. we heard a desperate pounding at the back door. Stephen rushed to see who it was. A young freshman was emotionally disturbed and deliberately attempting to take his own life. In our living room, (the only place we had for counseling), we laid hands on the young man and he experienced a wonderful transformation. It was early the next morning when he rose to leave. The "peace that passeth all understanding" (Phil. 4:7) was written across his face.

The wide cross-section of students that came from all over the United States and several foreign countries, coupled with their many backgrounds (some from Christian homes and others converted right off the street), magnified the emotional and spiritual problems we encountered. We dealt with young people who needed deliverance from addicting drugs or habits, those affected with anorexia and bulemia, and others involved with incest and sexual abuse at home. Over a period of months and sometimes years, we saw God change many lives into the image of His Son by His power. The day-to-day pressures were exasperating, but the long-range rewards were great!

The story of Zion is a marvelous epic that deserves a volume to record the accounts of the faithfulness of our God. One of my favorite chapels, as a student, was Monday morning with Rev. Mary Campbell, the principal, and Rosemary

Messerlian, dean of women. They took turns sharing the early beginnings of this work of faith and the great miracles God performed through the obedience of His servants. I sat on the edge of my seat, so as not to miss a word, and wondered where the time went when dismissal came.

God used a young woman named Christine A. Eckman from Guyana, South America, to begin a "faith school" (originally called "The School of the Prophets") for young men and women who could not afford higher education and training to enter the ministry. After arriving in East Providence, Rhode Island, she met and later married Rev. Gibson, the pastor of a new Pentecostal church. Together they envisioned and saw come to pass a Faith Bible School. The first year the school opened, there were three students, one of whom was an escaped convict. This young man was exposed and returned to the authorities.

Sixty-six years have passed since the first class graduated, and thousands of students have been ultimately touched by the commitment of Christine A. Gibson.

Stephen and I feel doubly blessed to have been dedicated to the Lord by this great woman of God during infancy. Although we did not know her personally, we sensed her fervor for God upon our lives.

Life at Zion was a tremendous challenge and source of spiritual growth, but for our family it was a time of unbelievable pressure. There was pressure to get to our classes and be prepared, to grade examinations, and to be "on call" at any hour of the day and night. We felt as though we lived in a glass house; there was never any privacy or personal family time. We were also houseparents to the ten senior men who lived upstairs. Eighteen hours a day our front and back entrances were used, and the pounding of feet going up and down stairs was heard. For one whole year a student, directly above where we slept, rolled out of bed and fell on the floor about three o'clock every morning. I would wake up and say, "Honey, there's Dave again. It must be 3:00 a.m."

Whenever I baked brownies or cooked a delicious meal, I heard the fellas come in the back door, stop, sniff the air, and say, "Sure smells good, doesn't it? Boy it makes me miss my mom's cooking!" Somehow the dining hall food wasn't quite the same. If I knew they were having a big exam the next day, I brewed a pot of coffee, baked some goodies, and carried them upstairs. The smiles on their faces, as they opened the door, were certainly worth the effort. Once a month we had the guys down for fellowship and they looked forward to strawberry cheesecake, French chocolate pie, or even a full-course Italian dinner. Believe me, there were never any leftovers.

One Monday morning, as I hustled to get ready for my first period class, I heard Leann call for my assistance. I hurriedly changed Jenell's diaper, hoisted her onto my hip, and walked in the direction of the cry for help. Before I reached the entrance to the kitchen, I noticed that my feet were dripping wet. I was sloshing through two or three inches of water by the time I reached the bathroom door. Leann lifted her curly blond head, threw her arms into the air, and pleaded, "Mom, please don't be mad at me. I was trying to go to the bathroom by myself, like a big girl...but when I flushed the toilet the roll of paper fell in and got stuck!"

I watched, horrified, as the water from the commode came gushing out over the floor like the geyser at Yellowstone National Park. I didn't know what to do first...call for help, put Jenell back in her crib, try to fix it myself...I had to do something immediately! Water was flowing out of the bathroom, across the kitchen floor, into the two adjoining bedrooms, and finally onto our new rust-colored living room carpet.

In desperation, I rolled up the sleeve of my dress blouse and plunged my arm into the swirling, awful smelling water and yanked out the soggy roll of paper. Thank God the overflowing stopped and the toilet finished flushing. I looked around me at the gallons of sewer water swirling around my black leather heels. I had no choice but to put Jenell down and begin the unpleasant task of attempting to clean up this mess.

I glanced at my watch. It was 7:45 a.m. In ten minutes I had to be in Songleading class, ready to teach, and appear presentable. Any moment one of our babysitters, assigned to help watch our children, would be walking through the front door. The thought came to my mind, "She is going to think I'm a terrible mother and housekeeper!" I grabbed as many clean bath towels as possible and quickly spread them over the floors. Leann and Jenell thought we were playing a new game, so they began splashing through the water and stomping on the soaked towels. I groaned in utter frustration as I realized my helplessness in stopping them.

With minutes ticking away, I scooped up a pile of the drenched cloths and headed down the basement stairs to put a load in the washing machine. I yelled over my shoulder, "Girls, now please, don't get into anything else! Mom will be right back."

I hadn't even added the detergent when I heard Leann screaming my name. "Mom! Mom! Hurry up! Jenell bit the tube of super glue and she can't breathe!"

Racing up the stairs, I cried out in disbelief, "What happened now? If I leave you girls alone for one minute, you get in trouble!"

Jenell held the deflated tube of glue in one hand. Gooey liquid was still oozing from the place where her teeth marks were, and she held her head back in an effort to catch her breath. The super glue had filled her mouth and was blocking off her airway. I held her head in my one hand, and with the other attempted to clear her mouth of the poisonous fluid. I reached down, placing my mouth over hers, and blew warm air into her lungs. The bluish hue on her face returned to a more natural pink. Her eyes, which had rolled back in her head, now focused again.

With tears in my voice, I inquired, "Sweetheart, are you okay? Oh, dear Jesus, you could have died! Why did you take the glue out of Mommy's desk drawer? Oh Lord, help me. I'm going to lose control of myself in a minute!"

I glanced at Jenell again. Something seemed strange. She was breathing all right...but...but...Oh no! Her tongue was stuck to the bottom of her chin and she could not speak! She walked around making strange grunting noises, trying to say words, but nothing would come out. I pulled gently at her tongue, but it was solidly glued to her chin.

I decided to call the Rhode Island Poison Control to see if there was anything more I could do. First, I got a recording that told me all the lines were busy and I must wait for the next free attendant. Shortly, a polite gentleman answered, "Yes, Ma'am, what can I do to help you?" I quickly explained the situation and I heard him chuckle on the other end. He replied, "Well, it sounds like you have everything under control. Just apply warm water to your daughter's chin...perhaps some Vaseline also. If her tongue does not loosen, then call your pediatrician." He hung up.

There was a knock at the front door — it was the baby-sitter. I shouted, "Come in at your own risk!" Surprised, she cautiously entered. One glimpse of the "disaster zone" and she immediately understood. I tried to call my husband at the administration office before he left for Church History class. When he answered the phone, I cried, "Oh Honey, you will never believe what has happened here this morning. Leann stuck a roll of toilet paper down the commode and tons of water has flowed all over our apartment. I tried to soak it up with towels, but while I was putting a load in the washer, Jenell ate a tube of super glue and her tongue is stuck to her chin. Can you come home and help me?" It poured out in one big breath.

Steve, who seemed to be in a state of shock, answered, "Honey, I'd love to help you, but the entire Junior class is waiting for me. Hey, I'll be praying for you...see you later." Silence...he was gone!

Sometime, while I was on the phone, Jenell's tongue had loosened and she was so relieved to be able to talk again, although her lips, teeth, and tongue were caked with crusty, dried super glue. I futilely attempted to explain the morning's events to the girl student and gathered up my teaching materials, in a last effort to make my class on time.

Suddenly, I realized something was wrong with my hand. In astonishment, I looked down at my fingers...they were completely fused together in a web-like fashion. In the frantic moment that I had cleared Jenell's mouth and airway, my own hand was covered with the sticky substance. Perplexed by the overwhelming circumstances, I finally gave way to tears. But then, a humorous thought struck me, "I'm going to Songleading class (where I wave my hands around in time-beating patterns) and no one will even notice if my fingers are glued together." I was absolutely right. No one even noticed.

Life at Zion was never boring to say the least, especially while trying to raise our children in the midst of a college campus. Jenell became the mysterious "phantom" of Missionary Manor, as she secretly did her devices and left the evidence behind. She loved to sneak upstairs into the men's dormitory, since it was considered "off limits" for our kids. But she always left a trail of trouble.

One young man had a beautiful doll on his bed given to him by his finance'. Jenell fell in love with that doll. When she went up for a short visit, she would ask Brian if she could keep it for just one night. But the answer was always no. One afternoon Brian came to the door with a naked, dirty, and very scraggly-looking doll in his hands. I teased him, "Is that your new doll, Brian?"

"No, it isn't mine," he responded. "I found this poor thing on my bed in place of my sweetheart's doll. Do you think Jenell switched them?"

We discovered that she had watched for Brian to leave for class and then the great "Houdini" made the change. It was incredible! Now the guys were on the look-out for Jenell.

There were other mystery cases to be solved. The case of the bag of Dunkin' Donuts with one or two bites missing from each pastry...and the index file cards for a term paper that were cut into "grass" all around the edges...and of course, the white-bottomed child who was seen streaking through the dormitory at two o'clock in the morning. The most amazing thing of all was the naked little girl seen swinging in the backyard over two feet of snow at about 3:00 a.m. How she unlocked all the doors and managed to climb through the snow without freezing to death...no one will ever know!

During our four years at Zion Bible Institute, a time of transition occurred in our lives. We knew that it wasn't the perfect situation in which to raise a family, but we believed that God had allowed us to be there for a character-building experience in our own hearts and to touch the lives of many young people. For Bryon, in many ways, they were the four best years of his life. The Lord gave him a special life-long friend — Jon Marc. He was the son of Nat, a talented musician and teacher, and his wife, Anne Marie, who was an executive secretary. They were our dear friends and colleagues.

Bryon and Jon Marc were buddies. They attended Dayspring Christian Academy in South Attleboro, Massachusetts, and were in the same grade. After school they rode bikes, played Atari and football, and pretended to be "spy agents" to investigate the hidden backgrounds of the students. Jon Marc had a keen understanding of Bryon's special problems and always did his best to make Bryon feel normal and accepted. Being an only child himself, he considered Bryon a real brother.

During his prayer time one evening, he inquired, "Mom, why was I born normal, and Bryon was born with a terrible skin disease? I don't understand why God hasn't healed him. I've prayed so many times. It just doesn't seem fair!"

"You're right, Jon Marc," his mother responded. "It's not fair that Bryon was born with a horrible skin condition. But then, life isn't always fair, is it?"

Bryon will never forget the afternoon that he and Jon Marc went bike riding around campus. He accidentally rode into a curb and flew over the top of his handlebars onto the cement sidewalk. His skin was torn and bleeding over most of his body. Jon Marc, who was quite a bit bigger in stature, ran over to Bryon and picked him up in his arms. He carried his bruised and hurting friend all the way home.

Life is not fair. There are many situations we cannot change. But God has given each one of us the same measure of time...each day is a gift from Him. How we use that precious gift is what matters most. Charles R. Swindoll in his book, *The Quest For Character*, shares "Today...that special block of time holding the key that locks out yesterday's nightmares and unlocks tomorrow's dreams."

*"So teach us to number our days, that we may present to Thee a heart of wisdom"* (Ps. 90:12).

# 9

# OUR CHRISTMAS ANGEL

Christmas in New England has always held a special place in my memories. Hyannis, the Cape Cod seaport town, was the place of my birth. Snow-crusted pine trees, steel gray ocean waves, salty mist that sprayed over barren beaches and deserted sand dunes along quiet coastal villages were all part of my vivid yesterdays.

On occasions when my family returned for a holiday visit, the excitement was the most intense when we crossed the Saga-more Bridge over the man-made Cape Cod Canal. For my two younger sisters and me, we were headed back home.

Now, almost thirty-three years later, my husband and I, and our four children, considered "little Rhody," the ocean state, our home. We enjoyed the full-time teaching positions on the staff of Zion Bible Institute. Being our alma mater, we felt a certain kinship and "specialness" about returning to New England. Stephen, born in the potato farmlands of Aroostook County — the northern-most part of Maine — was also content to be in the area again.

The Christmas of 1984 brought a special miracle that

would change our lives forever.

Classes had ended for the fall semester, and the three-hundred-and-fifty students joyously packed their few belongings to rush home for the holidays. The silent streets of Broadway, Gurney, and Leonard, and the red and white structures, library, Temple, and office buildings seemed strangely deserted. The ten senior men who lived on the second floor above us had vacated, and for the first time in four months we were enveloped with a welcome peacefulness.

Forgetting the stacks of Church History and Music Fundamental finals that had to be corrected, Stephen and I determined to spend some valuable time with our children and make the holidays festive. We tried to include everyone in our traditional activities. Bryon, age ten, was put in charge of unwrapping and sorting all the handmade tree decorations. Leann and Jenell, ages six and four, respectively, adorned one of Mommy's large aprons and helped to roll out, cut, and decorate the delicious Christmas cookies made from Nanny Sparks' all-natural butter recipe. Brent, the newest addition to our family, a bubbling one-year-old, kept busy by licking doughy beaters, taking ornaments "off" the tree, checking the surprises in all the stockings, and testing the blinking light bulbs to see if they were really "hot" like Daddy said.

Amidst the consuming busyness and constant child chatter there was still a gnawing ache inside. The children had presented us with their usual lists of "wished for" things to be under the tree. They realized that Christmas wasn't just brightly decorated packages, a vacation from school, and the madness of bargain shopping.

To encourage the real meaning of Christmas, we placed the crude manger, life-like characters, and little baby Jesus on a table in the living room. Daddy tried to juggle four squirmy kids on his knees as he read the first Christmas story from our family Bible...Luke, the second chapter. We also initiated a special project for needy youngsters in our church by packing a box full of baked goodies, handmade toys, crafts, and a favorite game from each of the children. Yet, we knew that deep inside each young heart was a certain longing for some of those "wished for" items under the tree.

Part of the uniqueness of Zion Bible Institute was the "faith policy" that was instilled in the students and exemplified by the faculty. Since its founding in 1924, Rev. Christine Gibson had never refused a student because he did not have the finances to pay for his education. Students were accepted upon the principle that as God supplied their personal needs, they would in turn give to the school. The faculty, secretaries, dietitians, landscapers, and maintenance workers did not receive a stipulated salary, but a small "sharing" after all the school bills had been paid. But with the responsibility of managing a home and caring for four children, that "sharing" was never enough.

This truth was poignantly realized as we passed by aisles of toys, dolls, and athletic equipment in the Toys 'R' Us department store. Glancing at our list and checking the price tags made the disappointment even more acute. Steve gently placed a warm hand on my shoulder and whispered, "Honey, you know we can't afford these toys...the children will just have to understand."

I sighed in agreement and together we chose other gifts within our budget. After the packages were wrapped with care, Leann and Jenell played a guessing game as to the contents of each box. The words seemed to pierce my heart, when one child remarked, "I don't see a gift big enough to be my cabbage patch stroller! That's what I really want."

On Sunday evening, December 23, there was to be a candlelight Christmas service in the beautiful Temple. Stephen was asked to deliver the scriptural message. After prodding him, he reluctantly confided that his text was: "It is more blessed to give than it is to receive."

I fought back the tears and acknowledged, "Yes, indeed. Our family knows what blessings are received from a giving heart."

I thought of how willingly we left our loving congregation and comfortable nine-room bi-level to come to a "faith school" and live in a cramped five-room apartment, making ourselves available for twenty-four-hour pastoral counseling

---

to the college students. The sacrifices were great...but the rewards were greater.

At exactly 6:00 p.m., one hour before the service began, we heard a diligent pounding on the outside front door. Caught in the middle of dressing the children and combing their hair, I ran down the hallway in my housecoat to answer the steady knocking. I threw open the heavy wooden door and a frozen gust of nordic air blew into my face. It had been snowing heavily all afternoon. The wintry blanket covered the campus like a picture postcard...in undisturbed solitude.

Standing in front of me was a woman, perhaps in her late fifties, warmly dressed in a dark blue wool coat and brown scarf, pulled tightly over her wispy gray hair. Her blue eyes sparkled and her gentle smile warmed my heart. In each gloved hand were shopping bags filled with beautifully wrapped gifts.

I wondered to myself, "Who could she be looking for?"

Interrupting my thoughts, she inquired, "Do you know where the Sparks family lives? Their names are Bryon, Leann, Jenell, and Brent."

I swallowed hard with disbelief and replied, "Yes, well...huh...they...I mean...the Sparkses live right here!"

"Wonderful!" she exclaimed. Her smile radiated heavenly joy. "These gifts are for your children!"

Frozen with astonishment, I finally choked out, "Well, who do we thank for these gifts...please tell me your name...and where you are from..."

Shaking her head, she firmly replied, "No, no...that's not important. When you look at the gift tags you will discover who to thank."

I picked up a gift and peeked at the card — "Love, From Jesus" it read.

I trembled with excitement and begged her to wait one moment while I ran to get my husband. He would certainly have to help carry the parcels inside. I found Stephen in the middle of shaving his face; white cream remained on one side of his chin. He wasn't anxious to go to the door, but I refused to take no for an answer. With some difficulty, I dragged a half-shaven, bare-chested man down the hall. He stepped ahead of me and gazed out into the cold.

"Honey, there is no one here. I'm sorry...but the woman is gone! The bags are here in the snow...but she has vanished."

As we stood together peering out into the quiet night, we noticed that there were no footprints on the stairs or sidewalk...no tire tracks in the street. The white dust lay untouched by human presence. A holy hush and divine wonderment filled our hearts. Suddenly, we knew that we had been visited by a very special Christmas angel...perhaps one of the angels that announced the Saviour's birth some two thousand years before.

I wished the gentle woman could have stayed and watched our youngsters on Christmas morning as they opened the "surprise" packages and found the exact things they had wished for. Their faces showed delightful astonishment to see a cabbage patch stroller, little pony stable, set of C. S. Lewis books, complete outfits of clothing (everything fit perfectly), and much more. Yet, in my heart I knew that our angelic visitor was very much with us.

Even now, years later, this Christmas is a memory our children fondly recall. At times, when we have experienced a tremendous need, someone always reminds us that God will take care of us.

"Remember our Christmas angel?" one of the children will reminisce. "If God can do a miracle once...He can do it again...and again."

He has.

*"Do not neglect to show hospitality to strangers, for by this some have entertained angels without knowing it" (Heb. 13:2).*

# 10

# THIN-SKINNED KIDS

When I heard the phone ring I cringed. It was 6:30 p.m. and I had just a few minutes to get ready for the Sunday evening service. As I picked up the receiver I wondered what emergency I would face now. There was a static crackling noise over the wires and the voice sounded strangely far away.

"Hello...hello...this is Nancy Daley. I'm calling you from Germany. Can you hear me?" the unfamiliar voice implored.

I spoke loudly into the receiver, "Yes, I can hear you...who do you wish to talk with?"

"I would like to speak with Mrs. Sparks. Are you Lillian Sparks?" she inquired.

Very surprised, I answered, "Yes, I am Mrs. Sparks, from East Providence, Rhode Island...but how do you know me?"

"I have just finished reading your book, *Tough Cookie*, which tells the story about your son, Bryon. It is a very moving story of courage and faith. I greatly admire you and your belief in God."

Inquisitively, I asked, "How did you get a hold of a copy of *Tough Cookie* in Germany?"

---

Nancy continued, "I am staying in Michelbach-Alzenau, West Germany for a period of three months at a private clinic called "The Vital Klinik." I have two-year-old twin daughters who have the same skin condition as Bryon. They are undergoing intensive treatment here. A friend of mine, who lives in New York City, happened to see your book in a local bookstore. She was so excited to find a book written about Epidermylosis Bullosa that she immediately bought it and mailed it to me here. After I completed the reading, I wanted to track you down. Do you have any idea how hard it was for me to find you?"

I voiced my agreement, "Yes, I know. Others have experienced the same problem getting in touch with our family. The address on the back of *Tough Cookie* is from our previous home, where we pastored in Middletown, Pennsylvania. Since the book was published we have moved to Rhode Island to teach in a Bible college. What a miracle you were able to locate us!"

"Believe it or not, I called your old telephone number, then the church, and finally the Middletown Post Office...who gave me your present address. I made all these long-distance calls from Germany! But I was determined to let you know just how much your story touched my life and also make you aware of the treatment center in West Germany for children with Epidermylosis Bullosa."

With a glimmer of hope, I asked, "Have your girls improved since they started on the treatment?"

Nancy sounded so enthusiastic, "Oh my, yes! Their blisters and open sores have healed...they can eat normally without choking...and some of their fingers and toes have unfused naturally. It is amazing."

"Can you tell me how much this treatment costs and how your trip has been financed?"

"I must admit the clinic is very expensive — approximately $10,000 to $15,000 a month, plus creams and medication for the skin. Depending on how severe the individual is, you must stay between two to four months. Thank God, my husband's company at IBM in Fishkill, New York agreed to finance our entire trip and then gave him two months off from work. I couldn't have done it without his help.''

My interest level was rising. "Nancy, be honest with me. Do you think this treatment would help Bryon?'' I inquired.

Nancy sounded like she was in the next room. "That's why I called...I know that if Bryon came he would improve tremendously.''

Bryon's dream came into focus and I pondered the possibility of God's using this clinic to bring healing for his skin and perhaps, someday, ten new fingers. It was too wonderful for words. The hot tears coursed down my cheeks unrestrained. My imagination had taken me a million miles away when I vaguely heard Nancy mention something about Thanksgiving.

"We will be home a few days before Thanksgiving,'' she was saying. "If you would like to come and see us, we live about four hours from Rhode Island...in Newburgh, New York.''

It seemed too good to be true. I put the receiver down and stared into space. Was I dreaming? No, I knew that I had just spent thirty minutes in conversation because the clock read 7:00 p.m. and I was late for church! Oh, my! Reality finally hit me, as I grabbed my Bible and coat and headed out the door and across campus to the Temple, to take my place at the piano. The chords of the opening song were being played. I quietly slipped onto the bench, unnoticed. Steve raised his arms to lead the congregation in worship. He caught my eye and gave me a knowing wink, which said, "Honey, so nice you could make it to church tonight!''

We visited the Daley family the day after Thanksgiving. It was November, 1981. Their twin daughters were adorable. I knew the care that was involved with Bryon and I couldn't comprehend the task of caring for TWO! The girls sat cross-legged on the floor and amiably played with Bryon. The first thing I noticed was how clear their skin looked. Nancy and Chris told us the entire story of their birth, hospitalizations, and treatment. We looked at many pictures, past and present.

We were very anxious to hear about the clinic in West Germany. Their tales came tumbling out one after the other. We learned about the "all-natural" diet, supplemental vitamin therapy, and rigid skin treatments given round-the-clock, every four hours. They told of the many friends they had made during their stay — other parents and children with EB. We listened to the good and the bad and tried to absorb the details. There were, of course, many sacrifices to be made in going, but the rewards seemed to outweigh them all.

We returned to Zion with new hope in our hearts for Bryon's healing. But one question loomed largely in our minds — "How would we raise $40,000 for this treatment while living at a 'faith school'?" We prayed about it together and then, committed it to God. We had a great God! He was well aware of our situation...and if He wanted Bryon to go to Germany, He would provide the finances.

* * *

Almost weekly, newspaper articles about the German clinic and its "thinned-skinned kids" were sent to us. The headlines in the *Chicago Sun-Times* read: Did they find a miracle cure...or is it another German fairy tale? It stated that many victims drawn by reports of dramatic cures for the inherited sickness known as Epidermylosis Bullosa (EB) had traveled to the small private clinic at the foot of a pine-covered hill in northwest Bavaria. There, near where the Brothers Grimm collected their famous fairy tales, a self-taught dermatologist claimed to be working miracles.

In an interview with the *Sun-Times*, Kozak, who wore a white clinical coat, said he began developing his methods twenty-five years ago as a treatment for his own skin condition, eczema. (This disfiguring skin condition is characterized by itching, blistering and scaling.) According to his brother-in-law and interpreter, Dan Enescu, Kozak was such "a monster" wrapped up in bandages that he apprenticed himself to two very important professors in biochemistry and biology in Rumania. Enescu, a urologist, said Kozak's disease made formal training at a university out of the question.

Working on his own, under the guidance of the two professors, Kozak said he found cures after more than five years, not only for eczema but for some forty skin diseases in all. Some doctors felt that they were receiving competition in their profession from a self-taught, ordinary person. Kozak told *Flacara*, a Rumanian trade union publication, "For me, the struggle with the opposition was more difficult than the struggle to find a cure for the disease." *Flacara* received hundreds of phone calls and letters of support from readers and eventually helped Kozak gain acceptance for his method through the political establishment. Kozak told the *Sun-Times* that in 1977, Rumanian President Nicolae Ceausescu conferred on him the title of "senior researcher first class," the highest rank in Rumania's scientific community. Kozak was placed in charge of twenty beds at the Fundini Clinic, one of the leading hospitals in Eastern Europe, near Bucharest.

Many families with afflicted children began to seek a miracle cure from the fifty-year-old Rumanian defector. Every year for six years, Carmelita Lee Vance took her twelve-year-old son to Lourdes, hoping for a miracle. Since birth, Bobby Lee had suffered from a disease that covered his body with painful blisters and disfigured his hands and feet with masses of dead skin, preventing normal growth. "Bobby couldn't walk when we came here," said Vance, who readily demonstrated how she could pull chunks of dead skin from her son's feet after four weeks of treatment. "Now he can walk and run, too. He's a lucky little boy that we found this place."

Accounts of other "miraculous" successes were numerous. A sixteen-year-old Canadian, who since birth was fed through a tube placed in his throat, ate his first crust of bread at the clinic. A nine-year-old girl who was near death from the effects of the disease when brought to Michelbach was no longer bedridden. A three-year-old boy from Corpus Christi, Texas, immobilized since birth by massive blistering, learned to walk.

Susie Bell, a seven-year-old, of Mississauga, Canada also sought the cure in Germany. She was born with no skin on parts of her body — the skin just fell away and she was red and raw. The doctors told her mother not to feel bad if she died, but their faith in God helped Susie to survive. Her feet were so covered with sores that she had to walk around on her knees. Her toenails were just "layer upon layer of a kind of crust." She had to wear special sandals or go barefoot. Susie improved greatly after her treatment at the clinic.

After his trip to Germany, nine-year-old Carlos Costa experienced the warmth of his mother's hug for the first time in his life. Before this time, Mrs. Maria Costa lived with the horrible knowledge that her loving touch could kill the boy who meant more to her than anything else in the world. At the very least, her touch would have left Carlos with bloody blisters because of his skin disease — and those blisters could easily have been infected. So while other children laughed and played, little Carlos lived like a mummy — his body swathed in cotton bandages. But since his treatment in West Germany, Carlos was given a new life. His sores almost vanished...and his mom now can cuddle and kiss him.

Every story was heartbreakingly the same. Those children afflicted with Epidermylosis Bullosa, a life threatening, rare genetic skin disorder, receive blisters and erosions at the slightest friction or trauma. Once blisters appear, they must be ruptured with a sterile needle and drained, often leaving a raw painful surface. The area is then cleaned and topical ointment is applied to minimize the high risk of infection that is always present. Then the area is wrapped with a nonadherent dressing.

The severe form of EB called the Recessive Dystrophic-scarring type shows generalized blistering and erosions which heal slowly resulting in scarring. The repeated scarring leads to fusion of the hands and feet resembling a "mitten effect." Blistering occurs most frequently in the mouth, tongue, and esophagus. "Webbing" of the throat and internal organs is common. Dental hygiene is difficult because brushing causes blisters to the gums. EB patients frequently suffer erosions of the corneas of the eyes.

A great deal of effort must be made to arrange the environment to reduce friction and trauma to the skin. Only soft clothing, shoes and toys can be used. Because of the difficulty in eating and the chronic blood loss from the blisters, the Recessive Dystrophic EB patient has difficulty in maintaining adequate nutrition. One of the principal treatments at the clinic was a restrictive, unconventional diet, which included slaughtered natural beef, breasts from year-old hens, well-cooked carrots, parsnips, parsley, homemade bread, cookies, and semolina. Patients were also given vitamin supplements and other nutrients. In addition, every four hours blistered areas were coated with salves and creams containing steroids, antibiotics, and other ingredients, then bandaged.

Many EB victims testify to similar frustrations due to infection and scarring of the esophagus and hands. Simple tasks like opening doors and bottles, putting money in a parking meter, doing buttons or zippers, and writing a letter become major projects. Some fear being locked in a restroom or being unable to use the telephone in an emergency. Without the support of family and friends, life would be impossible. The lack of independence in itself is a constant source of frustration. Others dream of the day when life can be a little more "normal."

For the first time in the life of a "thin-skinned" kid there seemed to be a ray of light — some hope of a cure. We were confident that if God wanted Bryon to go to Germany for treatment, He would open the right doors.

* * *

During this same period of time our family faced another financial crisis. Logos International, from Plainfield, New Jersey declared bankruptcy! We couldn't believe it! But that's exactly what the letter from the lawyers stated. *Tough Cookie* was doing so well under the publication and distribution of Logos Publishers. The book was making record sales each month. In July 1981 we had personally paid for the publishing of five thousand copies. Over two thousand of those were presold and quickly distributed. But Logos had mailed the remaining three thousand copies to bookstores across the country and around the world. When we contacted their Plainfield offices, we discovered that all of those books had been sold and the profits were lost in the bankruptcy law suit. We had the opportunity to go to court and try to get some of the profits, but it would involve thousands of dollars.

The perplexity of the situation grew worse. We didn't have the finances to go to bankruptcy court, so that was out of the question. But now we were completely out of books — two thousand were given to those who prepaid and three thousand, lost by Logos. Bookstores, churches, and many people began to contact us and ask for books. Even the Bible school students wanted copies to take home to their families for Christmas.

We contacted the new publisher — Bridge Publications, who had taken over Logos publications and assets, and they were willing to work with us in reprinting Tough Cookie. (The cost for five thousand new copies — $4,000!) We needed a financial miracle.

Bridge gave us the deadline as to when the monies were needed for printing to have the books before Christmas. It was only three days away! Steve and I knelt in the living room in front of the couch and presented this tremendous need to the Lord. It appeared so great to us, but we knew that to God, it was but a small thing. Philippians 4:19 tells us, "And my God shall supply all your needs according to His riches in glory in Christ Jesus." We claimed the promise in His Word!

The next afternoon, Steve was returning from teaching a Comparative Religions class and noticed a car parked in front of Missionary Manor. As he stepped onto the curb, a well-dressed young man in a suit and tie jumped out and extended his hand.

"Hi there, Pastor Sparks," he greeted. "You don't know me, but I faithfully attend Zion Gospel Temple and I sure enjoy your song leading."

After shaking hands, the smart-looking executive continued. "Do you have a few minutes to go for a cup of coffee and a pastry at Mister Donut's?"

"I always have time for a donut!" Steve replied.

Minutes later, while sipping a steaming cup of coffee and

munching on a Boston creme, the gentleman blurted out, "You're probably wondering why I asked you out. Last night I had a lot of trouble sleeping, and this morning during prayer God told me to bring a blank check and to write in the amount of whatever your family needs in the next few days. God told me you have a definite need. Right?"

Steve looked back in astonishment. He knew God could work miracles, but he sure didn't expect it to happen this way...and so fast. He answered, "You are the answer to a miracle that we need. Yes, in two days we must have $4,000 to pay a large commitment. Eventually, this will be a great blessing to our son, Bryon. My wife and I prayed about the finances last night and God gave us a beautiful peace that He would supply. YOU are the answer to that prayer."

The young man filled in the amount and handed the check to Steve. What a time of rejoicing we had when he returned home. Quickly, we phoned Bridge Publishers and put the check in the mail. We made the deadline on time. God was teaching us that He may not always answer when we want Him to, but He is never too late!

The miracle of the $4,000 was a spring-board for our faith in trusting God for an even greater provision — that of $40,000 to go to the treatment center in West Germany. With joyous anticipation, we looked forward to the blessings God had in store for us.

# 11

# A NEW BLUE BIKE

The Piedmont DC-10 rose higher and higher over the Boston harbor. Within two hours we would be landing at the Charlotte International Airport. I had to pinch myself...it all seemed like a dream: the phone call from the producers at the PTL Television Network inviting our family to appear on the program and share the Tough Cookie story, the all-expense round-trip provided for five days to sunny North Carolina, and stay at the PTL Mansion — a large brick colonial home where the television guests stayed, and the fact that millions of viewers would be watching our family. It was all mindboggling.

The flight attendant placed a delicious-looking meal in front of me, but the excitement in my stomach caused my appetite to subside. Bryon and his dad didn't seem to be affected the same way and quickly consumed the stuffed baked chicken, peas, and roasted potatoes.

After visiting with some close friends for several days, we went to the PTL Mansion where the original television studios were located. The facilities were now used for guests, special classes, and seminars. The former studio stood strangely empty and quiet.

Our hosts, Norman and Dorothy Bakker, Jim's brother and wife, gave us a detailed tour and explanation of the progress of the television ministry. Dorothy, a script-writer for the program, asked us many questions about Bryon's birth, early struggles, and answers to prayer. Occasionally tears filled her eyes as she jotted down our responses. Bryon had his own set of answers, which he interjected from time to time.

The three or four-story red brick Mansion was a splendid example of southern colonial architecture. The spacious rooms were decorated with exquisite taste in every detail. It was exhilarating just to walk from the sitting room to the grand dining room and breathe in the elegance. We knew this was a once-in-a-lifetime experience and we intended to enjoy every minute.

We thoroughly appreciated the tour through the new PTL facilities at Heritage USA, Fort Mills, South Carolina. We drove past the country store, lakeside restaurant, A-frame chalets, condominiums, Heritage Lake, and the Big Barn (which housed the Heritage Village Church and new television studios). Our favorite place was the Upper Room, built the exact size as the original upper room in Jerusalem. It was open twenty-four hours a day for prayer, counseling, and communion services. At various times special seminars or Bible studies were conducted there also. As you strolled down the "walk of faith" and entered the front doors, a very unusual presence of the Holy Spirit was felt.

Dinner was served in the grand dining room of the Mansion at 6:00 p.m. The other guests were Leonard Evans and his wife, the weekly Bible seminar teacher; Dino Karsinakas and his business manager; Laurie Brown, the daughter of Pat and Shirley Boone, and her husband. We were very honored to share the company of such well-known personalities.

Bryon stole the show as he picked up his fork between his clubbed hands and began to feed himself without the use of his fingers. He never missed a bite, but savored every tiny morsel. Dino, a well-known Christian artist, gazed intently at Bryon's contracted hands. Without a word, Bryon's life spoke volumes to the people sitting there. Because of the genuine interest, we began to share his story.

No one seemed to notice that when Bryon was finished eating, he slipped quietly from his seat and disappeared into another room. Everyone was actively contributing to the conversation, when we heard some dissident notes from the grand piano in the living room. All at once, everyone realized that Bryon was attempting to play "Jesus Loves Me" with his scarred hands.

Dino responded immediately by standing up and half-walking and half-jogging across the hall. As we listened, we heard the melodious notes of a trained musician and the high-pitched voice of a seven-year-old boy blend together in harmony. We joined them around the piano and, together, all the guests began to sing, "Jesus loves me, this I know...for the Bible tells me so."

We had bought Bryon a sharp new blue pin-striped suit and white shirt for his T.V. appearance the next morning. He was lacking only one item — a matching tie. We wanted to go to a store, but didn't have a vehicle. Leonard Evans and his wife graciously offered to drive us to the South Park Mall to look for a tie. We really enjoyed the time of fellowship and browsing from store to store. We eventually found a nice solid blue tie in the Sears Department Store.

The section next to the boys' clothing was the bicycle shop. While I paid for the tie, the rest of the group went to look at new bikes. Bryon was the most enthusiastic. "Hey, Dad! That's what I want for my eighth birthday more than anything else in the world!"

Steve looked at the prices, "Well, Son, that's a lot of money for just one gift. We'll see what happens. Okay?"

Bryon nodded his head in resignation and sighed, "Yeah, but if we trust the Lord, He could give me the money for a new bike."

"He sure could, Bryon!" asserted Brother Evans.

We strolled slowly through the mall and made a last stop at a candle and gift shop. I loved smelling the fragrances of the scented candles. All of a sudden, Bryon screamed with delight, "Mom...Dad...look what I found...a whole bunch of money!"

Under the counter was a rolled-up wad of bills and Bryon had spotted them. Steve examined the money and counted thirty dollars. We asked the cashier if she was missing any cash. She checked her drawer and everything was in order. Bryon began jumping up and down with sheer excitement.

"Now I can buy a new bike! Let's go get it right now!" he shouted.

Steve responded, "I know thirty dollars is a lot of money, but it's not enough for a bike. Son, it will only buy half a bike."

Undaunted, Bryon replied, "Okay. Which half can we go buy...the front or the back?"

Everyone began to laugh, including Bryon, as we realized how much Bryon wanted his bike. We left our name and number with the clerk, just in case someone reported the missing money. I know Bryon had his fingers crossed that no one would show up.

The following morning we were up early to be all prepared for our "big day." Bryon looked like a little man in his new suit and tie. If we were nervous or anxious it didn't seem to be contagious, since Bryon walked through the Mansion talking to the housekeepers, cooks, and other guests. Before we went downstairs to meet Norman Bakker, we heard the strumming of a guitar and singing coming from the room across the hall. As we peeked through the doorway, we caught a glimpse of Bryon sitting in the middle of a canopy bed along with Laurie Brown and her husband. They were all warming up for the program.

When I wrote our names in the guest book in the hallway, I noticed that the previous night Rex and Maude Aimee Humbard had slept in our bed. It was great to feel somewhat like a celebrity, even for just a day.

Hidden from view in the plush back seats of the limousine, we whisked by security and turned off the main road onto a private drive that led to the rear entrance of the

"Big Barn." The dressing rooms were just as I expected...plush and tastefully decorated. The program hostess, Pheobe, scurried around fixing coffee, orange juice, and breakfast pastries on a tray. Jeanne Johnson, one of the producers, was helping to put make-up on some of the guests. Bryon and Steve each took a turn in the salon chair, placed in front of the mirror with many lights. Their painted faces looked camera-perfect. Bryon was afraid to smile in case his face would "crack."

Uncle Henry Harrison made us feel right at home and like old-time friends. He sat on the couch next to Bryon and said, "Well, Son, we are so glad to have you at PTL. What are you going to tell those people out there about your life?"

Bryon smiled and answered, "That without God I wouldn't be here today!"

Everyone in the dressing room cheered with support.

The countdown had started. Only minutes were left before the band struck the opening notes of their theme song: "Praise the Lord. Now it's time to lift our voices, singing in one accord. Now it's time...to praise the Lord!" The band and the PTL Singers were practicing a last-minute song with Tammy Faye for the morning's program. The Speer Family, the featured guest musicians, were getting a quick sound level check with the audio department.

"Ten, nine, eight, seven..." Darryl, one of the head sound producers, was counting down. The music began and Uncle Henry announced, "Welcome to the PTL Show, starring Jim and Tammy Bakker!"

As they entered from the rear of the auditorium and came down the stairs, Tammy tripped and broke the strap on her bright red hi-heels. She tried to fix it, right on stage, in front of the T.V. cameras. We watched the program on a big-screen projector in a special waiting room. The minutes seemed to drag by. The Speer Family sang two or three songs. Jim talked some more. Tammy sang with the PTL Singers. Some announcements were made about their record and book sales. After what seemed like an eternity, Jim held up a copy of Tough Cookie and told the audience, "Today our special guest

Bryon sings "My Hands Belong To You Lord."

The Sparks family with David Mainse, "100 Huntley Street."

The Sparks on PTL Club.

Bryon talking with Henry and Tammy on the PTL Club.

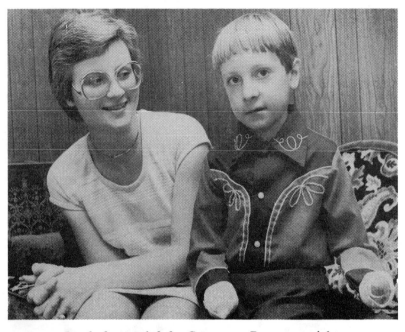

Just before we left for Germany—Bryon was eight.

Happy Fifteenth Birthday!

Keep signing those books Bryon!

"Off to school" Byron, Jenell, Brent, and Leann.

Bryon and Larry Bird.

Bryon and "the Big Guy"
—Eddie Johnson.

Eddie Johnson, Bryon, and
Freeman McNeal

Bryon, Bernie Kosar,
and Dad—"Go Browns!"

is a seven-year-old boy who was born with a rare skin disease. The doctors said he wouldn't live. Bryon, his mother, Lillian, and his father, Stephen, are here to tell the story. Let's welcome the Sparks family!''

Darryl pulled back a huge curtain and ushered us into the glaring lights. A thunderous applause greeted us, as we made our way across the living room setting. We greeted Uncle Henry and Tammy Faye with hugs and kisses and then shook hands with Mr. Bakker and Leonard Evans. There was a tremendous intensity of thought written across Jim's face as he glanced at the writer's proposed questions and then looked into the television cameras. His rapport with the audience was evident. In front of us, on a glass table, were frosted glasses of coke with ice that looked tempting.

Jim turned to Steve and asked, "You folks are teachers at a 'faith Bible school.' You have a son with a serious skin condition, yet you are living on 'faith.' Tell us what that means."

Steve explained about the founding principle of faith which was to provide education for students who did not have the finances to further their education. He also shared that it was made possible by the teachers' and staff's giving their services without any remuneration, only a "sharing policy."

Jim seemed totally dumbfounded by the "faith" concept. In a world of affluence and prosperity, one can imagine it was difficult to grasp. He mentioned the fact that PTL ministries had recently given Zion Bible Institute a gift of $50,000 to help with some outstanding deficits.

Turning his attention to Bryon, he continued, "Mom, tell us about Bryon's birth and why the doctors gave him no hope to live."

I had rehearsed in my mind a million times what I would say...and now all eyes were on me. My hands were clammy with nervous sweat and my mouth was dry. As I opened my mouth to speak, a wonderful peace came over me. I forgot about the millions of viewers, the people in the audience, the cameras, the producers, and the Bakkers. Suddenly I was at home in my living room just chatting with friends. With great ease and vividness, I unfolded the miracle of Bryon's birth.

I kept waiting for Mr. Bakker to interrupt me, but he was totally absorbed in the story. The audience was moved to tears as I recalled the nightmare experience when the nurse took Bryon's footprints, only to remove the skin from the bottoms of his feet. Steve shared his trauma of seeing Bryon for the first time. Thinking it was someone else's child, he prayed for the blistered, suffering infant to survive.

We told how the doctors asserted that Bryon would never walk because he had no skin on his feet. Then God performed a miracle, and he learned to walk. The same physicians watched Bryon run down their office hall with shoes on. The crowd broke out in spontaneous praise.

Jim's polished professionalism broke down. His eyes were moist and he struggled to contain himself. Tammy Faye and Uncle Henry were openly weeping. Jim attempted to collect his thoughts and asked, "What are Bryon's plans for the future? Does he have any dreams?"

"Yes, God has given Bryon a wonderful dream for the future," I replied. "You can see that Bryon's hands and fingers are contracted into useless mittens of skin. Even though three separate operations have been performed, none of them have been successful. About a year ago Bryon came into our room and told us that the Lord had given him a dream...his pajamas had fallen off and new skin covered his body...but best of all — he had ten brand new fingers to raise to the Lord!"

As the camera zoomed in with a close shot of Bryon's bandaged left hand and scarred, useless right hand, the studio audience exploded in applause and cheers. They were saying, "Bryon, you're a brave boy and we believe in you. One day God will bring your dream to pass."

Jeanne Johnson held up a cue card for Mr. Bakker to read. The title of Bryon's special song was written in black letters. Floundering for words, Jim asked, "Bryon would you sing a song for us?"

Bryon quietly responded, "Sure, I'd love to."

"Well, you and Mom go over to the music department and get all set up." Jim turned to the cameras, "Folks, this has been quite a story today. What faith and courage Bryon and his parents have shown. The doctors said he wouldn't live...and he's here today. They said he would never walk...and now he can run! He's trusting God for new skin and new fingers! Oh my! If Bryon can make it...YOU can make it too!" (Pauses as he reads the cue card.) "Here's Bryon Sparks to sing for us...'My ha...hand...hands...belong to You, Lord!' Let me tell you, if you're out there feeling sorry for yourself...you better get a hold of yourself! Here's Bryon to sing for us!"

Many people who were close friends of the Bakkers told us Jim was never that broken-up on a program. There wasn't a dry eye in the entire building.

While Bryon lifted his sweet voice in praise to the Lord, and Mom played the piano, Leonard Evans leaned over to Jim and told him the story about finding the $30 in the candle store. He mentioned how much Bryon wanted a new bicycle and he was believing in God to provide the rest of the money.

By the time Bryon finished the last note, his arms raised in surrender to the Lord, the crowd was on its feet, clapping, shouting, and wiping tears. We walked back over to the set. Jim was smiling from ear to ear. Every time he tried to say something the applause drowned him out. He finally gave up and waited for everyone to sit down.

"Bryon, the people love you!" Jim shouted. "Do you hear them clap? They believe in you, Bryon!"

When the noise subsided Jim turned to Brother Evans and said, "Pastor Evans, you were telling me a story about Bryon finding $30 last night in the mall. Tell us about it."

"Well, Jim..." Evans began. "Last night we went to the mall with the Sparkses to look for a new tie to match Bryon's suit. After we bought the tie we went into a candle shop. There under the counter, Bryon found thirty dollars rolled up. We asked the salesclerk and it didn't belong to anyone. So Bryon got to keep the money...and he's been wanting a new bicycle for his birthday. This money will buy him one-half of the bike. He's trusting the Lord for the rest."

Jim was ecstatic, "Well, I know a few people around here

who will make up the difference for a new bike. I will personally see to that! Bryon, don't you worry. You will have a new bike!"

Within a few moments we were off the air. There was a ten minute break of commercials and announcements. Scheduled during the next hour was a special telethon to raise funds. The producers needed the break to go over the material with Jim for the next program. But before anyone could stop him, Jim had run off stage and had returned carrying twenty offering buckets. He scurried up and down the aisles of the studio audience collecting money for Bryon. He finally came back to the set holding all of the buckets himself. The security personnel and producers were in a frenzy. They didn't know what to do. The countdown began for the second hour of programming.

Ten...nine...eight...seven...We were on the air again! Jim was standing on the set holding all the buckets. No one knew what to do. It didn't bother Jim...he told everyone about Bryon and the Sparks family and announced that he had just taken up an offering from the audience to buy Bryon a new bike. He handed the buckets to Steve and stated, "Here, Dad, you hold onto this. I'm sure there is enough money in there to buy a bike, a motorcycle, ice cream, or whatever else Bryon wants."

Tammy Faye began to sing a song and we were escorted out back to the dressing rooms. Steve and one of the security officers counted the cash—there was over $450.00! What a blessing! Bryon was beside himself with joy.

"See, I told you that if I trusted the Lord, I knew He would provide the money for the other half of my bike! Hallelujah! Praise the Lord!" Bryon shouted with glee.

The rest of our time at PTL was spent in many memorable activities. We ate lunch with Tammy Faye, Uncle Henry and Aunt Susan; visited the animal farm and went for rides; and viewed the entire morning's program later that day. Sooner than we wished, we were speeding across town towards the airport to catch our flight back to Boston. Back to Zion, the students, and two little girls waiting at home.

143

We walked into the terminal, checked our luggage and headed down the corridor to our gate. From out of nowhere a male voice yelled, "Hi, Bryon! You were great on the program yesterday. I'm rooting for you, Buddy."

We turned in the direction of his voice — it was a Piedmont ticket agent. We waved our thanks and continued down the hall. This was just a small sample of the response that came pouring in through letters and phone calls from across the country. "Tough Cookie" became a household word to many...and many prayed that Bryon's dream would come true.

One prayer was already answered...a new blue bike!

# 12

# ON THE WHITE LINE

At the age of nine I preached my first sermon. While visiting my aunt and uncle in Washburn, Maine for the summer, I was asked to speak at a youth service held in the Pentecostal Church. There were about one-hundred-and-fifty in attendance. The desire to preach God's Word grew stronger and at the age of eighteen, I entered Bible school to prepare for the ministry. This was in response to the call God had placed on my life.

I had many opportunities as a P.K. (preacher's kid) to speak in various churches my dad pastored. I taught Sunday School when I was thirteen, helped in children's church, and was a leader in our youth group. But the first evidence I had of God's anointing upon me to preach was at my Bible school graduation, when I was selected to be the class's valedictorian. It was a tremendous honor and an awesome responsibility. Our class motto was — "His." The Scripture I chose to speak from was Ephesians 1:18-19: "I pray that the eyes of your heart may be enlightened, so that you may know what is the hope of His calling, what are the riches of the glory of His inheritance in the saints, and what is the surpassing greatness of His power toward us who believe. These are in accordance with the working of the strength of His might..."

My three sub-points were

1. The Hope of His Calling
2. The Glory of His Inheritance
3. The Greatness of His Power

This valedictory address became a part of my life. God actually gave me prophetic words to say, that in the future, through Bryon, have been fulfilled.

I also worked towards receiving my credentials with the Assemblies of God denomination. When I was twenty I acquired my Christian Worker's papers and then as a pastor's wife, my license to preach. As news spread about the testimony of our son, and the forthcoming book, *Tough Cookie*, invitations began piling in from all over the mid-Atlantic states.

But I was not prepared for the deluge of calls and letters following our visit to PTL Television Network and the publication of the book. Steve and I had to go over each invitation to see if it would fit into our schedule of teaching, traveling with the Collegians, ministering in the Zion Temple, and caring for our children. Requests came to speak at Missions Rallies, Women's Conventions, weekend retreats, seminars, youth groups, International Aglow meetings, interdenominational prayer breakfasts, and church services. We finally decided that I could travel short distances during the month, but take only two extended speaking tours a year, which lasted about five to seven days.

One such tour was planned to Western Ontario, Canada. It would be my first time to speak in Canada and I had great expectations. Foremost was our appearance on "100 Huntley Street" with Rev. David Mainse. Mr. Ralph Bradley, the guest coordinator for the program, had phoned to make all the flight and hotel arrangements for Bryon and me to come. We were also scheduled to speak at several churches throughout Ontario and at a large women's missionary banquet in London. I felt somewhat "light-headed" by this small taste of being in the limelight. The Lord has a way, though, of reminding us who we really are and where our strength comes from.

Our USAir flight from Providence to Newark, New Jersey was uneventful. We arrived in plenty of time to check in for our connection to Toronto, where Mr. Bradley would pick us up and drive us to the downtown Ramada Inn. But as passengers began to get their boarding passes and enter the plane, I discovered that Bryon was put on "stand-by." I had a seat assignment, but Bryon was not guaranteed passage. Well, what was I going to do? Leave Bryon in the Newark International Airport alone while I flew to Toronto? No way! There had to be a mistake.

I told the check-in agent that Bryon and I had to be on that plane — we were scheduled to appear on Canadian National Television the next morning. I stood right next to the desk to make sure he didn't give away any seats. Most of the passengers had boarded the plane — just a few spaces were left. At the last second a hurried businessman in a three-piece suit walked up to the counter and slid a $50.00 bill into the agent's hand. "Here, keep this," he said. "Just get me a seat on this plane. I have an important engagement."

With unexpected boldness, I stepped up to the counter and looked the USAir employee right in the eye and said, "You promised me that seat for my son. He is handicapped and cannot travel alone. I trust you will use integrity in this situation."

Visibly shaken, the young man blurted out, "Well, of course, Mrs. Sparks! Here is your son's boarding pass. Sorry to keep you waiting...you can board immediately."

I took the card, grabbed our carry-on luggage, and headed up the ramp. Over my shoulder I could hear the agent explaining, "I'm sorry, Sir, but there are no more available seats. Please take this money. I do not accept bribes." We left behind one very disturbed gentleman. Bryon and I took the last two open seats on the plane.

We were in the air for only about an hour when the pilot spoke over the intercom to inform us of engine trouble. It appeared that one of the engines was leaking fuel oil and there was the possibility of a fire. The only choice was to land in the

Rochester, N.Y. airport and see if it could be repaired. Inwardly, I groaned, "Oh, no. More delays. Will we ever get to Toronto? Now what will happen?"

We landed in Rochester and for four hours they kept us in suspense. Finally, the decision was made — the plane was not able to fly. What were our choices? Stay overnight in Rochester and catch the first plane out in the morning or take a four-hour bus trip to Toronto. We chose the latter. Before we climbed on the bus I made two last-minute calls: one to Steve and one to Ralph Bradley.

We arrived at the Toronto International Airport at about 11:00 p.m. It was unbelievable that a two-hour plane trip had taken fourteen hours! But our troubles weren't over. As soon as we went to the baggage claim area we had the overwhelming task of sorting through three rooms filled with unclaimed luggage. Somewhere in this maze was our suitcase and boxes of *Tough Cookie* books. Miraculously, we spotted them in a far corner, underneath a pile of garment bags and sports equipment.

Next, we faced "customs." Unaided, I dragged the heavy boxes and suitcase and placed them on the table to be checked. A very unpleasant customs' officer confronted us. I'm sure he wasn't too happy about being kept later than usual to accommodate the passengers from Rochester.

"What's in these boxes?" he demanded.

I replied, "These are books about my son, Bryon. It is his biography."

"Are you going to sell them in Canada?" he questioned.

"Yes, I would like to. We will be speaking in several churches and appearing on the '100 Huntley Street' program tomorrow. It is important that I take the books."

Shaking his head, he retorted, "That's impossible. We will have to get special authorization for you to sell them. And then you must pay a 20% sales tax on each book, before taking them into Canada."

My heart missed a few beats. I felt sick to my stomach. "Oh Lord," I prayed quietly, "Please help us. We have had an exhausting day. The enemy has done everything possible to

---

prevent us from getting to Canada. If You want us on the program tomorrow — do something!''

At that precise moment an officer in a distinguished uniform walked up to us and said, ''Is there a problem here?''

''Yes, Sir. My son, Bryon, and I will be on the '100 Huntley Street' program tomorrow and we need to take these books with us...they're Bryon's story.''

His eyes lit up, ''Bryon? Is this the young man who sang on the PTL program last week?''

Dumbfounded, I fumbled, ''Yes, Sir. He's the one!''

The officer took Bryon's hand in his. Tears filled his eyes. ''Bryon, you touched my heart with your song. I want you to know I'm praying for you that you'll get your new fingers. Hey, boy...how's that new bike? Huh?''

''It's great...I love it!'' Bryon answered with surprise.

''Let these folks go through. They have my authorization,'' he motioned towards the other agent. Then he whistled for a skycap to transport our baggage to a beautiful limousine waiting outside. He wrote out a voucher and handed it to the driver. It was a free thirty-minute ride to the downtown Ramada Inn.

As I sank into the back seat exhausted, I whispered, ''Thank you, Lord. Your ways surpass my understanding. You never cease to amaze me by Your last-second intervention in our lives.''

At 7:30 the next morning Ralph Bradley met us for a quick breakfast and then drove us to the television station. Many of the employees took time out of their schedules to personally meet and talk with Bryon — especially David Mainse, the president and host of the program.

After a snack of orange juice and a Danish, talking with the writers, practicing with the sound technicians, and getting our make-up on, we were ready to go on the air. Once again Bryon was ready to sing ''My Hands Belong to You, Lord.'' Only this time an accomplished musician accompanied him. Mom had a chance to relax.

Bryon had his ''security blanket'' with him — it was his bedraggled and much-loved teddy bear, ''Fudgy.'' Fudgy was as old as Bryon and had slept with him every night. No way was Fudgy going to be left behind. His first television appearance was on the PTL show and now he would be seen on Canadian television. Bryon held him tightly under his left arm.

The program was very relaxed and personal, without any of the big band and Hollywood stereotype. The conversation with David proceeded very naturally. David, also, was moved to tears by the miracle of Bryon's birth and the many impossibilities he had faced. At one point, he got down on his knees beside Bryon and encircled him with his arm.

"Bryon, what is your teddy bear's name?" he asked.

Shyly, Bryon quipped, "Fudgy."

David inquired, "Well, what is so special about your bear?"

"Don't you know?" Bryon perked up. "He's the only bear I know that is born-again and filled with the Holy Ghost!"

David doubled over with laughter as the tears coursed down his cheeks. The audience joined in with joyous applause.

"Bryon, that's great!" the host chuckled. "I understand that next week you have a special event coming up...it's your birthday."

"Yes, and it's Fudgy's birthday too. We will both be eight years old," Bryon replied in a serious tone.

"The '100 Huntley Street' family and audience want to sing 'Happy Birthday' to Bryon and Fudgy," David excitedly announced.

Everyone joined in the singing to send birthday wishes. The atmosphere was one of pleasant spontaneity. Finally, David held the microphone for Bryon and he began to sing his song. Immediately a reverent hush descended upon the studio. Laughter turned to tears as Bryon lifted his fingerless clubs in praise. The people of Canada had opened their hearts to the "tough cookie."

One small girl, Susie, and her mother, Jean Bell, were especially moved to hear Bryon sing. Susie had a similar skin disease as Bryon and she had just returned from the clinic in Germany. When she heard Bryon was going to be on the program, she made a special effort to be there. After the show, we shared an exciting lunch together. Our conversation was saturated with questions about the German treatment. We were so pleased to see how well Susie appeared.

When David Mainse heard about the treatment in West Germany, he made a special plea to the Canadian people to help finance Bryon's trip. Eventually, over $15,000 came in for his expenses.

Later in the afternoon, Bryon and I met the Christian pilot who was to fly us to our next destination...London, Ontario. He had volunteered his services and plane for the entire time we were in Canada. We arrived at the smaller city airport in Toronto on Lake Ontario. There in the terminal we exchanged greetings, picked up our luggage and boxes, and headed out into a freezing spring rain. The thought crossed my mind, "Boy, wait till I tell everyone back home...my own pilot and plane...television appearances...Wow! This is great!"

The wet wind blew my suit jacket open and sprayed my legs. My hair, clothing, and hi-heels were drenched with water. I continued to slosh across the runway, trying to keep up with the pilot and juggle a suitcase at the same time. He was walking extremely fast. Now it was pouring. I was feeling less and less like a celebrity.

We approached the plane and it looked like a miniature toy. I saw two...maybe three seats. The only way to get in-...was to climb up the wing and crawl through the tiny side door and window. Bryon scrambled inside and disappeared in the backseat. Now it was my turn. With the pilot watching from behind, I struggled to grab hold of the slippery wing with my leather shoes. One...two...three...and I was on my knees, clawing my way over a rough sandpaper runner towards the opening. My pantyhose were ripped to shreds, my stringy wet hair was hanging in my eyes, and I couldn't imagine the view the pilot had from behind. As I collapsed into the right front seat, I sputtered, "and people think it's glamorous to fly!"

Within minutes, we were speeding down the runway and up into the air. Higher and higher into the cloudy sky. We were surrounded by dense, fluffy clouds on all sides of us. Condensation ran across the windows and over the wings. I felt like I could reach out and scoop up a handful of the white stuff and eat it like cotton candy. I tried to relax and enjoy the ride.

The pilot was a great conversationalist and explained many of the instruments on the panel in front of us. I noticed that there were two "steering wheels" — one in front of him and one in front of me. Casually, I remarked, "I wonder why there is an extra wheel in front of me?"

The pilot turned and looked at me with a twinkle in his eye, "Oh, don't you know? That wheel was put there in case anything happens to me...you can fly the plane!"

In total disbelief, I cried, "You've got to be kidding, I hope! I don't know anything about flying a plane."

I had been praying for myself, but after the plane hit an air pocket and plummeted slightly downward, I started praying for the pilot. I certainly didn't want anything to happen to him.

Then the thought dawned on me, "How are we going to find the airport, no less the runway, if we can't see an inch in front of us?" Cautiously, I questioned, "How is it possible for you to land with such poor visibility?"

The Christian friend explained, "This plane is my love...my lifetime hobby. I have been flying for several thousand hours and I know these instruments like the back of my hand. Visibility is no problem with the advanced navigational equipment and radar. I guarantee that we will not only find the runway, but when we touch down, the nose of this plane will be in the center of the white line."

It sounded fantastic, but appeared almost impossible. I certainly had my doubts. But after two hours in the air, we started our descent down out of the clouds. As we approached the runway, my eyes were glued to the nose of the plane. The first clear object I saw was the *white line* on the airstrip! He made a believer out of me. From that moment on, the pilot had my complete trust and faith in his aerodynamic abilities. I must admit, though, it felt good to be on the ground again.

The parents of one of my college classmates were to meet us in the London Airport. While we waited for them, Bryon played on the baggage conveyor belt...it was turned off. I saw the Catchpole family coming through the doors and ran to greet them. Suddenly, we heard a terrifying scream. The familiar voice sent shudders up and down my spine. I turned to look — sure enough, it was Bryon. While he was standing on the c⁰nveyor it sta⁷ted to Toek, causing Bryon to lose his balance and tumble forward. Catching his pants in the machinery, he was being dragged towards the opening, which slanted downward and out of the terminal. He was terrified.

I rushed to his side and pulled his pants out of the belt. Walking alongside the moving machine, I helped Bryon to his feet and he frantically grabbed my neck. His hands, arms, and shirt sleeves were already soaked with blood. I looked down at his legs...both of his knees were bleeding. Bryon was crying hysterically.

We tried to calm him down, but the pain was intense. I pulled some gauze bandages and cream out of my suitcase and attempted to wrap some of the open areas. A crowd of people, who had heard the screams, gathered around to watch. When I glanced up and saw that I had an audience, I felt the hot embarrassment rush to my cheeks. Some people had to turn away; the blood and loose skin made them sick.

Somehow, we transported Bryon to our friends' home. Once there, I spent several hours patching up his arms and legs. Bryon had been through this so many times, that he knew exactly what to expect. He was always grateful to have his own private nurse close by when he took a bad tumble. The nurse's name...MOM!

Later that evening, I was scheduled to speak at a large ladies' missions convention. I suggested to Bryon that he stay and rest at the Catchpoles. Nothing doing! He was up in a second, asking to get dressed, so he could come along. Even with hands, arms, and legs plastered with creams and bandages, Bryon painfully managed to climb up to the platform and sing for a crowd of four to five hundred women. When I told the ladies about Bryon's accident and his determination to sing, they responded with a grateful applause. Bryon touched their hearts.

During the week, we also met a wonderful couple, Marlene and Calvin Stiller. Calvin was a kidney-transplant specialist, who worked at the London University Hospital. Because of his position, he was on many committees and in many benefit organizations. When they learned of our desire to take Bryon to Germany for treatment, they pledged to help finance his trip if there was no other way. This gave us the hope that the $40,000 was not out of the question.

We were excited about returning to East Providence. Steve was to meet us at the airport and we had lots of wonderful stories to tell him. Our flight home went exactly as scheduled...a little different from a few days before. We exited the plane and started down the rampway. A handsome, blond-haired, well-dressed man stood at the bottom of the incline waiting for someone. It was Steve! And he held a beautiful bouquet of flowers in his hand. I could hardly believe my eyes...but yes, they were for me.

I wondered, "Did someone die? Or has something happened to the kids? I hope not." Showing my surprise, I blurted out, "What's the occasion? Are these flowers really for me? What happened while we were away?"

"Whoa! Slow down," Steve requested. "Let's go for some coffee and I'll tell you the great news. You're not going to believe it...it's absolutely a miracle!"

Sitting in Valle's Steak House, adjacent to the airport, I demanded, "Come on, Honey, tell us the news. We can't wait one more minute!"

With an immense grin, Steve began to unfold the events: "You remember that when we sent the PTL Network and the Bakkers a thank you letter, we also mentioned the possibility of going to Germany for special treatments? Well...at 10:30 this morning I received a call from the producers telling me that Jim was going to read our letter on the air, and that they were sending our family a check for $40,000! Bryon's treatment will be paid for! The money is in the mail today!

"When I heard the news...I cried and laughed all at the same time. The secretaries in the office thought something terrible had happened to you and Bryon. I kept saying...'40,000

...Oh, Lord....40,000...I can't believe it!' The ladies thought your plane had crashed from 40,000 feet!''

My mouth hung open in amazement. I couldn't move or speak...I was in shock. The words went over me like waves, and then the reality started to filter into my senses. My eyes became moist as I grasped the magnitude of God's love and concern for our family. Here we were teachers at a faith school, receiving no income, and God was sending us $40,000. It was difficult for the human mind to conceive.

Steve interrupted my thoughts: "I was so excited after the phone call that I ran over to the Temple where the students were having chapel services. I walked right up front and whispered the news in Brother Hockhousen's ear. He let me tell the story to the entire student body. The place went spastic! Kids were crying, praising God, and jumping up and down for joy. It was quite an experience."

* * *

Late that night, as I lay in bed thinking about the events of the week...and that day...I recalled my first experience flying in a small propellered plane. The feelings and fears were vivid in my memory. It seemed that the Lord spoke to me, "Lillian, your life has been like that small plane...flying in dense clouds. You haven't been able to see what I am doing in your life, and you wonder what the future holds. But just as the pilot trusted his instruments to bring the plane down out of the clouds and land it precisely on the white line, so it will be the same with your life. The fact that you are still in the clouds and you don't understand everything...doesn't matter. For one day the clouds will be cleared away, and if you trust Me completely, your life will be in the center of My will. You will be right in the middle of the *white line.*"

*"In the same way, we can see and understand only a little about God now, as if we were peering at His reflection in a poor mirror; but someday we are going to see Him in His completeness, face to face.*

---

155

*Now all that I know is hazy and blurred, but then I will see everything clearly, just as clearly as God sees into my heart right now"* (1 Cor. 13:12; TLB).

# 13

# THE VITAL KLINIK

The land of castles and cathedrals saturated with romantic Western culture was soon to become a reality. It was July 1982 — almost a year since we first heard about the "miracle" clinic located in the rural farmlands, just thirty miles southeast of Frankfurt, West Germany. The possibility of having Bryon treated in this skin disease center seemed like a million light-years away. The articles from *People* magazine, newspaper clippings, letters from other children with Epidermylosis Bullosa, and meeting the Daley family encouraged us to keep our hopes alive.

Three-year-old Leann grabbed my arm and squealed with delight as TWA's L1011 jumbo jet lifted off from Kennedy's International Airport. The terrific force thrust us back in our seats, and I heard Bryon and Leann hold their breath. This would be their first overseas flight.

The airline hostess placed a delicious tray of sirloin beef tips, mushrooms and rice in front of me. The gurgling sound from my stomach told me it was time to eat. I glanced at my watch. It was 12:00 midnight. I tried to remember the last time we ate. Besides grabbing a quick sandwich in the airport cafeteria, we hadn't eaten since breakfast in Rhode Island! Because of the congested air traffic over Kennedy, we had flown around for an extra hour-and-a-half waiting for a terminal to park at. Missing supper made every bite taste better.

A feeling of intense loneliness swept over me, as I thought of leaving eighteen-month-old Jenell with my parents for two long months. I saw a mixture of confusion and questioning in her blue eyes, as she clung to Pop-Pop's neck and continued to wave her little hand, long after we had walked down the ramp towards gate 22. She seemed to be asking, "Why are you leaving me, Mommy? You will be right back, won't you?"

I brushed the tears from my eyes. I wanted to reassure her that everything would work out as we had planned, but there were many questions about the future. This meant learning to trust God one day at a time. A lesson that we were experiencing repeatedly.

We knew God had miraculously opened the door for our family to go to Germany. There was no doubt in our minds. The gift of $40,000 from the PTL Television Network and the many donations from "100 Huntley Street" viewers, churches, and friends had made it happen. Our hearts were filled with praise to God for He does bring to pass the dreams that He plants within our hearts.

Leann interrupted my thoughts by imploring, "Mommy, where is my blanket? I can't go to sleep without my blanket!...And where did you put my nightie?...Isn't everyone going to get ready for bed?...I'm so tired."

She had a difficult time understanding why she couldn't stretch out across Bryon, Daddy and me, like in her bed at home. But believe me, they don't make planes for stretching out! Bryon didn't give a hoot about resting; he was too wound-up. He had already been up to the second floor to visit the pilots, got a set of official TWA wings, and was now watching the movie with Dad. All the window shades were drawn to darken the cabin because the sun was beginning to come up in the east.

Sitting on my right was a good-looking, blond-haired

young man about twenty-six, from Michigan. Bill was keenly interested in Bryon and our trip to Germany. For him it meant a month of tourism pleasure along the Rhine's towering peaks and fairy-tale forests. He had noticed Bryon's hands and inquired about his condition. Our conversation then led to God's provision for our trip and the book, *Tough Cookie*. He paid for a copy and began to read it during the flight.

It still amazes me how God opens the door to share our faith with absolutely no effort on our part. Lifestyle evangelism, for the Christian, should be as natural as eating or sleeping. It is a way of life.

It was only 3:00 a.m. but they began serving us a continental breakfast, which consisted of orange juice, a hard roll, and strong coffee. How little did I realize that this would be my diet for the next ten weeks. I would actually look forward to that hard roll and small amount of preserves every morning. The American way of life was six hours behind us. In thirty minutes we would land in the Frankfurt Main International Airport and our lives would never be the same.

Frankfurt has the busiest airport in Europe and is a great commercial and industrial center in Germany. Immediately the "foreignness" began to sink in, as we heard the sounds of different languages, saw the various styles of dress, and were pressed along by the crowds of impatient and harried travelers. The gigantic colorful billboards advertised foreign products, airlines, and sex. There were adult book shops and "health" spas around every corner. Our senses strained to take in all the new sights and sounds, plus keep our bearings.

The summer of 1982 promised to be hot and humid. It was both hot and humid on July 3, 1982. Somehow we made it through customs, rented a small Fiat, and found our way to the Holiday Inn at the Main Tanus Zentrum north of Frankfurt. Once in our room, we showered, changed our filthy crumpled-up clothes, and collapsed on our beds. Sleep came easy after being awake for thirty-six hours.

The next day was July 4 — which meant nothing to the Germans. I thought of the celebrations back home. Probably my parents would take Jenell to the fireworks show, and it would be her first time to really be awed by the colors and sprays of lights. She would scream with excitement and fear, wanting to enjoy it but afraid that the loud noises would hurt her.

For two days we took in as much countryside as possible. We drove to the Weisbaden spas, ate sundaes at a Milch Kur, strolled along the Mainz on the Rhine, and then dined on the outdoor patio of the Newhof Inn in New-Isenberg. We tasted bonnensuppe (soup made of beans and sausage), kartoffelsalat (potato salad spiced with bacon and onions), weiner schnitzel, and schwarzwalder kirschtorte (the world-famous cherry cake from the Black Forest). It was delightful! Steve ordered a side of cauliflower at one small restaurant and they brought him a "whole head" covered with melted cheese and ham. There was plenty for the entire family!

On Monday morning, July 5, after a scrumptious break-fast buffet at the hotel, we headed in the direction of the Klinik with only a German map and our noses to lead us. At several points we stopped and asked how to get to "Michelbach-Alzenau." My four years of high school German was quite useful as the local countrymen shouted foreign directions and waved their arms. I quickly learned to write the name on a piece of paper and show them how it looked, rather than trust my own pronunciation.

Steve enjoyed driving on the autobahn with "no speed limits" in force. But he was sure to keep to the right as the Mercedes came out of nowhere, flashed its headlights, and passed us going about 150 kilometers. The cars were only a blur as they flew by.

The emerald green pastures, speckled with cows and horses and white-washed cottages bedecked with bright flo-wers, surrounded us on every side. Out of the corner of my eye flashed the bold white letters: VITAL KLINIK. They were printed on the roof of a two-story, L-shaped, motel-type struc-ture on the left side of the road. We buzzed past before I could shout, "Stop, Honey! There it is!" We were so relieved to be at our destination.

The doctors were expecting us and we had a busy afternoon getting settled. The first thing I noticed was the cleanliness of the facility. Our small room with two beds, four white walls, adjoining bathroom, and the ceramic tiled patio was spotless. It wasn't the Hilton, but it was comfortable. Bryon and Leann liked the down feather comforters covered with starchy white sheets. They jumped on top of the beds and sank into the fluffy softness. Mom and Dad carried up suitcases and boxes, and then attempted to make it feel like home.

On the first floor of the Klinik there was a large dining room with windows that opened onto the front porch and a playground in the back. Next to the dining room was a small receptionist's office, lobby, rest rooms, the doctors' offices and examining rooms. On the second floor were about thirty patient rooms. Where the wings of the "L" came together, there was a small treatment room. The walls were made of white stucco plaster; the floors were tiled with ceramic and grey marble. A quarter of a mile down the road was a championship horse farm. The unmistakable "fresh-air" drifted through all the open windows. There were no screens or air-conditioners...anywhere!

Next to the Klinik was a rose-colored, two-story guest house, called the "Pension Steumuhle." Frau Freda, the owner, was a pleasant grandmother in her middle sixties. She immediately fell in love with spunky, curly blond-haired Leann. Steve and Leann rented a lovely, quiet room overlooking the farmlands, in the Pension. It would be their home for three weeks while they were in Germany with us.

Dr. Enescu, a small man with dark hair and a quick step, greeted us and took Bryon's medical history. His English was perfect. We learned that he spoke five different languages fluently and understood another two languages. His dark eyes darted occasionally from the windows to the several doors leading to the examining room and to the lobby, as though he was expecting someone. Finally, another woman entered the room and he introduced us to Dr. Radelescu. She took us to one of the examining rooms and asked Bryon to undress. I helped him take off his clothes and they proceeded with blood, urine and culture samples. Dr. Enescu came in and took pictures of Bryon's open sores, deep ulcers, and contracted fingers and toes. When everyone was done stabbing and poking, Bryon was glad to get his clothes on again.

It was 2:00 p.m. and time for "mittagessen" — the big meal of the day. We walked into the dining room and all the eyes focused on us — the newest members of the clinic family. Everyone was especially inspecting eight-year-old Bryon, who had the tell-tale signs of EB. In the far corner of the room was a long table with twenty or more patients, wrapped with bandages and wet compresses covering their faces and hands. These individuals were the "eczema group" — mostly from Germany or European countries. Then scattered throughout the dining hall at smaller tables of three or four were the families of the EB children.

Instantly, we sensed a strong bond of understanding and companionship between Bryon and the other children. It seemed that their spirits reached out and touched one another.

We sat next to the MacCaffrey's from Saskatchewan, Canada. Barb, twenty-six, and her brother, Kenny, sixteen, were accompanied by their mother, Stella. Conversation came easy as we shared similar EB stories and told how we came to the clinic. Barb was thin and had no fingernails but otherwise bore none of the usual markings. Kenny's fingers were afflicted and he had devised a special way to feed himself and write.

There were many others...two-year-old Jessica and her mother, Elaine, from Indiana...ten-year-old Jeff from Newfoundland, Canada...Amanda, age three, from South Carolina...Bor, age three, and his mother, Ineke, from Holland...and ten-year-old Petra from Stuttgart, West Germany. There were others with impetigo, scarladerma, elephantitis, and various skin conditions.

We all sat together in the dining hall savoring stuffed cabbage, chicken soup, boiled potatoes, and yogurt. The smaller children sat on the floor and played. Various languages were spoken. Occasionally, laughter was heard and some turned to see who the instigator was. No one seemed to mind the hundreds of flies that swarmed through the screenless windows and covered the walls, tables, lights, and food. Some used their hands, others waved switches of paper to shoo the pests away. The insects were especially attracted to the patients wrapped with creams and gauze. They persistently lighted upon them while parents brushed them away. Soon it became a game to see how many flies one could "terminate" during a mealtime. I remember the leading contender held the record of 48!

We learned immediately that there were two kinds of diets: normal and special. Parents and friends who were not patients received the "normal" diet, and ALL others with skin conditions received the "special" diet. Bryon started his special diet at lunch which consisted of carrot soup, natural yogurt, boiled long-grain rice, fresh beef, salad with lemon juice, chamomile tea, and "heppinger stilleswasser" (mineral water). For supper the menu was the same. Breakfast or "fruhstruck" included hot cream of farina, fresh rolls, unsalted butter, and tea. The "normal" diet really wasn't all that different except we were allowed coffee, preserves, cabbage and other meats and vegetables. After a few days every meal tasted the same. Surprisingly, I forgot about pancakes, sausages and eggs, and actually found myself looking forward to the strong German coffee, fresh rolls and butter every morning.

The "treatments" started around the clock, every three to four hours. Bryon was a sweetheart, even when they dragged him out of bed at 2:00 a.m. and then again at 6:00 a.m. during the night. Everyone warned us that the diet and treatments were difficult to adjust to at first. They also hinted that the patients usually got worse physically before they began to get better. I didn't understand what they meant until I watched Bryon begin to break down with blisters, open sores, infection, fevers, nausea, and bleeding. Our main purpose in coming was to help Bryon get better. For six weeks we experienced overwhelming frustrations as we watched Bryon's body weaken and poisonous infection drain out of his system. The only way to live through the pain was to take one day at a time.

After the results from the lab tests returned, Dr. Enescu brought Bryon's jars of vitamins to the room. He had to take one pill during and one right after each meal. That meant six pills a day. The "pills" were made of communion wafer material about the size of a quarter. The two pieces of wafer were fitted together and held the vitamin powder. The children held these wafers on their tongues until they started to dissolve. When the powder burst into their mouths, they would grab a drink of tea and wash it down. It was the worst-tasting stuff in the world. Bryon said it was, "Awful, absolutely awful!"

We had taken a case of *Tough Cookie* books with us. As soon as we made these available, parents and patients were sitting in the lobby, dining room, and outside on the porches, reading Bryon's book. This became a tremendous open door for us to share our faith in God and witness about the miracles that had taken place in our lives.

During the warm summer evenings, after the kids were in bed, many of the parents gathered on the verandas to play games, share experiences, and sometime cry...from the extreme pressure and strain caused by caring for an EB child. Very few had any religious background or faith to rely upon. Most were single-parent families where one of the mates chose to bail out from the emotional merry-go-round. Our family was a glimmer of hope, that life could still have meaning...and normalcy...and purpose.

In a few short days our lives settled into somewhat of a routine. In between meals and treatments we made short getaways in our compact red Ford Fiat. Germany was waiting for us and we had a grand time discovering it. Frau Freda took us to a nearby village where there was a Benzing department store. The first item I purchased was a German coffee-maker for our room. We also stocked up on chocolates, cookies, laundry soaps and a rack to hang our clothes on. The Frau helped us to rent a typewriter so that I could work on my correspondence, lessons and a new book. This provided me with hours of valuable work time.

In the city of Hanau, a site for one of the largest U.S. military bases, we discovered an indoor shopping mall, similar to those in the States. There were several great restaurants, dairy bars, shops, game rooms and a theater. The kids enjoyed riding the escalators up and down, while Steve and I shared a dessert. In Hanau we found our first American fast-food restaurant — Wendy's! We couldn't believe our eyes. Boy, did those double cheeseburgers and fries taste good! Bryon never said a word while we stuffed our faces and slurped on frosties. He just sipped his carrot soup from the clinic.

About a week after we had settled in, our dear missionary friends, Eddie and Ruth Washington from Kaiserslautern, visited us. They brightened up our whole day with gifts of peanut butter, orange and apple juice, soda-pop, and candy. They had spent more than twenty years in Germany working with the military and their families in establishing local Pentecostal churches. The Washingtons were a tremendous help in indoctrinating us to German customs and culture. We spent the afternoon visiting outside under the shade trees, playing games with the children, and talking about common acquaintances. Then we drove to nearby Alzenau and enjoyed a delicious dinner of "weiner schnitzel" (veal) and fresh cold asparagus with a mayonnaise sauce poured over it. Bryon, of course, took two thermoses of carrot soup and noodles mixed with beef. It was a treat to be out for the evening with Christian friends who could speak English. Our friends invited us to visit them and requested Stephen to speak at their churches. We promised them that we would see them again.

Finally the moment arrived when I had the "awesome" experience to master the "waschbeg" — a primitive form of a washing machine for clothes. Everyone in the clinic had to take turns with the "waschbeg" as there were no laundromats anywhere and the clinic had no such facilities for the patients or their families. This contraption looked like an oversized orange ice chest; a box with a motorized lid that sat in the middle of the tub.

I was determined to learn how to use this machine as it was the only means of providing clean clothes for my family. The first step was to handfill it with water from the tub, sprinkle in detergent, put a few articles of clothing inside, cover it with the lid and turn it on. The box shook and jerked several times to the right and then stopped. Then it repeated the action in the left direction and stopped. After several minutes of shaking and jerking it completely stopped. Next, the water was drained out into the tub and clean rinse water was poured in. The whole process was repeated. Then came the most fun of all — wringing every piece of clothing out by hand and hanging them on a make-shift line on the balcony outside our room. The absolute 'pits' was to go through all those contortions, only to have a sudden wind and rain storm blow your laundry all over the balcony and down onto the ground. It was the perfect activity for a boring day. It certainly was a great experience in the school of patience. We had a lot of laughs at ourselves and our clothes, after a few weeks of putting them through the "waschbeg."

Leann had no problem adjusting. The tow-headed boy, Bor, from Holland was her best friend. Language didn't seem to be a problem for these three-year-olds as they played on the gymset, chased each other through the fields and picked strawberries together. One afternoon I looked down from our balcony to see Leann jumping up and down on one foot, chasing after Bor, and screaming for him to stop. The Dutch boy seemed delighted to have Leann's total attention as he waved her missing shoe in the air and attempted to throw it over the fence and out of reach. Leann hopped up to the fence just in time to retrieve her shoe. Then they both burst into a siege of giggles and ran off in another direction. Leann seemed oblivious as to the real reason we were at the clinic. She was happy to know that Mom and Dad were there.

One morning at breakfast, very unexpectedly, Leann looked up at her daddy with those big blue eyes and stated, "Daddy, I love you...well...a little bit...but Mommy, I love you way up to the sky!" She raised both hands in a sweeping arch that reached to the heavens.

Bryon's treatments and new diet seemed to be progressing nicely. He learned to eat the food and really enjoy it. His favorite was the freshly-baked bread and homemade butter. He inhaled about five to six rolls a day and loved to wrap them in napkins to take back to the room for a snack.

His over-all skin condition had improved — it looked less red, there were fewer blisters, some of his toes were separated, and a lot of dead skin had peeled off. The "nurses" (girls with no formal education, but on-the-job medical training) were very kind to the children. They worked on three or four patients at one time in a crowded, closed-in room. The entire treatment took about forty-five minutes. New blisters were broken with a sterile needle and drained with a piece of white cotton. All the open sores were cleaned with vegetable oil on a cotton ball, covered with antibiotic cream, cotton squares, and bandaged. White Vaseline-type cream, called "body-salbe," was rubbed over all the red rough areas. The gauze was tied on — no tape was used.

The nurses taught the children German songs, phrases, and stories. Many times the chorus of happy voices was heard down the hallways. Sometimes the nurses and kids played jokes on each other. Following a treatment one afternoon, Bryon stood in the doorway of our room totally naked except for his bandages, and cotton balls stuck to his chin and head — which resembled a German Santa Claus. He paraded up and down the halls, while the girls squealed with glee. They loved Bryon's favorite teddy bear, "Fudgy." To make him officially German they nicknamed the bear — "Chokolady" (chocolate).

It was difficult at times not to let the many little irritating inconsistencies with schedules and foreign prejudices get the best of us. Often the girls did not show up for work and they were understaffed. This put a strain on everyone and caused the treatments to be off schedule by six to eight hours. The nurses and most of the employees were habitual smokers, and even smoked while doing the children's treatments. The doctors' lifestyles were totally unstructured — staying up all hours of the night, drinking and partying in the offices, and then not showing up for several days. Professor Kozak was supposed to check on Bryon's condition every day, yet for periods of three to four days he did not appear. Perhaps he was on a business trip or working in another hospital — we never really knew.

We also felt some anti-American sentiments at times, especially when the German patients were taken for treatments ahead of Americans or Canadians, even when one of our children was scheduled to go first. The same preferential actions were obvious in the dining room, where the Germans were served on glassware, while the Americans and Canadians received plastic dishes. When we stepped in line to get our plates, the German people were served first, even if it meant pushing in front of others and cutting in line. Only small things...I realized...but when you are a foreigner and away from home, it can play a game on your emotions. I struggled to overcome criticism and a growing frustration at those who were serving us. I knew a bitter attitude would only destroy my spirit...I would eventually be the loser, not these people. I could not change the conditions, but I could control the way I responded to those conditions.

There were many things we did to help us forget the daily pressures. One of our favorites was to take a walk in the coolness of the early evening through the pasturelands and surrounding farms. We saw many of the young boys herding sheep and cattle, while the girls worked in the gardens with their mothers. We discovered an enormous beehive hanging from a large sprawling tree. From a safe distance we watched the constant flurry of bees coming and going from the millions of nearby clover blossoms.

On one of our walks down a paved bicycle trail, we stumbled onto a delicate yellow flower, poking its head and leaves through the black cement. There it stood in the middle of the concrete path, stretching its face towards the western sun. How was it able to push through such a hard surface and still appear in such beauty? The four of us stood quietly and studied the plant in amazement. It was a tiny miracle, showing the handiwork of God. If this little flower could survive through adverse circumstances, so could we withstand the constant irritations at the clinic. Someone has said, "Bloom where you are planted" — that was definitely meant for me.

Another escape was the "Frankenstuben" — the cozy country inn across the way. Down a paved road, under the highway overpass, and adjacent to a large sports arena was our family "hideaway." Besides great German cooking, there we experienced the most delightful ice cream treats in Europe. Three or four scoops of your favorite "eis," drenched in fruit and sauces, then topped with mounds of real whipped cream and gourmet wafers, was sure to make you forget life at the clinic for at least a few minutes.

After Leann and Bryon were safely tucked in bed, Steve and I would rendezvous at the Frankenstuben for a late night "date." Sometimes we felt like teenagers again, trying to sneak a few moments alone, after giving our entire day to treatments, washing clothes, and entertaining the children. It would be eleven long weeks before we would really feel married again.

On a few rare afternoons we escaped the clinic to explore the surrounding fairy tale countryside. The Schloss Castle in Aschaffenburg and the Ronneburg Schloss were our favorites. The Aschaffenburg Castle was built like a medieval fortress in a square structure, surrounded by a moat with a draw-bridge and inside courtyard. Three floors of antiquated paintings, tapestries, costumes, and artifacts kept Leann and Bryon's attention for hours.

In Ronneburg, the castle was situated on an elevated hill overlooking the neatly laid-out rows of crops and farm houses. Once inhabited by the Huguenots and others who sought religious freedom, now it was a place for visitors to explore the towers, dungeons, and underground passageways. The servants' quarters had been remodeled into a fine dining room and inn. Their black forest cherry torte was the best I've ever tasted.

We spent one Sunday afternoon at the Frankfurt Zoo, gazing at the lions, tigers, monkeys, polar bears, and elephants. The animals didn't care that we couldn't speak German...they just stared at us no matter what we yelled at them. It was an extremely hot day and the "eis" at the cafe sure satisfied our taste buds. It would have been a perfect day if we hadn't gotten lost on our way back to Michelbach. For three hours we drove around Frankfurt following signs for Route 3,

---

169

which pointed in several directions. There were no signs giving north and south indications, nor the name of the farthest destination.

There are two things that really annoy Stephen...being late...and getting lost. Well, we managed to do both of them in one afternoon. The sight of the clinic was a welcome landmark to four tired, hot, and weary explorers. Enough of touring for one day.

A great place to goof off on a tepid summer day was the local "schwimm bad" — swimming pool. Alzenau had two "bads" — a man-made lake and an olympic-size pool. It was interesting to see how Leann reacted to the other children who were all bathing nude. Within five minutes she had taken off her swimsuit and was splashing in the water with the other youngsters. Being a proper mother, I endeavored to keep her covered. But Leann wasn't going to be "different" from everyone else...so off came the swimwear. I finally gave in to the apparent custom.

The children became the least of my concern as I noticed that the older generation was not fully clothed either. Sitting on a blanket, while wiggling our toes in the sand, we watched one elderly woman bob spasmodically up and down in the lake. Finally the possibility dawned on us that she could be in trouble. Screaming in German, while gurgling water, she went under for the last time. Steve bolted off the blanket and dove into the water. After what seemed like an eternity, he appeared above the surface, pulling the woman with one arm and stroking with the other. Close to shore, he collapsed. I ran over and turned the heavyset woman on her side and pushed water out of her stomach. She began to choke and cough. Other people joined us. Apparently some were relatives, and they began to speak to her. The poor woman had almost drowned. Within a few minutes she revived. Grateful for being rescued, she turned and grabbed Stephen in one enormous bear hug, one he will never forget. The Frau kissed him on both cheeks and said, "Danke sehr...danke sehr" (which means thank you).

Nearly three weeks had passed since our coming to Germany. On our third Sunday, Steve left to minister with the

Washingtons in Kaiserlautern at the military base. I moved a crib into our already crowded room for Leann to stay with us. I tried to keep the children busy so that we wouldn't think of the loneliness of being separated. We made pastel-colored butterflies with straws for antennas and pasted them on our bare white walls. Bryon had bought a few posters and had received a pile of cards from friends at home...so we became interior decorators. It definitely made our room and spirits brighter.

The kids knew I missed their daddy, so they tried extra hard to be good. Leann and I walked into the village of Michelbach and had a shopping excursion. I bought a typical German basket to remind me of how the women carried them to the villages every day, where they bought meat, vegetables, and bread. Leann wanted a pretty green watering can to sprinkle all the flowers at the clinic. Then I spied a blue and red plastic drink holder for Bryon to carry his herbal tea. We also tucked in our basket some tasty cookies, cheese, and a few blooming plants from the "blumen."

Later in the afternoon, while we were "supposed" to be napping, Leann ate my entire "milch" chocolate bar and bit the erasers off my pencils. She looked as guilty as someone who was caught with his hand in the cookie jar. Her face was covered with chocolate, but she shook her head "no." No, she didn't eat the candy! What a little monkey.

Monday morning at 11:45 a.m. Steve walked into our room. I didn't expect him until late in the day. I think he really missed us and made an effort to get back early. Knowing that he would be leaving for home in just five days gave him extra incentive. He wanted to stay longer but he had made a commitment to speak at the Southern New England Youth Camp...he couldn't back out now.

Thursday, July 22, was our last day together. We packed it full of activities. We drove to Hanau, visited the indoor shopping center, ate at Wendy's, and found a large Kaufhof department store. We bought a lot of souvenirs for our friends at home. Then we topped it off with an evening alone for dinner. Some of the parents volunteered to watch Bryon and Leann for us.

It was an evening to be remembered. Gentle warm rain rolled off the windshield...we hardly noticed. The million lights from the city of Frankfurt seemed endless from the Henninger Turm's revolving restaurant. During dinner we viewed the city in three complete turns. The clinic, Bryon's condition, pressures, separation, and all that lay ahead...melted away for a few precious hours. As we looked into each other's eyes by candlelight...nothing else existed...just the two of us. Words flowed. Some thoughts were shared, others were sensed. That night we fell in love all over again.

I awoke the next morning with a gnawing ache of loneliness. The point in time I dreaded had come. My honey had to go home to the States...to Rhode Island and Zion Bible Institute. Back to responsibilities and jobs that had to be done.

Leann looked like a little "madchen" in her red flared skirt, white cotton blouse, clogs, and small wicker basket. Daddy and Leann stood under the sign for Gate A-13 at the "flughafen" (airport) and I took their picture. It was time for them to board the Lufthansa 747. Everyone tried hard to be brave as we said good-bye. Then Bryon reached up to hug Daddy's neck and I heard the sobs, "Daddy, don't leave...I'm gonna miss you, Dad."

I blinked hard as they pulled away and walked down the ramp and out of sight. We sat and watched through the windows until the jet backed out and headed towards the runway. We waved furiously, just in case they could see us standing there with our noses pressed against the glass. My heart actually hurt. Tears fell in rivets down both cheeks and I didn't care who saw them. Bryon was asking questions...I couldn't answer him. I had tried to be brave for him; now he was being brave for me. "It's okay, Mom. You still have me," Bryon assured me.

The ride to the clinic was strangely quiet compared to a few hours earlier when everyone had tried to get into the conversation. The Pension, the Frankenstuben, the play ground...and the wooded trails...all reminded me of Steve. Every time someone asked me a question, I started to cry. I had to get a hold of myself, for Bryon's sake at least. He needed me to be strong. The only way I could survive the next six weeks was to bury myself in work and help Bryon get better.

I caught up on mountains of correspondence we had received through television appearances and the *Tough Cookie* book. Then I started to outline and make preparations for a sequel. At first the inspiration came hard, but then chapters and titles began to fall into place. At that point I didn't know that it would take eight long years to complete the manuscript.

Just up the road a piece was a large horse farm. One Sunday morning we noticed a line of cars and trailers moving like a steady procession of army ants towards the farm. We wondered what event was taking place. Petra, age 10, and her father, Rudolph, who roomed directly across the hall, suggested we take a walk up the road and see for ourselves. Much to our surprise, we discovered that they were holding an international horse tournament.

Flags, cars, and multitudes of people lined the road. Stands selling German sausage, sauerkraut, and beer were crowded with hungry patrons. We found an empty spot along the white wooden fence and climbed up to get a good view of the events. Perfectly groomed horses and uniformed riders moved through the maze of jumps, ditches, and obstacles. Each was graded and given a score. During the intermission they featured a unique dog show with German Shepherds. It turned out to be a delightful afternoon.

Quite a few older women arrived from Ontario for treatment at the clinic. They all fell in love with Bryon. Margaret Price, a retired school teacher, had scalerderma, which caused a large hole in her head. She covered the open sore by wearing a white frosted wig. We delighted to hear her tales about the mischievous youngsters she had taught. One night as we were getting ready for bed, Bryon piped up: "I know why Mrs. Price has a hole in her head...the kids in school drove her crazy!"

Bryon and I could hardly control ourselves. We doubled over in laughter and buried our faces in our pillows. We giggled until the tears ran down our cheeks. We tried not to wake everyone, but it was a relief to let out all those pent-up emotions and frustrations. Laughter is definitely the best medicine for lonely hearts.

Another antidote for boredom and loneliness was the "Children's Magic Show," produced by Helen Gonzales, Bobby Lee, and Bryon Sparks. The whole clinic was invited to the premier showing. Chairs were crowded into the lounge and waiting rooms as parents, patients, and nurses waited anxiously. The magicians kept the audience spellbound for an hour with their tricks, illusions, and the famous 'disappearing act.' They all received a standing ovation.

Often waves of homesickness flooded me. It was a fight to keep from going under. So many customs and differences made the ache more poignant. Especially the diet. The dining room served the same kind of food every day. For breakfast the menu was hard rolls, butter, and coffee. For lunch...boiled potatoes or rice, beef and carrots in a stew. For supper...hard rolls, lunch meat, and head cheese. Nothing ever changed.

One evening as we entered the cafeteria, I began to grumble and complain about the food. I muttered to Bryon, "Well, I wonder what we will have for supper tonight? Oh, yes, hard rolls, lunch meat, and cheese."

Sarcastically, I added, "They shouldn't have gone to so much trouble. Doesn't this look appetizing?" I threw a roll, meat, and cheese on my plate, and slumped down into my seat. I thought about what I would have if I were back home. Ummm...veal Parmesan, broccoli with cheese, baked potato with sour cream...and strawberry cheesecake — New York style! My glands began to salivate and I knew I was delirious with hunger.

Bryon hadn't said a word. He kept shoveling more heaping spoonfuls of meat, noodles, and carrots in his mouth. Finally, in exasperation, I slammed down my fork and exclaimed, "I don't think I can eat one more roll or I'll choke!"

Bryon gently lifted his head and looked at me. "Mom, I've been eating the same food for six weeks, and I'm not complaining!"

---

My bitter attitude was broken. I felt ashamed of myself. Bryon was right — he had been through a lot and yet he hadn't complained once. I asked the Lord to forgive me and then thanked Bryon for being so honest. "In everything give thanks" ...even for hard rolls, lunch meat, and head cheese.

For several days Bryon's skin seemed to get worse. New sores opened up and infection was draining from his body. I became very concerned. One morning he awakened in a feverish sweat, nauseated, and lethargic. Several of the other children had contracted staph and yeast infections and were confined to their rooms. Kenny McCaffrey, from Saskatchewan, had .been marooned to his room for ten days. Had Bryon picked up the same bacteria?

I went down to the doctors' offices and requested that Professor Kozak examine Bryon. They agreed. I wrapped Bryon's naked thirty-pound body in a clean sheet and carried him to the examination room. Kozak closely studied all of Bryon's new lesions and took cultures of the pus-filled areas. I tried to explain to Mr. Enescu, our interpreter, the dismay I felt over the breakdown of Bryon's skin and the tremendous pain he was experiencing. As Mr. Enescu repeated my words in Rumanian, Mr. Kozak nodded his head to show that he understood. He was very calm about Bryon's condition and even seemed pleased...like he expected this to happen. I thought to myself, "How can he be so calm about this...almost stoic...towards Bryon's pathetic condition...his pain...and apparent infection? Why doesn't he do something to relieve this suffering?"

As if he could read my thoughts, Mr. Kozak placed his hand on my shoulder and replied, "Mrs. Sparks. No problem. No problem."

I wanted to scream at him, "What do you mean there is no problem! There is definitely a problem here. Anyone can see that!" It was futile. They turned and walked away conversing in German or Rumanian, dismissing us from their discussion. Helplessly, I wrapped Bryon in the sheet and carried him back to the room.

But Bryon's treatment did change. Because of the serious

infection he was not allowed out of his room. His clothes and bandages were removed and special antibiotic creams were rubbed over the open sores every two hours, day and night. His condition worsened. He lay on his bed hour after hour listening to the tape recorder, unable to feed himself or go to the toilet without help.

The days seemed to drag on. Besides feeding him, rubbing cream over his sores, keeping the flies and insects away, and changing his sheets, I tried to read stories and play games as a diversion from the unbearable agony. Almost his entire body was covered with blisters and infection. I wondered when this nightmare would end. Certainly we hadn't traveled thousands of miles for Bryon to die in a foreign country.

Pavel Kozak was a known expert. Scrapbooks in the waiting room testified to his miraculous treatments. Pictures of "before" and "after" were convincing enough to make people believe that he had results. Born in Rumania, he was afflicted with a severe case of eczema at the age of nineteen. For four years he lay in a hospital bed; his skin was cracked and open. It was then he determined to become a biochemist and dermatologist to help cure skin diseases. His lifetime pursuit led him to the University Hospital of Bucharest: where he treated over one hundred thousand patients. His fame spread throughout Europe. Many people wished to receive his treatments, but the Rumanian government would not allow him to treat anyone outside of his country. Heartbroken, he decided to leave his homeland and defect to Germany. It was here he began a new life.

Living in Frankfurt with his wife, Maria, and their two boys, Alexander and Peter, Kozak had a dream of starting his own clinic. Through Mr. Enescu, his brother-in-law, he had the opportunity to work at the small private clinic — "Vital Klinik" — in Michelbach. Now patients could be treated from all over Europe, Canada, and the United States.

Yet knowing all these facts did not make the pain any easier to bear as Bryon continued to suffer. Torn with doubts and overcome with fear, I tossed sleeplessly in my bed. Finally, about three o'clock I slipped out of my covers and retreated to the bathroom. I closed the door behind me and turned on the bath water. The dam of frustrations, uncertainties, and unanswered questions broke wide open. I sobbed uncontrollably. Crushed, I bore my soul before the Lord.

"Lord," I cried, "Please show me in some small way that You care about us. Speak to me, Lord, so that I have the assurance that You haven't forgotten us and left us alone. I need to know that somehow You are going 'to work all things for our good.' "

I tried to regain my composure as I turned off the water and dried my tears with a towel. I stopped and listened. I thought I heard music coming from our room. I slowly pushed open the bathroom door and stepped into the darkness. It was Bryon. He must have heard me crying and sensed my hurt. The words filled the room and floated out into the night..."Great is Thy faithfulness...Oh God, my Father...There is no shadow of turning with Thee...Thou changest not, Thy compassions, they fail not...Great is Thy faithfulness, Lord unto me...Great is Thy faithfulness...Great is Thy faithfulness...Morning by morning new mercies I see...All that I needed Thy hand hath provided...Great is Thy faithfulness, Lord unto me."

Tears streamed down my cheeks. Bryon's song of hope was exactly "the word" I needed from the Lord. If my buddy could sing while lying on a bed completely naked, covered with bleeding sores, then I could put my trust in God one more time. The same God that gives "songs in the night," also brings "joy in the morning."

Ten weeks had passed since we first left for Germany. So much had happened. It was August 27, 1982 and we were going home. The last two weeks were the most difficult, as the infection drained from Bryon's body and the new pink skin began to form. But today that was all forgotten, while Bryon ran through the clinic saying good-bye to all his new friends. For the first time in his life, he wore regular shoes. Painlessly, he jumped from step to step and bounded across the front yard. His body was covered with beautiful new skin. Only one open sore remained. Bryon's dream of healing was coming true.

Mr. Kozak joined us for pictures and smiled approvingly

at his young patient. Bryon gave him a grateful hug. Kozak placed his hand on my shoulder and reaffirmed, "Mrs. Sparks. No problem." (I had learned that these were the only words he knew in English.) But it didn't matter...for with God there was "no problem."

> *"With men this is impossible, but with God all things are possible" (Matt. 19:26b).*

# 14

# THE HIGHEST PRAISE

The highest praise,
More than spoken words
    It's what my heart would say;
All I have to offer You in my small way,
Is to give my life to You.

The highest praise,
Not to see, and yet believe
    You died for me;
Sometimes in the night I thank You silently,
For all You do.
The highest praise...
    Is to give my life to You.[2]

The first time I heard these words was on a recording done by the Brooklyn Tabernacle Choir under the direction of Carol Cymbala. They sang with such an urgency and heart-felt enthusiasm, that I was immediately drawn to their style. Most of the songs were written by Carol herself. I liked the freshness of words and upbeat contemporary rhythms. The Collegians responded immediately to the Tabernacle's music and many of the songs became a part of our repertoire. Each time the choir put out a new album, we were anxious to listen to the selections.

After several years of appreciating their music, we had the delightful experience of having a choir exchange with their church. Jim Cymbala, the pastor, his wife, Carol, and their best soloists came to Zion Bible Institute to minister with us. In one afternoon, Carol and the soloists taught our Sanctuary Choir five new songs (without any music) and we presented them that evening in a sacred concert. It was dynamic!

A month later the Collegians were invited to minister in their church and sing with their anointed choir. Located in downtown Brooklyn, on Flatbush Avenue, this renovated movie theater was the perfect place to blend diverse social, racial, and national backgrounds. Their building, which seated about two thousand, was packed three times on Sunday. Pastor Cymbala admitted that the secret of his church's effectiveness was the Tuesday night prayer meeting, which at times had over two thousand in attendance.

Through our music ministry exchange, God gave us two precious new friends...Jim and Carol Cymbala. Our family continued to minister there and the people grew to love Bryon. During one weekend of services, Bryon sang and shared his testimony at a children's rally. A Puerto Rican boy, about eight years old, named Reynaldo, sat on the front row with his other brothers and sisters. Immediately, I recognized something familiar about this boy. He too, was covered with bandages. As I looked closer, I saw the unmistakable symptoms of Epidermylosis Bullosa.

The Children's Ministry Team, along with puppets and clowns, had held rallies throughout the city, announcing

Bryon's coming. Reynaldo's father identified himself and made the team aware of his son, who was confined to a hospital. The team members made a special effort to bring Reynaldo and his whole family to the crusade. It meant communicating with his social worker and getting permission for his release from the hospital.

Our special joy was to see Reynaldo and his brothers and sisters come to the altar for salvation after Bryon finished singing. There is a disease that is worse than EB — that disease is called "sin." Sin destroys our heart and robs us of eternal life. We saw God perform a miracle in Reynaldo and his family...they left with clean hearts, free of sin!

* * *

Many wonderful letters came in from across the United States, Canada, and from around the world. *Tough Cookie* was being read in Australia, New Zealand, Japan, the Philippines, England, Italy, Yugoslavia, Germany, Netherlands, Israel, Zimbabwe, Barbados, Alaska, Yukon Territories, and many other countries too numerous to mention. A few students helped me to answer each letter individually.

One letter arrived from a young woman who had attended Bible school with us. I didn't recognize her married name, but as I read her story the pieces fit together. Susan was in her early thirties, the mother of two small girls, and the wife of a hopeless alcoholic. When she married John, he seemed like a good fellow and hard worker. But after a few months she discovered that he had a drinking problem, and consequently abused her and the children.

During the ten years they were married, Susan had left John many times to live with her mother. The constant drunkenness and beatings had broken down her emotional stability. At times she was close to a nervous breakdown. Susan never knew when her husband would stumble through the front door in a rage, lashing out at anything and anyone in his path. Alone, late at night, she lay perfectly still, listening for the front door to open, the heavy footsteps, and the fumbling noises in the dark.

Susan tried to pray, but she wondered if God even heard her. It seemed like an imaginary dream, that years before she had attended Bible school and felt God's calling into the ministry. Things had radically changed. She stopped going to church, married a man who was not a Christian, and forgot about God's plan for her life.

After one of John's drunken rages, Susan decided to leave permanently. While John was gone, Susan and the children began to pack their things. In the midst of rushing around, she heard a knock at the door — it was her neighbor!

"Hi, Susan," her friend said. "I heard John come home last night, and I prayed for you and the children. Is everyone all right?"

"Yeah, we're okay." Susan looked down at the floor. "We're leaving again. Maybe I'll stay with my mother a while and then get a place of my own."

Her neighbor reached out and touched her arm. She said, "I thought you might be leaving, so I came by to give you this book to read, *Tough Cookie.* The author, Lillian Sparks, spoke at our church last night and she mentioned attending Zion Bible Institute. Isn't that where you went to school, Susan?"

"Yes, but that was ages ago. I haven't kept in touch with anyone from Zion. No one will remember me."

"Well, I thought you might like to read Lillian's story about her son, Bryon. Their family has been through a real struggle, but God has been their strength. Perhaps it will encourage you." Her friend handed her the book and turned to walk across the street.

Susan stared at the cover...the young boy's eyes seemed to look into her soul. She sensed that he, too, had been through suffering in his life. But she also saw a joy and contentment that she didn't know. Forgetting the disarray of her home and the suitcases scattered about the living room, she sank down into a chair and began to peruse the pages. Miraculously, the girls found something quiet to play with. Unnoticed the hours flew by. Susan knew only one thing...she couldn't stop reading.

Finally, Susan finished the last page. Tears streamed down her cheeks. She knew what she must do...recommit her life to Christ. In the center of the living room carpet, she knelt in prayer. With heart-rending sobs, she asked the Lord Jesus to come into her heart again. A million pounds of anxiety and guilt rolled off her shoulders. She felt clean...and free, for the first time in ten years. She was deliriously happy, crying and laughing all at once. The children didn't understand what had happened to their mom, but they were thrilled when she tightly hugged them and told them how much she loved them.

Almost immediately, Susan knew she couldn't leave. God spoke to her heart and gave her a wonderful assurance that He was going to do a miracle in her husband's life. For the first time in years she had hope again.

Susan put away all the clothes and placed the suitcases in the closets. It was Saturday, and she knew John usually came home intoxicated. So she bathed the girls early and put them to bed. Before she crawled in between the covers, she knelt beside her bed and thanked the Lord for changing her life. She felt the same peace and assurance she had felt earlier that afternoon.

Susan normally had difficulty falling asleep because of the gnawing fear that John would soon return. So when she heard the front door, she jolted upright in bed. She couldn't believe it...she had been asleep. Her heart pounding, she listened for the familiar sounds of disorientation and stupor. Suddenly, she heard childish screams and realized John had gone into the girls' room. Susan tore out of bed and across the hall. John had pulled one of the girls onto the floor and was lashing her in the face with the back of his hand. Susan was terrified.

"Please, John...don't!" Susan agonized. "Don't hurt her ...she's sleeping."

Surprisingly, John stepped back and all his anger melted away. He stumbled down the hall and into the living room. Susan heard him open another can of beer and fall into a chair. After tucking her daughter back into bed and trying to soothe her, she endeavored to get some rest herself.

The next morning, Susan rolled over and glanced at the

clock. It read 7:30 a.m. Her nose picked up the scents of fresh coffee brewing and bacon frying. That's impossible, she thought to herself. Unless I really went to my mother's house in the middle of the night and I don't remember. She pulled on a housecoat and hurried into the kitchen. She froze in shock. "Oh dear God, I've died and gone to heaven...this can't be happening." Standing in front of the stove, with an apron tied around his waist, there was a freshly shaved and showered man cooking breakfast...it was John! That in itself was a divine miracle. Never in their ten years of married life had he ever made coffee or fixed breakfast.

"Stop standing there, like a gaping baboon," John shouted at her. "Get those girls out of bed and dressed...we're going to church this morning!"

Susan jumped at his command and quickly obeyed before he changed his mind. "What happened to John?" she wondered. "This is unbelievable! Overnight I have a new husband." She was dying to ask him "why" about everything, but held it inside, for fear that the wonderful bubble would burst.

Seated in the car, en route to church, Susan couldn't hold it in anymore. "John, what happened to you?" she blurted out.

Hesitating, John replied, "Well, I was drinking last night and I don't remember how I got home. But when I woke up about at three in the morning, I saw this 'tough crumble' book...or whatever it's called...lying on the table. I was absolutely sober. So I picked up the book and started to read. Man...what a story! That family has some faith. I mean...the way they trusted God after all they had been through...it's amazing..." His voice trembled. "I don't known much about religion, but I knelt down and asked God to come into my life. And if the pastor gives an invitation for salvation at church this morning...I'm going right down front!"

Susan bit her lip. She was shaking from excitement. God had done a miracle in John's life...just as He promised. Now she prayed that the pastor would make a call for commitment. Her heart beat wildly with anticipation.

At the close of the service, when the Pastor asked if there

was anyone who would like to give their life to Christ, John, Susan, and their two girls walked to the altar. Many tears were shed that day as God brought restoration grace into a broken family. His love softened the stony hearts and replaced them with hearts of flesh...new...clean hearts.

The story didn't end there. Several months after I received Susan's letter, our Collegian Choir visited their church. Unknown to me, this family was sitting in the audience during the entire concert. Following the altar call, I caught a glimpse of a man and his wife, each holding a child in their arms, making their way towards the front. The woman looked strangely familiar. They walked up to me and introduced themselves. Susan referred to the letter she had written to me months earlier. The light went on. I recognized who she was...a former classmate from Bible school.

Both of them glowed with the love of Christ...like neon signs. The words tumbled out...about John's miraculous deliverance from alcoholism...their marriage saved from divorce...rebuilding their home...counseling for the children...and thanks for writing the "tough cookie" story which ultimately changed their lives.

Words cannot express the sense of awe and humility I felt at that moment. Awe at the greatness of our God and how He continued "to work everything out for good." Even Bryon's years of suffering was used as an instrument of good. I also felt humble because He chose to use me in His all-knowing plan. My heart wanted to burst with thanksgiving and gratitude for being included in His intricate plan.

These experiences gave new meaning and purpose for Bryon's life. Often we received phone calls from other parents who had children with EB or some other handicap, requesting prayer and advice for their situation. Distance was not a factor. One call came from the mother of a Mongoloid child, who was both deaf and blind. Tearfully, she explained that she and her husband had decided to put Matthew in an institution...his care was overwhelming. Meanwhile, a friend of theirs loaned them a *Tough Cookie* book to read over the weekend. By Monday morning they reversed their decision — they would keep their son. They phoned to express their thanks for sharing Bryon's struggles and day-by-day care. It gave them courage and hope for the future.

We had the opportunity to meet another gentleman, whose life nad been radically altered by Bryon's testimony. David was an ex-priest, in his middle thirties, who lived in the Harrisburg, Pennsylvania area. We met Dave at a book-signing party, sponsored by Waldenbooks in the Capitol City Mall. He stood off to the side during the autographing and television interview and watched throngs of people shaking hands and talking with Bryon. At closing time, the store manager said to me, "Mrs. Sparks, I have someone who would like to meet you. He read your book only a week ago and it has changed his life."

We shook hands. The handsome, dark-haired man asserted, "Yes, it's true. Just a week ago I read your book and I accepted the Lord Jesus as my Saviour. But the story starts a long time ago...when I was just out of high school. I had such a desire to serve God, so I entered the priesthood. For a year I struggled to find fulfillment and happiness, but it wasn't in religion, liturgy, forms, or rituals.

"Eventually I left the church and fell in love with a beautiful girl. We lived together, and subsequently, had two children. I realized I was living in sin, but I felt trapped. I was devastated by the fact that I had failed God. I was condemned... no good...worthless.

"Out of work and unable to support my family, I reached rock bottom. I began to contemplate suicide. First it was just a thought and then it became a consuming force. Several times I made an attempt...but my girlfriend found me in time.

"One week ago, I came to this mall, trying to think of a way to end it all. I walked from store to store. Finally, I happened to enter this bookstore. When I looked behind the cash register, I saw an old friend from high school. In desperation, I began to tell this 'almost-stranger' my whole life's story. As I turned to leave, she handed me your book, and said, 'Here, Dave, this is a new book that just came in. I read some of it and it is just what you need.'

---

"I took the book home, not believing that it would help me. As I went to bed, I thought I would scan through a few pages. Several hours later I had finished reading the whole thing. It was amazing.

"It was page 35 that changed my life. I will never forget it, because that's exactly how old I am. You described my life in detail — the unfulfillment, unhappiness, searching, longing, and even attempting to take one's life — it's all there. I said, 'Does this lady know me? Has someone told her about my ugly past?' At 3:00 a.m. I knelt beside my bed and invited Jesus Christ into my life...as my personal friend and Saviour. What joy and peace filled my heart...it was indescribable.

"I hope that you don't mind, but I tore that page out of your book. I have it taped to my wall where the light switch is. Every morning and night I want to be reminded of the person I used to be. You described him on page 35 in your book. Thank you, Mrs. Sparks. Your faith has changed my life."

What a marvelous working of God's perfect timing. "In His time...He makes all things beautiful" the praise chorus reminds us. The test is to wait for God to perfect His work in us. That "perfecting" is a painful process.

A few months ago my husband preached a sermon entitled, "Faith on Trial." His text came from 1 Peter 4:12,13 — "Beloved think it not strange concerning the fiery trial which is to test you, as though some strange thing happened to you, But rejoice inasmuch as ye are partakers of Christ's sufferings, that, when his glory shall be revealed, ye may be glad also with exceeding joy" (Scofield).

He spoke of the severe test that the disciples faced in Matthew 14:22-33. The same element that could have helped them, hindered them — "a contrary wind." Until then they were secure and comfortable, but God wanted their attention and sent the wind. When fear overtook them, Jesus met them right where they were, for He is the "master of every situation."

He reminded us of three things: faith can grow in the midst of weakness or strength, failure can come at the peak of success, and victory can come again even after defeat. Peter was "beginning" to sink. Perhaps no one but the Master saw him failing. We know one thing — Peter walked back to the boat after sinking. There's hope, even after failure!

* * *

Perhaps the many letters and calls prompted this occurrence...one night I had a dream about heaven. I knew I was in eternity, my body was transformed. My greatest desire was to see Jesus and then my loved ones. I walked over green grassy mountains, through colorful flower gardens, and finally on a crystal highway that led towards a glimmering city. There was a long line of people at the main gate, and I wondered what or who they were waiting for. As I got closer to the front of the line, I saw a handsome young man — it was Bryon! My eyes brimmed with tears...Bryon was totally healed. He radiated the love of God. Adults and children were shaking his perfectly formed hands and thanking him for his courage. Because of his testimony and courage...they had found Christ.

The vivid intensity of this vision caused me to awake from sleep, and sit up in bed. I spent the rest of the night in prayer and praise, thanking God for His gift to us...Bryon. Perhaps the Lord allowed me to take a peek in one of heaven's windows to get a glimpse of what God has in store for those who are found faithful. He has prepared a "crown of righteousness" for all those who have "kept the faith" (2 Tim. 4:7,8).

I related this dream to Bryon one day, trying to encourage him to keep up the good "fight of faith." Bryon replied, "You know that for each soul we win to Christ, we receive another star in our crown?"

I added, "Yes, the apostle Peter tells us, 'And when the Chief Shepherd appears, you will receive the unfading crown of glory'" (1 Pet. 5:4).

"Wow!" Bryon exclaimed. "Just think of all those people who have given their hearts to the Lord because of my testimony. That will be quite a few stars to put in my crown. Hey, Mom...there's only one problem. Do you think my head will be big enough to hold up such a large crown?"

———

"Bryon, I'm sure the Lord will have a way of solving that problem," I chuckled to myself.

*"That the proof of your faith, being more precious than gold which is perishable, even though tested by fire, may be found to result in praise and glory and honor at the revelation of Jesus Christ" (1 Pet. 1:7).*

# 15

# BROKEN THINGS

*"Verily, verily I say unto you, except a grain of wheat fall into the ground and die, it abideth alone: but if it die, it bringeth forth much fruit. He that loveth his life shall lose it; and he that hateth his life in this world shall keep it unto life eternal" (John 12:24,25; OB).*

During our four years as teachers in Zion Bible Institute we went through many life-changing experiences. One such lesson was the meaning of true "brokenness." We discovered that real brokenness occurs as we yield our wills to His will. This process is often painful and humiliating, but it is the only way that the proud "I" can be bent into the "C" — "Not I, but Christ" (Gal. 2:20).

Roy Hession in *The Calvary Road* explains that brokenness is the beginning of revival as the life of the Lord Jesus is poured into human hearts.

"Being broken is both God's work and ours. He brings His pressure to bear, but we have to make the choice. If we are really open to conviction as we seek fellowship with God (and willingness for the light is the prime condition of fellowship with God), God will show us the expressions of this proud, hard self that cause Him pain. Then it is we can stiffen our necks and refuse to repent, or we can bow the head and say, 'Yes, Lord.' Brokenness in daily experience is simply the response of humility to the conviction of God. And inasmuch as this conviction is continuous, we shall need to be broken continually. And this can be very costly, when we see all the yielding of rights and selfish interests that this will involve, and the confessions and restitutions that may be sometimes necessary.''

Steve felt overwhelming frustration at the lack of pastoral ministry. A "shepherd" at heart, he missed feeding and nurturing his flock. He had hoped for some pulpit ministry and pastoral courses for instruction, but those doors were never opened. Sitting on a shelf for four years and watching others "minister" was a tremendous breaking experience for him. My heart ached as I watched him in his private pain. I wanted to reach out and soothe the hurt, but the experience was so deeply spiritual there were no words or expressions that could comfort.

As a young girl I remembered my mother's sound advice in confronting life's unanswered questions — "You can either become bitter or better. The choice is up to you." The temptation was always there to become calloused and embittered by unfair circumstances and "no-win" situations. But God was faithful to remind us that He was bringing His pressure to bear in our lives and the choice was up to us.

One evening following supper, as Steve prepared to lead our family in devotions, Jenell (about six years old) raised her hand to ask a question. Steve laid the open Bible on the table, raised his eyebrows, and responded, "Yes, Jenell. Do you want to say something?"

Jenell's hand went down and her chubby cheeks glowed

with enthusiasm. "Daddy, I was wondering if we could do something special for devotions tonight? You know every once in a while we go into the living room and get down on our knees and really seek God. It's been such a long time since we did that...and I think we really need to 'cry-out' all our sins!"

If you knew Jenell, you knew that she had a lot of "sins" to cry out! God used Jenell to touch our hearts and we found ourselves on our knees for the next two hours, crying and praying for one another. It was one of those family "high-water marks" that left a definite impact on each one of us.

Not long after our special prayer time, Bryon came home from Dayspring Christian Academy one afternoon in tears. Bryon sobbed, "Dad, I have to talk to you alone...this is really important."

So Steve took Bryon into our bedroom and closed the door. I heard their muffled voices, tears, and finally, prayers. I wondered what could have happened to Bryon to cause this heartbreak.

Later that evening as we climbed into bed, I mentioned the incident to my honey. He gently chuckled as he recalled his conversation with Bryon. Bryon had related how some of the boys from his fifth grade class had made fun of him and called him names. He put up with their jesting all morning, until he felt totally humiliated and angry. Bryon said, "I just couldn't stand it anymore, Dad...I was so upset...and I just glared at them...and then I did something terrible...I cursed at them. I know it was wrong, but I was so mad."

Bryon broke into sobs, "Oh, Dad, do you think Jesus will forgive me? I'm so sorry for what I said." Steve said that they knelt beside our bed and asked Jesus' forgiveness for the angry, unkind words that were spoken. Then Steve inquired, "Bryon, you don't have to tell me if you don't want to, but I was wondering what you actually said."

Bryon's head hung down. His voice quavered as he replied, "I know it was just terrible, Dad. But they made me so angry that I shook my fist and shouted, 'Okay, guys. Shut up! Shut up!'" The tears continued to stream down his little face. "I know Jesus has forgiven me and I promise to tell the boys tomorrow at school that I'm sorry."

Bryon was learning that the Lord Jesus cannot live in us fully until the proud self within us is broken — the "self" which wants its own way and tries to stand up for its rights. At last this self must bow its head to God's will and admit it's wrong — surrendering personal rights so that Jesus might be Lord of all. It was a painful dying to self and self-attitudes.

This "surrendering of self" reminds me of Leann's stubbornness of will when she was only three. Every afternoon I encountered a "battle of the wills" as I attempted to lay her down for a nap. It wasn't that she needed the nap, as much as I needed her to lie down. That's when I put my house back together and had an hour of luxury time alone. But no matter how many times I put her in bed, she continued to scramble out and make havoc of her room. Finally, I announced that a spanking would follow if she refused to stay in bed.

After several minutes of questionable quietness, I heard her call my name. "Mom!" she pleaded. "Please come in here for just a second. I need to talk to you."

Reluctantly, I pushed open the door and knelt down beside her bunkbed. "Okay, sweetheart," I asserted. "This is the last time Mommy is coming in here. What do you want now?"

Leaning over to whisper in my ear, she retorted, "Mom, I want you to know that I may be lying down on the outside, but inside I'm STANDING UP!"

I suppressed the immediate response of laughter as I left her bedroom, but the reality of her statement hit home — what a picture of human nature! This is the reason we are not likely to be broken except at the cross of Jesus. The willingness of Jesus to be broken for us is the all-compelling motive in our being broken too.

Another unexpected surprise was waiting for us just around the corner. We had lived in Rhode Island for two-and-a-half years and our children were growing up. Bryon was ten years old, Leann almost five, and Jenell just over two. We were quite contented with three children — they were certainly a handful with all our other teaching responsibilities.

---

194

But one evening as I tucked Bryon into bed and he said his prayers, he added one extra request that caused me to take notice. He ended his petitions with — "And please, Lord, give me the desire of my heart — a baby brother."

Startled, I announced, "Bryon, don't be foolish. Mom and Dad are very happy with the children God has given us. We love you, Leann, and Jenell. We really don't have a desire for any more babies."

But Bryon would not be deterred from expressing the intent of his heart. Every night he concluded his prayers by asking for a brother. This began to unnerve me because I recalled the many times God had answered Bryon's requests.

When Bryon was only three we spent the summer of 1977 in St. Christopher's Hospital for Children in Philadelphia, Pennsylvania. It was during this time that Bryon had two extensive hand surgeries performed in an attempt to separate his contracted fingers. After opening his right hand they covered his palm and each finger with pig skin, shipped in from Texas.

As Bryon awoke from the anesthesia and discovered pink furry skin with little black spots covering his hand, he was horrified. That night as I prayed with him he simply stated — "Lord, You know that I am thankful for my new fingers...and the doctors and nurses who are helping me...but, Lord, I have one problem...I can't stand this pig skin...please don't let it work...thanks, God. Amen."

"Bryon!" I cried, "Please don't pray that way. We want the pig skin to work so that new skin will grow underneath. Eventually it will come off. Don't worry, Honey."

Bryon protested, "But Mom, I'm not going back to pre-school with pink furry skin and little black dots! No one will even sit next to me. They'll think I'm a pig!"

Nothing I said could change his mind. Within three days the pig skin had dropped off and the doctors didn't try again. Somehow I knew that God was listening to Bryon's prayers this time too. Just two weeks after he had first mentioned a new brother, the smell of coffee made me nauseous. When the familiar episodes with 'morning sickness' and dry heaves became a reality, I knew Bryon's prayers were being answered.

What joy filled the Sparks' home on November 19, 1983 when eight-pound-two-ounce Brent David Sparks came into this world. Especially for Bryon. He gave up all the extra space in his room for a cradle, changing table, toys, and baby paraphernalia. He lay awake at night and watched his brother's chest rise and fall in sleep. When Brent cried, he gently rocked the cradle and sang to him. He truly loved his new brother — he was an actualized dream come true.

Since that time we have cautiously reminded Bryon not to pray in that direction again! "Four and no more" was our motto in 1984. We warned Bryon that if he was tempted, we were sure to find a one-way plane ticket for Siberia! (Just kidding!) Bryon promised to keep this in mind.

What an interesting year it proved to be. I attempted to keep up with my normal schedule of teaching, directing the choir, and traveling during our spring and summer tours. I only missed one service when Brent was born. As soon as he came home from the hospital, I bundled him up in a large wicker "Moses" basket and carted him with me everywhere. Thank God he loved to travel — he could sleep through anything. What a darling baby!

Before Brent was born we had laid the ground work for a special missionary tour with the choir to the Island of Sicily, located off the coast of Italy. Not all of the choir members were able to go, only those who raised the $800.00 for airfare and expenses. It was a real sacrifice for many, as they gave up an additional two weeks of their summer jobs which were waiting for them, and time with their family and friends. It also meant going through months of intense missionary training, a course in right relationships, and learning all of our songs in Italian. God put together a great team of twenty-three first-time missionaries. The events that occurred during those fifteen days changed all of our lives. We learned in graphic illustrations the vivid meaning of "true brokenness."

Nat Saginario, the "mini-missions" director with the Christian Churches of North America (CCNA), made all the arrangements for our ministry — the flights, contacts with the missionaries, accommodations, and financial support. He also instructed us in a course designed for short mission's trips. The book, *The Calvary Road*, by Roy Hession was a key guide in our study of right relationships and attitudes in the body of Christ. Nat focused on the change that would occur in our lives, not how many lives we would change while we were in Sicily. Although the missionaries and Italian people were greatly blessed by our ministry, we were the ones who reaped the most benefits.

One of our private jokes was the fact that none of us had any personal rights: "No Rights!" Everyone was so faithful to remind the others when they were in distress or going through a rough time, that they had "no rights!" We also had to learn to trust one another without reservation, especially those in leadership. Even when the request or command seemed unreasonable or defied our natural instincts — we were taught to obey explicitly. Both of these lessons proved to be "life-saving" while we were in Sicily.

On June 10, 1984 we flew out of Logan International Airport in Boston, aboard the Italian carrier "Alitalia." Excitement was at a feverish high. Some of the young people had never flown and they crammed to get a good view from the window seats. Steve, Bryon, myself, twelve young men, and eight young ladies made up the team.

Our first confrontation with "travel hazards" occurred when we landed at the Leonardo da Vinci Airport, at Fiumicino, on the outskirts of Rome. It was 9:00 a.m. Sunday morning and we expected to make a connecting flight to Catania, one of the most important towns in Sicily. Our missionary friends, Nino and Chris Mortelliti, were waiting for us. Our first service was scheduled for that evening at 6:00 p.m. in a large movie theater in downtown Barcelona. But, to our dismay, all the employees of Alitalia had gone on strike for twenty-four to forty-eight hours, until negotiations were made.

The airport was deserted. No one was available to give us information about connecting flights or time schedules. By twelve noon the last agent had left the airport. The only employees remaining were those in the small shops and cafeteria, where we had a light lunch. Attempts to contact the missionaries were futile. There was nothing to do but wait.

We laid our garment bags on the floor and took turns "napping," trying to catch up on the night's sleep we had lost. Some wrote letters, others read, and some students even witnessed to other stranded travelers. About 5 p.m. we had group devotions to encourage ourselves in the Lord. The sounds of song and praise drifted through the terminal. Many gathered nearby to watch and listen with genuine interest. We committed our situation to the Lord. We had already missed our first service. Yet, God's timing was always perfect and we had to trust Him.

Throughout the day flights arrived from all over the world, but absolutely no flights departed. A few stranded passengers snowballed into thousands of hungry, tired, and displaced persons. Everyone was watching the flight boards to see when the next flight was scheduled to leave. Finally about 10:00 p.m. there was an announcement over the loudspeaker — the possibility of a flight to Catania! We grabbed our carry-on luggage and ran to the gate...along with five hundred other travelers. There was no way that we all were going to fit on one plane. Foreigners pushed and shoved to get to the front of the line, screaming strange syllables and words. The overwhelming thought of getting all the team members on the same plane seemed impossible. I silently whispered a small prayer.

For almost three hours we stood at the gate, bodies pressed against bodies, until the very air was choked with perspiration. Bryon sat on the floor between our legs, his back against some of the luggage. A feeling of hopelessness stuck in my throat. I knew God wanted us to minister in Sicily, but I didn't know it would take such a sacrificial effort to get there.

At 1:00 a.m. (Monday morning) an agent began to accept boarding passes and allow passengers to board the bus which transported them to the carrier. In a moment's panic I realized that the booth was several aisles away from us and there were hundreds of people ahead of us. I whispered to the young men to squeeze through the crowd and try to save us seats on the plane. The fellas climbed over seats and people, and I saw them wave as they disappeared through the doorway to the transport bus. "Oh God," I cried, "Don't let us get separated...may we all get on the plane safely."

Somehow we managed to by-pass some of the mob and found ourselves packed like sardines on the bus. Unable to move or breathe, I held myself steady by clutching an iron bar hanging from the ceiling, waiting for the doors to open and let in the fresh air. Stumbling out into the blackness of night, everyone made a frantic scramble for the front and rear stairway ramps to the plane. There were no seat assignments — only total chaos. A tremor of fear went through me — I looked for Bryon — he was gone! Losing some composure, I began to call his name. No answer.

I reached the steps and hurriedly ascended into the plane. Suppose Bryon was still in the bus, or worse yet, still back in the terminal! I ran up the aisle, crying out his name. In the last seat, next to the window sat Bryon, looking very calm and relaxed.

"Bryon, how did you find your way onto the plane?" I asked.

"Well, Mom, I got off the bus and I couldn't find you. So I followed the people to the plane and all of a sudden one of the guys grabbed me and helped me find a seat. God took care of me. I wasn't afraid."

It was a miracle...every single member of the team made it on the plane! We were scattered everywhere, but we all had a seat. When the plane was full, the doors were closed, and hundreds were left behind. It was 2:30 a.m. — our second night without sleep. We arrived in Catania about 3:30 a.m. and the weary missionaries and workers were still waiting for us. Customs were closed for the night so we were unable to retrieve any of our luggage and equipment until 9:00 a.m. I asked for two volunteers to stay behind with one of the Christian brothers and the luggage. Tom Burns and John Battaglia unhesitatingly stepped forward. I wanted to kiss them both. The rest of us piled into two small cars and a van to travel the two hours to Barcelona — our mission's headquarters.

We had three hours to sleep, shower, dress, and then eat before we appeared on national Italian television. Our luggage arrived one hour before our T.V. appearance. John and Tom went to bed totally exhausted. In spite of our faltering Italian and weary bodies, God used the program to touch thousands of people with the gospel.

Sicilia, or better known as "Sicily," was one of the most beautiful islands in the Mediterranean, and also the largest. It was a land of mythology, where a belief in the supernatural played an important role in everyday life and where religious festivals were peppered with ancient rites and customs. Her people were steeped in traditions. There were vast stretches of beautiful scenery, from volcanic Mount Etna to endless sandy beaches. Fishing villages dotted the coastline. We enjoyed many of these sights and new experiences during our ministry tour.

Our missions training in proper relationships and "no personal rights" became an important part of our day-to-day survival. It was difficult for our girls to remove ALL make-up and jewelry, don "head-coverings," and wear nylons at all times (even in one hundred-degree weather) — but they adjusted. The young men also had to remove their jewelry, go without showers, and dress in suits and ties to minister. It was a real breaking of "self" and at times individuals just exploded into tears. We learned to support one another in prayer and encouragement. Slowly our lives were changing...no longer "I" but "Christ" was seen.

One of the problems was the shortage of water. Every home was allotted a certain amount of water each day — their water tanks were filled every morning at exactly 6:00 a.m. This water was used for cooking, washing, cleaning, and bathing. When it ran out — there was no more water until the following day. With all twelve of the young men, the missionary family, Steve, Bryon, and I staying together in the church — we had a problem! We learned how to take two-minute showers. One minute to get wet, turn the water off, soap-up, and one minute to rinse off. If someone took an extra minute — another team member went without their shower that day.

Another frustration was the "hurry-up-and-wait" syndrome. We would get up at five or six o'clock in the morning and have the whole team ready to go by eight, only to sit and wait for several hours while errands were run and cars repaired, or the missionary had left for an appointment. Then we would drive twice as fast to make-up for the lost time. Almost everyone learned to make good use of this "wasted" time by studying, reading, having personal devotions, or practicing their Italian.

As team leader, I knew I had to set an example to the group in my relationship with the missionaries and how I handled stressful situations. I thought I was doing a "fair" job when the Lord decided to teach me a greater lesson in "no rights."

A week after we arrived in Sicily, we were scheduled to minister in Palermo, the capital and principal seaport. That Sunday morning dawned hot and humid and promised to reach into the low hundreds by midday. After a three-hour drive, we attempted to set up our generator, sound system, and risers in a narrow windowless, store-front building. Already, people were jammed on the rough wooden benches, filling the aisles, and spilling out into a crowd on the street. The building's capacity was about one hundred fifty, but approximately four hundred people packed into every available, breathable space. The choir hardly had room to stand on the risers and minister.

Difficulties arose from every direction. The only toilet facility in the building broke and we had to pass buckets of water through a small courtyard window to get it to flush. Most of the lady team members stood in a bucket-brigade for over an hour. In the beginning of the service our generator ran out of gasoline and two boys had to drive to the nearest gas station for a refill. Because of the lack of ventilation and intense heat, many of us were on the verge of collapsing during the concert. As soon as it was possible, we pushed through the crowd and stumbled out onto the street, drinking in the somewhat "cooler" air. Steve had to remain inside to preach the Word while Nino interpreted. We prayed for God to give him strength.

Yet our distress was not felt by the people of Palermo, for over one-half of the congregation stood to receive Christ as their personal Saviour at the end of the service. It was impossible for us to pray with them individually — we joined our hearts while standing outside the small church — the Holy Spirit touched lives where we were not able.

Most of us had perspired so profusely that our clothes clung to us as though we had just stepped out of a shower. Families from the congregation had volunteered to take us home for dinner. Two by two the assignments were given out until just Steve, Bryon, and myself remained. A man and his wife stepped forward and motioned for us to come with them. With some effort, we smiled and followed them down the street to their car. Exhaustion overtook us as we struggled to carry the briefcases (containing passports, monies, and important documents), a container of special food for Bryon, a cosmetic case, and garment bags.

When we arrived at their car — the smallest Fiat Panda I'd ever seen — I wondered how the five of us would fit! But before I could protest, their two sons and maternal grandmother appeared on the scene. Much to our disbelief, they all intended to squeeze into this much-too-small vehicle. Dismay clouded my face. Steve and I stared at each other and shook our heads.

They motioned for me to climb into the back seat — I reluctantly followed their directions. Then the mother and grandmother climbed in on either side of me, their plenteous hips covering mine. The boys scrambled in too and sat on my knees. There was no place for the luggage to go, so it too was handed in and placed on our laps, making a wall of people and cases up to the ceiling. The two front seats were pushed back and I felt a tremendous pressure of sweaty bodies and baggage against my chest. Instantly, breathing became a conscious effort and I silently prayed that the ride to their house would be quick. Little did I know that it would be a forty-five-minute drive through the hot, congested streets of Palermo before we reached our destination.

Each woman had her arm around my neck and no matter

which way I turned my face was buried in an armpit. The boys had to go to the bathroom and they wriggled restlessly on my tingling knees. One boy couldn't hold it...I felt the wetness drip down my leg. The pain in my head, chest, and legs became unbearable. The women screamed to each other in liquid Italian. Steve attempted to communicate with the father, while holding Bryon on his lap in the front seat. The two windows were open, but none of the fresh air reached the back.

I remember thinking, "I could die in this car and no one would ever know...or care! Lord, I know You asked us to give up our own personal comforts and rights...but our lives too!" A blackness like a warm dark cloud floated over me and I slipped into unconsciousness.

The next thing I felt was an intense pain in my legs and chest, as the bodies were peeled off and fresh air blew in to revive me. The first thought I had was, "I'm still alive. Thank God!"

It took me several minutes to get my legs and arms to move — they were paralyzed. I dragged myself out of the back seat and hobbled into an apartment building to wait for the elevator. They lived on the fifth floor. The look in Steve's eyes told me that he had never seen me in such a pathetic state. When the iron-grated elevator door opened, I estimated that there was enough room for three or four of us. I was wrong — again! They allowed our family to back in first and then all five of them pushed and shoved until the only place left for our arms was above our heads. The brother handed in our luggage and we held it up in the air.

The elevator door closed and we inched our way up to the fifth floor. It seemed like an eternity. Finally we made our way to their apartment. The refreshing coolness created by the marble floors and walls was a welcome relief. In stark contrast to their antique, battered-up car, their home was lavishly immaculate. The desire to splash cold water on my face and peel off my urine-soaked pantyhose was foremost in my mind.

The Italian Senora showed me to the "toilette" and I gratefully closed the door. There was no lock. I put my face down in the sink and ran refreshing water over my hands and face. I realized the urge to use the bathroom had come and gone hours ago. I peeled off my pantyhose and collapsed on the commode. Moments later the boys pushed open the door and proceeded to wash their hands in the sink. They were shortly followed by their father, who seemed not to notice that I was in an embarrassing predicament. I pulled my dress about my legs. Totally humiliated, I wondered what I would say to these people at dinner. This lack of respect for personal privacy overwhelmed me.

Somehow I made it through dinner and the rest of the afternoon. Then the time I dreaded had come — our trip back to the church. Surely, these folks noticed how uncomfortable we were and some would volunteer to stay at home. I contemplated how I would feel with seven courses of homemade pasta, salad, shrimp, lasagna, coffee and desert, swimming around in my stomach, while crunched in the back seat.

I tried to drop a subtle hint by saying "Chi' Amore" and "Grazia" to everyone. But much to my dismay ALL five followed us to the elevator. At this point let me insert — that if you had been watching a movie you could now play it in reverse and see exactly what happened to us on our return trip. It was incredible! All eight people squashed into the elevator ...hands up...luggage handed on top...into the back seat... ladies climb in ...boys on my knees...luggage up to the ceiling...seats pushed back...and the forty-five minute drive to the church! Only this time the temperature outside was several degrees hotter, we were all stuffed with a big dinner, and I never passed out.

As we neared the church, I saw through a small side window a beautiful gray Mercedes Benz pull alongside us at a red light. In the back seat were two of the male team members. They looked refreshed and were relaxing in apparent luxury. When they saw Brother Sparks and Bryon up front they shouted, "Hey, how ya doing? Where's Sister Sparks? We don't see her!" Steve motioned with his hand towards the rear of the car, but try as they did, neither of them saw where I was buried. Their elegant car swiftly passed and went on ahead. When we arrived at the curbside in front of the church, I heard a lot of commotion on the sidewalk. Once again we began the process of unloading bodies, luggage, kids, women, and last of all — me. When I climbed out of my own private prison cell and tried to stand up, all the members of the mini-missions team, in one voice, yelled — "No Rights!"

I felt the hot tears of humiliation and exhaustion sting my eyes. I felt a lump swell in my throat that tried to choke any words I had to say. I knew my response at this moment was a key in the successfulness of all the training and teaching we had instituted...plus our missions work at hand.

Struggling to speak, I managed, "Yes, that's right. I have no rights, except to know Christ, and Him crucified!" Silence fell over the entire team. The smirking laughter turned to solemnness and teary eyes as we loaded up for our next destination.

I can't say for sure that it was *this* experience in particular that created a "turning point" in our ministry, but there was a tremendous change in the lives of the team members. Later that evening as we sang and preached in an open-air amphi-theater in Raffadoli, we saw about four hundred come forward for salvation. Steve reemphasized the fact that the call was for a first-time commitment. Nino Mortelliti turned and replied, "Yes, Steve, they did understand...these people are respond-ing for the first time."

I learned that brokenness is a constant choice. Every time someone hurts and slights us, we immediately have the choice by means of God's grace to humble ourselves or we can resist it and stiffen our necks again with a disturbed spirit. But I have also discovered that there is no prayer that God is so swift to answer as the prayer that He might break us.

Someone has said, "It takes broken soil to produce a crop, broken clouds to give rain, broken grain to give bread, broken bread to give strength (Mark 6:4). It is the broken alabaster box that gives forth perfume (Mark 14:3); and it is the broken body of Christ that provides healing and salvation for mankind."

Bill and Gloria Gaither expressed it this way:

Something beautiful, something good;
All my confusion He understood;
All I had to offer Him was brokenness and strife,
But He made something beautiful of my life.[3]

*"The sacrifices of God are a broken spirit; A broken
and a contrite heart, O God, Thou wilt not despise"
(Ps. 51:17).*

---

[3]"Something Beautiful." Words by Gloria Gaither. Music by William J.
Gaither. ©Copyright 1971 by William J. Gaither. All rights reserved. Used
by permission.

# 16

# NIHIL SINE DEO

A warm salty breeze caressed my hair in the morning sun. The azure-blue Mediterranean Sea stretched beyond the scenic inlets and hidden caves along the Costa Brava, known as the "wild coast" of Spain. I glanced at the speedometer and was amazed that traveling at 120 kilometers seemed very natural. The "autopista" curved like a snake towards the snow-capped French Alps in the distance. Highway A-17 was a fine motorway from Barcelona to the quaint Spanish town of Figueras, located in the province of Catalonia — the gateway to France.

I glanced over my shoulder...Bryon was soundly sleeping on the rear seat. Only an hour before we had completed the nine-hour excursion on a TWA 747 from New York's Kennedy Airport to Barcelona, Spain. Bryon and I were old "pros" when it came to international flying. We knew exactly what to expect. The flight from Pittsburgh to New York was only two hours. Then we had a four-hour break, long enough to browse through newsstands and gourmet cookie shops and eat some Haagen Das ice cream. At 7:20 p.m. we departed for our overseas destination, with only one stop in Lisbon, Portugal.

At 9:00 p.m. we enjoyed a delicious meal of chicken Parmesan, followed by a hilarious movie and a short two-hour nap. At 2:00 a.m. we ate a continental breakfast, and at 4:00 a.m. (10:00 a.m. European time) we were on the ground.

The stark difference of culture was immediately evident as we disembarked the plane and were escorted to the terminal by heavily-armed militia. At the passport control we received cold official stares and a brisk wave of the arm to signal our admission. Once inside the main building, we stared in disbelief at the mounds of garbage and waste spread across the entire floor. People didn't seem to be disturbed by this appalling condition — they walked around it, over it, and some even "waded" through it. Days later, I discovered that the airport maintenance personnel had gone on strike, which accounted for this shocking welcome.

We made the proper arrangements to secure our rental car and pushed our luggage cart past a dozen more armed guards and through the main entrance. Like a giant winding caterpillar, bright yellow taxi-cabs formed a single line along the curb and for several miles down the road. I was amused to see the drivers playing cards, washing their vehicles, or taking a siesta in their front seats. This certainly wasn't Hometown, U.S.A.!

It was June 3, 1986, and we faced a summer that we would remember for the rest of our lives. The fact that we were in Spain and on our way to the new clinic — called "Clinic Cal Deu" — was a miracle. My mind replayed the series of events which had brought us to this moment.

After four years of teaching in Zion Bible Institute, God opened a wonderful door of ministry for our family in Warren, Ohio. Rev. Oliver Dalaba, senior pastor, from Warren First Assembly of God, happened to visit Zion Gospel Temple one Sunday morning when Steve was preaching as a fill-in for the pastor. A couple of months later, he contacted Steve and invited him to be the Associate of Pastoral Care. It was a definite answer to prayer.

July 1985 found us amidst boxes, furniture, and play equipment...and then the wearisome task of moving twelve hours away. We loaded the largest available Ryder rental truck, and then had to attach a small U-haul trailer on behind to hold all the "left-over" stuff. We had to leave some things in Rhode Island.

I remember the untiring personal sacrifice of one of the students. Phil Drayton, a native from the island of Barbados, had been in the Collegians for two years and was part of the mini-missions team to Sicily. We asked for some students to help us pack, but everyone was involved in "summer work weeks." Yet, after a full day's work on the campus, Phil came by and worked late into the evening to help us pack.

On the last day (Saturday) he stood in the pouring rain for six hours putting together a car-top carrier and taking apart, piece by piece, our lawn furniture and swing set. Then he tied all the parts to the back of our Ryder truck. Never a word of complaint. As we said good-bye, Phil threw his arms around my neck.

With tears in his eyes, he cried, "Sister Sparks, I will never forget you. Your life has touched mine." And with a twinkle, "By the way...No Rights...remember?"

We would never forget the years of ministry and personal investment in the lives of many young people during this time. Many of those individuals are in full-time pastoral and missionary work today. To God be the glory!

Our family life drastically changed as we settled into the busy routine of pastoring once again. Only this time to a much large constituency — about nine hundred people. Steve thrived on the challenge of pastoral counseling, Bible studies, home fellowship groups, and visitation. It was the true fulfillment of his calling.

Then an unexpected shock came, when just nine months later, Pastor Dalaba resigned. He moved to Michigan, where he had accepted a senior pastor position. Within just a few weeks, we found ourselves candidates and then, the newly-elected senior pastor and wife at First Assembly. It was an awesome responsibility. God was our total confidence.

Our first Sunday as the new senior pastor was April 6, 1986. The following week, I received a phone call from a Canadian friend, whom we had met in Germany at the Vital Klinik.

Tom was a thirty-one-year-old man with Epidermylosis Bullosa. Professor Kozak had saved his life, even though the Canadian doctors had given him one week to live. With heartfelt gratitude, Tom was investing his life to aid other EB victims in finding new health. Tom had been through about thirty hand surgeries and knew the frustration that Bryon felt.

Tom's call brought the good news we had been praying for — a hand surgeon who might operate on Bryon's fingers. His name was Dr. Alberto Morelli, from Busto Arsizio, Italy. We learned that a nine-year-old girl named Enza had just returned from Italy with all ten of her fingers open and useful. Hope grabbed our hearts. It almost sounded too good to be true.

The Vital Klinik from West Germany had moved to Cabanellas, Spain — a small farming community situated near Costa Rosa on the Mediterranean Sea, just twenty miles south of the French border. This new location provided the perfect spot for treatment and rehabilitation. We learned that there was an opening for Bryon in June, if we were able to make the trip. We made the necessary arrangements and plans were laid to leave on the third.

My parents volunteered to keep Leann and Jenell for at least a month. A family in the church, the Rosenbergs, assisted in caring for two-year-old Brent. Everything was falling into place. But we still needed a financial miracle to pay for our airline tickets and the clinic bills — which were estimated in the excess of $35,000! We knew our God was faithful...and we anxiously looked forward to His divine provision.

During this time we received a call from "Heritage Update," a program that was aired on the PTL Television Network. They were interested in doing a follow-up story on Bryon's progress. When they discovered our plans to make a trip to Italy for the purpose of hand surgery...they were ecstatic! Within a couple days, they organized a reporting crew and flew a private plane into our small Warren airport.

For two days they were welcomed guests in our home...interviewing, taping, and catching glimpses of a "normal" day in the Sparks' household. They caught Bryon making a few baskets in the back yard, the children playing on the swings, Mom doing treatments, and Bryon in his fifth-grade classroom. It sure was an exciting time for all of us.

A week later the "Heritage Update" film clip was aired on the PTL Satellite Network. The response from the partners was tremendous. Many viewers had followed the "tough cookie" for years and wanted to be a part of the miracle. We received a check for $20,000 from the Heritage Church...three weeks before our departure. The wheels of God's marvelous plan were set in motion.

The days passed like lightning and it was time to say goodbye to Steve (and Daddy). He stood at the gate and waved as we walked down the ramp and out of sight. From our small window on the plane, we saw him searching for our faces. His eyes lit up when he made contact with ours. As the plane pulled out of the terminal, I had to fight back the tears. It seemed like we were always saying farewell...and it hurt. Hopefully, in a few weeks, Steve would join us for Bryon's hand surgery.

I hummed the melody to a favorite chorus..."In His time, He makes all things beautiful...in His time." This song certainly rang true in our lives. Bryon's lifelong dream was unfolding before our eyes. In His time, and in His way, He was perfecting His plan for us.

Bryon's light snoring brought my mind back to the highway and the exit sign which read: Figueras/Rosas 20 km. I drove up to the toll booth and fumbled in my purse for the correct amount of pesetas. Six hundred pesetas seemed like a big amount to pay for a toll. It took me a while to adjust to the rate of exchange.

The center of Figueras was a hubbub of activity. Inland from the Costa Brava, this town was the site of the imposing eighteenth-century fortress Castle of San Fernando, once the headquarters for an army of ten thousand men with hundreds of horses. Today, scores of small foreign cars seemed to dart out of nowhere, honk, speed in front of us, and then disappear just as quickly. Defensive driving was essential for survival.

I parked my Seat across from the town square and walked into the nearest bank — "Banco de Zaragoza." I had two words written on a piece of paper — they were my only directions to find the clinic. Hotel Duran. Thankfully, one of the bank officers knew how to speak English and gave me precise directions to the hotel.

I walked through the double glass doors and across the marble entryway of the hotel...sitting in the lounge was Professor Kozak. Even after four years, I immediately recognized the white-haired, bespectacled gentleman.

"How do you do?" he inquired politely. "And how is my boy, Bryon?" he added, standing to his feet. He embraced Bryon in a big bear hug and ruffled his hair. He seemed pleased that we had come to his new clinic for treatment.

Borus, the clinic's handyman, instructed us to follow him in the large white van, and soon we were buzzing along the country roads. Neat rows of wheat and corn stretched for miles on both sides. White stucco farmhouses, with red pottery roofing, dotted the landscape. The far-distant French Alps capped with snow, poked through the clouds. I pinched myself. It didn't seem possible that we were actually in this land of romance and castles.

Clinic Cal Deu was actually an elegant Spanish villa, that had once been owned by a famous German consulate. It was easily seen from the road, as it perched on the top of a small hill. Flags from many countries stood in perfect semaphore across the front lawn. The narrow dirt road led us through two stone pillars and into a small courtyard. The villa itself was a magnificent work of architecture with its arches, fireplaces, marble living room, grand mahogany staircase, and in-the-ground pool. Surrounded by patios, open porches, fruit trees, flower gardens, and a barnyard full of chickens and turkeys, it was an impressive property.

Mama Kozak greeted us with loving enthusiasm, and then showed us to our small (but meticulously clean) room. Two beds with crisp white sheets, a small night stand, and a treatment table with a roll of white paper were the total decorations. It was completely devoid of color. Nothing mattered to us except a warm meal, clean clothes, a hot bath, and BED! We had been awake for almost forty hours and we were exhausted.

Life in the clinic quickly settled into a routine. Breakfast was served between 8 and 9 a.m. which consisted of semolina, toast, and herbal tea. (Parents were allowed some of the bitterly-strong Spanish coffee.) The morning included "treatment time," laundry duty (scrubbing all our clothes in a sink and hanging them among the fruit trees), and cleaning our rooms. Lunch was served anywhere from 1 to 3 p.m. — it was never the same schedule. The children occupied themselves by playing Word Yahtzee, working on a puzzle, going for walks, or playing a gentle game of foot soccer. Supper was ready between 7:30 and 9:00 p.m., followed by coffee and a pastry on the open second-story patio. One more treatment was done later in the evening, after the heat of the day, and then it was time to "hit the sack."

Meals were worth waiting for — everything was made fresh daily in the clinic's small kitchen. "Paella" based on either seafood or chicken, served on saffron rice with green peppers, peas and any other vegetable that the cook had on hand, was a traditional lunchtime favorite. A good standby for the evening meal was the "tortilla espanola" — an omelet made of eggs and potatoes. "Pane" and "fruta" (bread and fresh fruit) were placed on the table at every meal. My favorite was a "cafe' con leche" (half coffee and half hot milk) and a sweet pastry for breakfast. At least I knew we weren't going to starve during our stay in Spain.

Besides Professor and Maria Kozak and Borus (the driver and maintenance man), there were three hard-working Spanish girls who did just about everything to keep the clinic operating — cooking, laundry, cleaning, gardening, and even some landscaping! Delores, tall and big-boned, was quiet and shy. Sarah, short, with black cropped hair, was quite spirited and even a little sassy at times. Reddish-brown haired Maria was a gentle person filled with love for the patients. She knew both Spanish and French fluently and was able to speak to those who were French Canadian.

Professor Kozak held our first "parent-staff" meeting two days after we arrived. With the help of Nicole, a mother from Quebec, Canada, the basic ground rules were laid down.

Nicole was able to understand "most" of what the professor said because the French and Rumanian languages are very similar. I was somewhat shocked at the rigidity of the rules in comparison to the carefree lifestyle at the German clinic. Basically, these issues were presented:

1. Meal times were to be observed strictly. No one would be served after hours. (Even though we waited sometimes hours for the food to be prepared.)

2. No parents were allowed in the kitchen, for sanitary reasons.

3. No one was allowed to visit another patient in his or her room. Conversation had to be kept to a minimum.

4. At the end of every day the garbage in our room had to be burned in a trash container — to prevent contamination from infected bandages.

5. Patients' clothes had to be sent to town for cleaning to prevent the spreading of germs. (This was never possible. The cost was astronomical!)

6. No one was allowed to go into Figueras for shopping or eating. No one was permitted to bring back snacks or treats to their rooms — this was a source of temptation for the patients to "cheat" on their diets.

7. If you had a vehicle you were not allowed to offer "taxi" service to the other patients or parents due to problems with insurance. (This was extremely frustrating, as many did not have any means of transportation without my help.)

8. Curfew was at 10:00 p.m. Everyone was expected to be in their rooms and in bed. (The doors were locked at 10:00 p.m. and we were not allowed to visit with any others, even though certain "favorites" were allowed to visit loudly outside, even late into the night hours.)

To many of us from the United States, these rules seemed like a prison, but to the Europeans, it seemed to be the status quo. I felt almost "trapped" and stripped of the freedoms we enjoy so liberally. That "old man" inside of me wanted to rebel and demand my own way, but the gentle prodding of the Holy Spirit reminded me why we were there — for Bryon's well-being! Not for myself. It was as if someone was continually whispering in my ear: "No rights!"

The original plan for Bryon's treatment was to stay in the clinic for two weeks to build up his strength, then go to Italy for two to three weeks of surgery, and then return to the Clinic Cal Deu for a couple weeks of recovery. Altogether we were looking at possibly six to seven weeks. This plan was to change a hundred times during our stay...sometimes even day to day. When Professor Kozak first examined Bryon's overall physical condition and his hands, he announced emphatically, "No surgery for six months!" He held up six fingers to reinforce his statement.

My heart sank. Steve was supposed to join us in Italy in just two weeks for Bryon's hand surgery — now that didn't seem possible. But two days later the Professor called an interpreter friend of his in Barcelona and asked her to speak to me.

In essence she conveyed, "Mr. Kozak wants Bryon to stay at the clinic for a least one month's treatment. If all goes well, then he can go to the hospital in Milan for his first 'intervention' (surgery). The first intervention is very important. Bryon's hands are filled with infection and they must be opened so that Kozak can treat the inside. Before his surgery he must have tests and x-rays. There must be no infection in his body at the time of surgery."

She explained, "Mr. Kozak's methods are much improved from those he used in the German clinic. Everything will be different — the creams, pills, diet, and method of treatment for faster results."

Bryon was scheduled to go to the laboratory in Figueras the next morning for tests. He wasn't exactly thrilled to get up at 6:00 a.m. and get ready for the ride to town, but we managed. After the blood tests, x-rays, and fluid extractions from his little "clubs," we spent the rest of the morning shopping. We found a delightful toy store and purchased a soft kick-ball, pencil case, and computer game to help with boredom at the clinic. We also stopped at the Hotel Duran and enjoyed a "cafe' con leche" and warm glass of milk with cookies.

Shortly after we returned from town, Daddy called to decide when he should come to see us, if at all. Finally, we made plans for a ten-day visit to help break up the monotony. At that time we had no guarantee of the hand surgery in Italy. We began to count the days on the calendar for Daddy's arrival in Spain.

One evening about twelve midnight we received a phone call from our church receptionist and good friend, Charlene. She was so excited that she had forgotten about the six-hour time difference. The Lord had given her a wonderful vision and she wanted to share it with us. She began to cry, "I was standing in my kitchen at the counter...mixing a cake...when all of a sudden Bryon appeared before me with his Celtics cap on. He was praising the Lord and holding all ten new fingers up in the air! I just wanted you to know that we are believing God for a miracle...don't get discouraged. God is faithful. He will bring to pass what He has promised!"

Charlene's phone call was just the spiritual "boost" we needed. What an encouragement! When she heard that we might stay longer than we expected, she was ready to pack her suitcase and jump on the next plane to come and be with us. Charlene was one in a million!

The Lord knew we needed this "word of encouragement," for the following day Mr. Kozak informed us that the laboratory tests results had arrived: staph infection and fungus. Bryon's arms and legs were leaking fluid and pus due to the serious infection in his body. The medication was forcing (literally "pushing") the infection out of his system. This caused his skin to come off and many areas to fester into open sores, but it was the only way to expel the poison and cleanse his body.

We passed the time by playing computer games, working on word puzzles, taking walks in the country, visiting with other patients, and counting the hours until Daddy landed in Barcelona.

Two-year-old Christy from California and six-year-old Chad from Florida returned to the States with their mothers. There were a lot of bitter feelings about unpaid clinic bills and a disagreement as to the length of their stay — but they chose to leave anyway. There was an obvious relief when this group had vacated. One of the mothers had been involved in an affair and had often come back from Figueras inebriated and unable to care for her child. Unfortunately, these individuals cast a shadow of mistrust and ill-feeling over the minds of the Professor and the staff for ALL Americans and Canadians. It was a barrier that we confronted on a daily basis.

Maria Kozak, affectionately known as "Mama Kozak," had a genuine love and concern for the EB children. In sharp contrast to her husband, Pavel, who was often given to bouts of anger or total withdrawal, she remained strong and calm through every calamity. Maria was up before dawn working in the kitchen to prepare the meals for the day. Sweat gleamed on her brow as she placed a steaming bowl of fresh chicken-vegetable soup in front of Bryon. When he sipped the broth from the spoon and exclaimed, "Very good! Ummm!" — a broad toothy smile erupted across Maria's face. This was her reward — to make the children happy and to see them improve.

Life had not been easy for Maria. One of five children, she had grown up in Communist-controlled Rumania. At the age of twenty-nine, she first met the Professor in the Bucharest University Hospital, while being treated for a skin disorder. Pavel cured her condition within two weeks. They fell in love and a short time later they were married. Eventually, they defected from their homeland, seeking a place where the Professor could set up a treatment center. Frankfurt, West Germany became their new home. Their sons, Peter and Alexander, grew up in West Germany. For several years while Pavel had no clinic, Maria worked in a factory to support her family. Now they were separated — the boys remained in Germany with a relative and the Kozaks were in Spain at the new clinic. Tears filled Maria's eyes when she spoke of her sons so far away.

* * *

Steve arrived on June 12 — a beautiful Thursday morning. His plane was an hour late, and he looked totally exhausted, but it was great to see "Dad." We had only one week together so we endeavored to make the most of it. Every day was an adventure. After taking a day to recover from jet lag, we spent the afternoon at the seacoast resort of Rosas. Bryon enjoyed the game of mini-golf and the go-cart rides. Our favorite pastime was to walk along the white sandy beaches, look out at the endless blue Mediterranean, and savor every bite of our banana splits at a nearby cafe'.

We tried to take our excursions between lunch and supper, so that Bryon could still receive the special diet and his treatments. The next day we drove to the inland lake of Baynoles — which will be the site of the water sports for the 1992 Olympics. We relaxed in the hot sun during a one-hour boat cruise around the lake. Many private boathouses and swimming clubs decorated the shoreline. And of course, we had time for some "gelato" (ice cream) before we returned to the clinic.

Bryon also relished the moments spent with Dad playing Word Yahtzee, doing search-a-word books, or chasing each other with a kickball. Steve became the "life" of the clinic in his attempts to speak Spanish, compliment the staff, and tell jokes to the patients and their parents. He even volunteered to take three of the mothers to the once-a-week open market in the center of Figueras. They laughed and talked all the way there and back — he never understood one word they said, but he sure had a great time.

Sunday, June 15, was Father's Day. We planned a trip into France for the afternoon. Within thirty minutes we crossed the border and passed by a large Aztec-type pyramid which was part of the Welcome Center. In the sprawling city of Perpignan we spent several hours touring one of the most splendid palaces, dating back to medieval times. Later we drove along the French Riviera and stopped in the little coastal town of Canet. We had forgotten that all the banks and money exchanges were closed on Sunday and we had great difficulty changing our currency. The waiter at a local restaurant misunderstood my order and brought two cups of coffee. He refused to take one back and I had to pay for both of them. Besides getting lost on the way back and putting up with people ignorantly staring at Bryon, we had an enjoyable day.

The best day was our trip to Marineland in Malgrat. The shows were comparable to the Sea World in Orlando and were translated into four languages. Bryon rode the miniature train and browsed through the gift shops.

Professor Kozak did not share the same feeling we had about sightseeing. In fact, two days before Steve returned home, he confronted us with the help of Stephanie, a young woman visiting from Rumania who could speak perfect English. Kozak laid down some very stringent rules about our trips and Bryon's treatment.

Mr. Kozak asserted firmly, "If you want to go to Italy for surgery on Bryon's hands, then I need strict obedience and discipline from you. No more trips. No more eating out. The next five days are very important in preparing Bryon for the surgery. The infection is draining out of his hands and the staph and fungus must be under control before we go to Italy."

It was hard to swallow, but I knew Kozak was our only link to Dr. Morelli. I didn't want to ruin this all-important chance for Bryon. In a way it was better that Steve was going home — because it was a greater temptation to break the rules with him there. Reasoning this in my mind was very logical, but it still didn't ease the terrible hurt when we had to say good-bye. Bryon stood on the dining room balcony, tears streaming down his cheeks, sobbing, "Daddy, don't leave me. Please don't go!"

Part of the hurt was the uncertainty of the future and all the unanswered questions. Would Bryon get rid of the infection? Would we be able to go to Italy? Would Dr. Morelli operate on Bryon's hands? Would the surgeries be successful?

How long would we be away from home? The only sure answer was to trust God.

The days melted into one long continuous day. Without my calendar I would never have remembered what day of the week it was. I poured myself into writing letters, reading books, working on my new manuscript, and typing letters for the clinic. Since I knew how to type and was able to speak English, I was chosen to be the official correspondent with all the prospective patients. At least it kept me preoccupied, leaving little time to think about my husband and three other children at home.

The nights seemed to be endless with the barking dogs, intense heat, and the "army" of insects which flew through our screen-less window. We didn't have much choice; either close the wooden shutters and die from heat exhaustion, or open the shutters and be attacked by strange flying critters. Bryon and I were the official "SWAT TEAM." We swatted everything that "buzzed" and hit our walls. In the morning we surveyed the casualties — splattered over the walls and scattered on the floor. What a mess!

After Peter and Alexander Kozak arrived from West Germany, there was even more late night activity. The commotion from outdoor tennis matches, parties, loud television programs, and "rough-housing" with the dogs was heard until one or two o'clock in the morning. I lay on top of my starchy sheets and tried to concentrate on prayer or verses of Scripture. To block out some of the noise, we played Christian music on our tape player.

I quoted this passage continually: "Thou wilt keep him in perfect peace, whose mind is stayed on thee, because he trusteth in thee" (Isa. 26:3; Scofield).

I woke up one morning with incredible pain in my jaw and the right side of my face. At first I thought it was an ear infection. Then I realized it was an abscessed molar. Maria, one of the staff, suggested I go to a dentist in town. (The only one!) After sitting in a waiting room filled with people for three hours, the nurse told me to come back at six o'clock that evening. Finally, the dentist x-rayed my tooth and confirmed my fear — it was an abscess. It was my first experience with a primitive-type root canal. He drilled out the old filling, took a large needle, swiftly punctured the cavity into my root, while he pushed on my face until the infection poured out. What agony! I had to leave the root open for a week to let the poison drain out. It was a small compensation, but at least I had some relief from the pain.

Lora, a pretty, dark-haired young girl in her early twenties, from Ontario, was a constant companion for Bryon. After Steve left, she spent many hours playing word games with him. Even though she had scarlederma, she showed very few outward signs of the disease. Ginette, a gray-haired French-Canadian woman in her forties, also with scarlederma, became our dorm-mate. She was a close friend and a source of moral support when things got rough. As a dedicated Catholic Christian, Ginette had a genuine faith in God and His miracle power. We shared many conversations about the Lord and the Word of God. On more than one occasion we embraced each other in desperate prayer. Thank God for placing this special friend across the hall from us.

There were others also who became a part of our lives. Frank and Maria had two girls, Sondra and Jennifer, ages seven and four respectively, who were both affected with a severe case of Epidermylosis Bullosa Dystraphica. Imagine caring for two children with EB! They had sold their home in Toronto, Ontario to raise enough money to come to the clinic. Both girls had difficulty eating which caused them to choke and gag constantly during meal times.

Tina and Guido arrived from Milan, Italy with their sixteen-year-old daughter, Sonia. Her form of EB had affected her feet so that she was unable to walk without help. Her fingers had grown together into useless clubs. But her spirit was bright, and she had a great sense of humor. Bryon had another friend.

One morning Frank and Maria and their girls were suddenly moved out of their room and Borus transported them to the Hotel Duran. There seemed to be a lot of confusion and hurt concerning the reasons why they had to leave. Later that day, Maria Zuli and her eleven-year-old son, Alexander, arrived from Rome. I learned from Sara and the other staff workers that the Zuli family was a big financial benefactor for the clinic. Now the pieces fit together. The Zulis were given the "red carpet" treatment. Very shortly, I discovered that none of the rules applied to them.

Alexander had a very mild form of EB, which affected only his hands, feet, and knees. He had already been to the hospital in Milan for hand surgery. Now he was preparing to return for his second operation. The Professor hinted that there was a slight possibility for Bryon to see Dr. Morelli at the same time, depending on his progress.

To accelerate the healing process, Mr. Kozak began giving Bryon antibiotic injections three times a day. This was not a pleasant experience. Every time Bryon saw the Professor coming with a needle, he cried, "No shots, please no more shots!" But the injections did help to fight the terrible infection in Bryon's body, especially in his hands. The first four weeks of treatment produced only open sores that oozed with pus, but the fifth week proved to be a turning point — sores began to heal and new skin formed.

Bryon's bright spirit was an encouragement to everyone in the clinic. No matter what he went through, he always had time to crack a joke or sing a song. Although we never discussed it, there was a real anti-American feeling expressed from some of the other patients and especially Kozak's sons. Bryon detected this immediately and decided to do something about it. Late in the evening during his treatments, he sang "The Star-Spangled Banner" at the top of his lungs. With all the doors and windows wide open, the sounds of our national anthem were heard all through the clinic and over the surrounding countryside. The children and their parents gathered in the hallways and at the final blustery note, applauded and yelled, "Bravo! Bravo Bryon!" Bryon really caused quite a commotion!

After the children were asleep, Ginette, Tina, Maria, and myself enjoyed sitting out on the upstairs balcony, sipping coffee, and conducting international language lessons. We learned a little Rumanian, Spanish, Italian, and English mixed together. Sometimes we had to act out a "word" or "phrase" to get the correct meaning. When the "light" finally came on, we laughed at our silly charades.

A few days before the Zulis left for Italy, the Professor came into our room. He motioned for me to follow him out onto the hillside flourishing with fruit trees.

"Mrs. Sparks," he began in his broken English, "When I was eight years in Rumania, God gave me a dream. He got my attention by showing me a dream of this clinic in Spain. I looked everywhere — Germany, Canada, Bermuda, Italy, the United States — but it was not the dream. Then when I came to Cal Deu, which means 'House of God,' I knew this was the right place."

He pointed to a tree that had been cut down, but now new leaves were sprouting all around the trunk. "This is life!" he exclaimed. "People said to me, 'Nothing will grow there...it is no good. The land is not good for growth.' But they were wrong. Because this is the 'house of God.' "

My eyes filled with tears and I wondered, "Does he really know what he is saying? Does he understand the full meaning of his words?" I then asked him, "What does 'Nihil Sine Deo' mean, which is printed on your clinic stationery?"

Faltering for the right words, he stated, "Nothing without God!"

My heart leaped within me. "O Lord!" I cried. "This man who knows nothing about Your great love and compassion, and knows You only through a form of godliness, is speaking truth into my life. Your word tells me: 'I am the vine, ye are the branches: He that abideth in me, and I in him, the same bringeth forth much fruit: for without me ye can do nothing' " (John 15:5; OB).

As we walked back up the hill to the clinic, the sun was dropping behind the mountains. The Professor grabbed my elbow and stated, "Mrs. Sparks, you must get your plane tickets tomorrow to fly to Italy. Bryon is very good...yes, he is ready for surgery. We leave July 6!"

Mr. Kozak was right...Nothing without God!

# 17

# CASA DI CURA

Bethesda was a special bathing pool in Bible times where sick people received healing as the angel troubled the waters. Jesus often visited this "place of mercy" during the Passover feast of the Jews. Bethesda was a spring-fed pool surrounded by five porches, located in the city of Jerusalem. Sick folks waited on these porches to step down into the waters which were troubled on a regular occasion by an angel — who was a special messenger of healing from God. John writes about it:

> *"In these lay a great multitude of impotent (helpless) people, of blind, halt, withered, waiting for the moving of the water. For an angel went down at a certain season into the pool, and troubled the water..."* (John 5:3,4a; OB).

Those who were sick of the diseases of this life took the pains to travel far and had the patience to wait so long for the cure. Such was the impotent man who lay beside the Sheep Gate — the place of sacrifices. He had spent thirty-eight years with this infirmity. He had lost the use of his limbs and could not walk. He had probably thought many times that he must have been born to suffer. His life seemed ruined. Every time the angel troubled the water, someone else got into the waters before him.

But one day Jesus came by! Jesus saw the impotent man lying in his hopeless condition and asked him: "Wilt thou be made whole?" (v. 6).

The impotent man answered Jesus by saying: "No man careth for my soul!" Every time the waters were troubled someone beat him to the pool. Many times he was only a step away from his healing.

Jesus said, "Rise, take up thy bed, and walk" (v. 8). These divine words were the vehicle of divine power. Immediately, the man took the gift of faith and was healed. He took Christ at His Word and received healing.

Casa Di Cura was also known as the "house of cure" throughout modern Europe. People traveled for many miles to receive treatment for incurable orthopedic maladies. Dr. Alberto Morelli had inherited his father's practice of forty-five years. Now approaching his eighties, the elderly professor was a world-renowned hand surgeon. He had operated on sixty children with Epidermylosis Bullosa. The disease was not foreign to him.

True to Mr. Kozak's promise, we left for Italy on the morning of July 6, 1986. We flew into Milan's Forlanini-Linate Airport, which was about thirty miles from the hospital. The Casa Di Cura was located in the bustling city of Busto Arsizio, just forty miles south of Lugano, Switzerland. Relatives of the Zuli family met us at the plane and took us out for a lovely Sunday dinner.

The restaurant was on the first floor of the Hotel Astoria, just a few blocks from the clinic. The meal consisted of prosciutto di Parma (Parma ham), minestra di fagioli (butter bean soup), fettuccine crema (pasta with cream, butter, and Parmesan cheese), cappuccino (coffee with milk), and Zuccoto (chilled, spongy chocolate cake). It was wonderful!

Room 105 was to become our "home" for the next three

weeks. It was a spacious room, with a marble floor, ten-foot ceiling, two firm beds, some furnishings, a tall window over-looking the narrow street, and a private bath. It was adequate. Down the hall was a small cucine (kitchen), where we could prepare the special diet of semolina, tea, rice, carrot soup, and bread. The milk had to be bought fresh every day at the supermercado (grocery store) and the Hotel Astoria provided fresh baked bread.

The next day we met Dr. John Manupassa, the staff plastic surgeon, a native of Indonesia. Because he had learned English during his medical studies in England, he became the primary interpreter for us. His quiet manner and confidence was a source of encouragement in the difficult days ahead.

Bronzed and strikingly handsome, the younger Dr. Morelli made his appearance also. He seemed genuinely interested in helping Bryon. He held Bryon's small contracted clubs in his hands and examined them closely. In silence, he gently shook his head.

After an endless pause he spoke, "I have seen many children with Epidermylosis Bullosa, but these hands are the very worst. The surgery will be most difficult — perhaps even impossible."

His eyes met mine. I felt the rush of hot tears and replied, "Dr. Morelli, you are our last hope. This is the only place of cure that we know of...please help us...at least try!"

With great sympathy, he answered, "I'll do my best."

We couldn't ask for anything more. We had to believe that God was in control of Bryon's hands.

The rest of the day was filled with x-rays, blood tests, and E.K.G. tests. Bryon almost flipped out when the technician started attaching all kinds of wires, clamps, and machines to his body. His greatest fear was that his skin would be ripped off. I tried desperately to explain the problem, but they didn't seem to understand. Finally, when the technician saw a piece of flesh tear away with the clamp, the light went on. Very apologetically, he corrected the situation and took the readings another way.

July 8 was surgery day! I called Steve the night before, so

---

227

that he could be praying for us during the day. The operation was scheduled for 2:00 p.m. No eating or drinking was allowed that day.

After Bryon's treatment I walked briskly into town to exchange currency, pick up a few sleeveless undershirts, some groceries, and a new Mario Brothers computer game. I rushed so that Bryon would not be left alone too long. When I burst through the doorway with my arms full of packages, my mouth fell open in utter amazement. Very nonchalantly, Steve was relaxing in the over-stuffed leather chair in the corner of the room.

"What are you doing here?" I screamed with delight!

"Well, the Lord did a miracle," he answered. "Our church took up a large love offering for Bryon's expenses during the morning service on Sunday. Then afterwards, an elderly lady walked up to me and handed me a check to pay for my airfare. I called our travel agent yesterday, right after I talked to you on the phone. I wanted to be sure Bryon was scheduled to have surgery before I made the trip. I had exactly two hours to pack and make it to the airport before my flight...and now I'm here!"

It sounded like a fantasy...but I was so glad it was true. Steve was with us for the day of surgery and the next ten days. The Lord knew I desperately needed the moral support, since I had already been away from home for forty days. It was a definite answer to prayer.

Bryon was supposed to go for surgery first; Alexander second. But somehow the schedule got turned around and they came for Alexander first, which meant that Bryon had to wait another long two hours. Finally, Luisella, the head nurse, gave Bryon two shots; one for sedation, one for pre-anesthesia. Immediately, Bryon started to get that "spacey" look, his eyes were open, but he couldn't communicate. Dominic, a male orderly, helped to lift Bryon onto the transport stretcher and wheeled him away.

There is no feeling like watching your child being taken away from you, to be cared for by other individuals, and knowing that you have absolutely no power over what happens to him. This is a true picture of submission. Releasing someone you love into the hands of Almighty God.

Steve and I watched him disappear into the service elevator and went back into room 105. A delicious tray of cappuccino and biscuits were waiting for us. For a long time neither of us said a word. Then Steve suggested, "Honey, I think we should pray for Bryon right now. I know God didn't allow us to come this far without a miracle. I feel in my spirit that this operation will be the answer to Bryon's dream. Don't you?"

I quickly nodded my head in agreement. The next hour we spent in quiet intercession to a God that we knew answered prayer. Prayer is the power source for every Christian — and we were plugging into that divine power. Someone has said, "All of life, especially the spiritual life, is like an echo — giving me back exactly what I put into it."

Unknown to us, a battle of decision was being waged in the operating room. Dr. Morelli had made an incision around Bryon's right wrist, and then he pulled off all the outer layer of scar tissue and dead skin covering his club. When the doctor saw how entangled the bones, blood vessels, tendons, muscles, and nerve endings were, he stared in disbelief. The two assistants said, "Dr. Morelli, you are a great hand surgeon, but this is impossible! Forget about the operation. Bandage his hand and send him home."

But something inside the great surgeon impelled him to make one more attempt. Very carefully, he made a small cut along Bryon's palm, where the ends of his gnarled fingers were. He took his own gloved hand and inserted his fingers deep into the incision beneath the small stubs. He instructed his assistants to hold onto Bryon's wrist and palm, so that he wouldn't literally pull his hand off his arm. Dr. Morelli placed his knee against the operating table and then exerted tremendous force on those fused fingers. All of a sudden, nine years of contracture gave way — all five fingers opened up! What a miracle!

The physicians were so jubilant about the release of the fingers, that they didn't even notice that Bryon was sitting up on the operating table...wide awake!

---

He asked in a shaky voice, "What are you guys doing?"

Shocked beyond words, the doctors stood motionless for a few seconds. Then they looked at the anesthesiologist, who was supposed to be doing his job. Quickly, he gave Bryon another dose of ketamine to put him to sleep again. During the remainder of the surgery they inserted five-inch steel pins in each of his fingers, covered his raw hand with antibiotics, and packed the fingers with gauze and bandages. It looked like a gigantic tennis racket hanging from his body.

Because of the tremendous trauma, loss of blood, and length of the operation, the doctors decided to do only one hand at a time. (In a few months we were able to return for surgery on his left hand.)

Dominic walked with me to the "sale operationale" (operating room). Bryon was crying out in pain and calling my name. He had an intravenous line going into his neck by his ear. I noticed some of his skin was torn from his chest and neck due to the electrode monitors. I rubbed his hair and whispered his name.

He tried to open his eyes and started to cry, "Mommy, Jesus gave me five new fingers. I woke up on the operating table and I saw them...they are beautiful, Mom! God is giving me my dream!" He drifted off into temporary oblivion, the tears still on his cheeks.

My heart was bursting with praise! God does answer prayer. Dr. Morelli came out in the hallway and gave us the "thumbs up" sign that everything was okay. "Buono, Bryon, buono!" he said with a smile. Steve was waiting for us in the room and rejoiced to hear the good report. We were far from the completed miracle — but we were on our way!

While Steve went to the Hotel Astoria to get settled in, Bryon took a long nap. I wet his bloody lips with cotton soaked in chamomile tea. When he woke up, he began asking for food. He was starved! Next, he wanted to get out of bed and sit in the lounging chair. When Dr. Morelli came in to check on his condition, he exclaimed, "Bravo, Bryon! You are amazing!" Bryon was sitting up, trying to feed himself by using both of his elbows.

The next few days we all concentrated on helping Bryon get better. Some days were more difficult than others. Like the day after surgery, when the lab technician wanted Bryon to walk down two flights of stairs and across the courtyard to the laboratory — just to get a tube of blood! Bryon passed out on the floor as soon as he got off the bed. So they brought a wheelchair. Just one problem — the wheelchair couldn't fit in the elevator and we couldn't lift it down the stairs. Between lifting Bryon and half-carrying the wheelchair, we finally made it to the lab. By that time Bryon was screaming from the pain of moving his hand and knocking it into objects. The hospital personnel realized the terrible trauma this caused, so the next time they needed a blood sample, they came to the room.

Two days after surgery they changed the bandages on Bryon's hand for the first time. Dr. Manupassa allowed me to stand in the hallway and watch the entire procedure. The fingers were quite swollen and bloody, but I counted all five individual digits sticking out from his hand. It was utterly amazing. His 'pinky' was the smallest.

The hardest part of the bandage changes were the two pre-medicated shots: one for his saliva to dry up so he wouldn't choke and one for sedation. Bryon's thighs were covered with dark blue bruises from the injections. After the second treatment, Bryon came back to the room, still heavily under the influence of ketamine. As he drifted in and out of consciousness, he shared the deepest secrets of his heart.

"Jesus, You're wonderful," Bryon began to talk to the Lord. "You're lovely...I worship You. I praise You. Thank You for giving me five new fingers...and for giving me the strength to endure the pain. I know how You felt on the cross because I have pins and needles in my hands too. Even if my other hand never has surgery, I still thank You for giving me five fingers. I worship You with my new fingers...

"Thank You for my family...for my dad who makes me laugh...and my mom who has so much patience to care for me...for Leann, she's seven...Jenell, she's five...and Brent, he doesn't understand what's happening, he's only two-and-a-half...

---

"I can't wait to see You, Jesus. Then I will be perfect. No more blisters. No more surgery or hospitals. I will have ten perfect fingers...Thank You for dying for me...You paid a great price. Please take all the sin out of my heart...make me clean...so You and Fudgy (Bryon's worn-out teddy bear) can live in there. I want to make sure I'm ready to go to heaven...

"Lord, I love You...You are No. 1 in my life. You will always be No. 1! Lord, You are more beautiful than silver...Lord, You are more precious than gold...Lord, You are more costly than diamonds...I desire that nothing keep us apart!" (Bryon's version of an old chorus.)

The tears streamed down my cheeks as I hurried to write in my prayer journal all of Bryon's expressions. To think that such pure, genuine thoughts came from my son, while he was subconscious, was incredible! During a very difficult time in his life, praise still flowed from his young heart. "Oh God," I cried, "teach me more about trusting You through Bryon's life."

Steve bought Bryon two new games at a nearby toy store: magnetic checkers and photo memory. They spent hours sitting on Bryon's bed, engaged in serious competition. It was always — "Oh, Dad, just one more game. Please?"

Once in the middle of the night, Bryon sat up in bed and yelled, "What jumps can I make, Mom?" Then he lay back down and was sound asleep. I chuckled to myself and thought, "No wonder he beats Daddy. He plans his strategy while he's sleeping!"

The ten days Steve stayed in Italy passed by all too quickly. He had to go home to Leann, Jenell, and Brent. They needed him too. We had a difficult decision to make before he left — would I be able to speak at our Ohio District's Ladies Retreat during August 9-11? Our time schedule was completely altered from our previous plans. From what Dr. Morelli indicated about the length of recovery and then an additional two weeks at the clinic in Spain — there was no way humanly possible I could make it. Steve had to call Roberta Crabtree, our district Women's Ministries President, and let her know I was not able to speak. What a disappointment! I had looked forward to this special speaking engagement for a year. I had studied and prepared for months. But Bryon had to come first. I knew God would honor my decision.

Thursday, July 17, was a rough day. We had to say goodbye to Daddy. When it was time for Bryon to go up for a dressing change, Steve kissed us farewell. As they wheeled Bryon down the hall, he begged, "Don't leave me, Daddy...I love you...please don't go!" Boy did it hurt!

An hour later, when we came back to the room, two notes were waiting for us, one on each of our pillows. Bryon's read:

*To My Buddy:*

*Hi son...I love you. You are the most "bravo" tough cookie in the whole world. You are so special to Mom and Dad.*

*I know it hurts to be away from each other but Mom and you need each other too. Take good care of Mom for me, okay?*

*Practice your memory and checker games...don't beat Mom too much. I love you, Buddy.*

*See you soon...Daddy.*

And one for me:

*Dearest Sweetheart,*

*I love you. Thank you for letting me come and share this time with you. I really tried hard to be unselfish. I hope I was a blessing to the both of you. That was my desire.*

*Please remember that many people are praying for our family. God will hold us safely in His arms. Hold me tight at nite. Think of me...I'll be thinking about you.*

*I love you, Stephen.*

---

A new box of kleenex was opened. I looked in the waste can...there in the bottom were crumpled up tissues. I picked one up and put it under my nose...it smelled just like my honey. A fresh flood of tears fell down my cheeks. I knew I had to be strong for Bryon...it wasn't easy.

Bryon was great at helping me forget the loneliness. He was able to turn a serious situation into a comedy. After one of his dressing changes, and still a little groggy from the anesthesia, he began to get impatient. "Hey, let's get this show on the road! Why can't we go downstairs yet? Dr. Morelli, where are you? You are the best doctor in the whole world...yup! Dr.Morelli is 'numero uno' — He's No. 1 all right!" The surgical staff was in hysterics, especially those who understood a little English. For the rest, Dr. John did some impromptu interpretation.

Another evening I was bringing in my clothes from the makeshift line outside the window, when I noticed that my one and only pair of white pantyhose was lying in the street. There were car tire tracks across them. In the darkness it looked like a ghostly aberration. The hospital doors were locked at nine o'clock, so the only way to get out was to find the night nurse. Bryon and I trudged down the hall, calling, "Senora, Senora." But there was no answer. We decided to try the third floor.

The third floor was filled with older patients who had hand and foot surgery. When they heard Bryon and I yelling, they all came out of their rooms and followed us. Some were on crutches, and others had big bandages on their hands or feet. Finally, Gina appeared out of the treatment room, all in disarray. I tried desperately to explain what happened, but to no avail. In utter frustration, I motioned for her to follow me down the stairs. By this time we had caused quite a commotion. To my dismay, not only Gina, but all of the patients from the third floor decided to come too!

Like a huge parade we arrived at the entrance to the hospital. Gina took out her keys and unlocked the front doors. At that moment, one of the staff doctors pulled up to the curb to park. With wide-eyed amazement, he watched as I walked out of the hospital and into the street, trailed by a small army of invalids. When I reached my tire-striped pantyhose, I held them up in the air and pointed to my clothesline two stories above. Everyone broke out in a round of applause and cheers! It was the greatest entertainment they had all week. What a night!

A few days later, Bryon I decided to go down to the main floor for a cappuccino, hot milk, and a cookie break. Once we were in the compact elevator, we noticed that someone had pushed the button for the third floor. When the door opened, a man leaning on a cane with a heavily bandaged foot, was being pushed and shoved by two little Italian grandmothers. The ladies maneuvered him inside the elevator, but then had to let him go because there was no room for either of them. Bryon and I were backed into the far corner, against the wall.

At this point, the heavy-set gentleman began to scream for help. Apparently, he changed his mind and didn't want to get on the elevator after all. But by now — the elevator door began to close shut. The two ladies started to pull him out, but his injured foot and cane were stuck in the doorway. He responded with painful cries. In desperation, one woman yanked his foot out of the pinned position and they all collapsed on the floor as the door closed. The end of the cane was still stuck in the elevator. Bryon and I descended...we heard the cane break off...and then we burst into uncontrollable laughter. It was too much to bear...like watching an old Charlie Chaplin movie. Needless to say, it made our day!

We waited downstairs for over an hour for them to appear — but they never showed up. For days afterwards, all we had to do was mention the man with the cane and we were rolling on the floor. It was great therapy.

Bryon's hand healed beautifully during the three weeks we stayed at the Casa Di Cura. Then it was time to say good-bye to Dr. Morelli, Dr. Manupasse, Dominic, Luisella, Elizabetta, Rita, Francesa, Gina, and all the others who had taken care of us. We had to go to the clinic in Spain for two weeks of rehabilitation before returning to the States. We also needed an extra supply of creams and vitamins to take with us.

The day before we departed, I had to change all of Bryon's bandages with Dr. Manupassa's personal instruction and approval. The last two dressing changes were done without anesthesia. Dr. Morelli came in to check out Bryon's new fingers and to say farewell. For some strange reason, he held his hands behind his back. Then suddenly he asked: "Bryon, do you want to go home with those pins stuck in your fingers?"

"No way!" Bryon asserted.

Swiftly, with great agility, Dr. Morelli reached for the first pin with a pair of pliers and pulled it out.

"Ohhhh my!" cried Bryon.

"Did it hurt?" asked Dr. Morelli.

"Well, sorta!" replied Bryon.

Before Bryon could resist...one, two, three, four...the rest of the pins were out! Beads of perspiration glistened on Bryon's forehead. He was glad it was over.

On Saturday, July 26, we flew from Milan, Italy to Barcelona, Spain. The day began at 3:18 a.m. By six o'clock we were riding in Dominic's car, listening to rock music and fighting cigarette smoke. When we arrived at the airport all of the passengers were lined up at ONE counter. We waited for over an hour just to check our baggage. Then the nightmare began.

A mob of rude, loud, smelly people jammed the gateway to the bus — our means of transportation to the plane. The crowd was oblivious to small children, babies, pregnant women, and the handicapped. Even the airline agents were cold and indifferent. Body by body we were packed like sardines in a can, into the bus. People stared at Bryon, looked horrified, and then turned away. No one tried to make room, offered a seat, or attempted to help.

Bryon looked so pathetic with all his bandages and one arm that looked like a huge boxing glove. He was knocked, pushed, banged, and stepped on...but silently endured the pain. Finally, we stumbled off the bus and there was a mad scramble to climb the stairs to the plane. We were the last ones to board.

At our seats, 8L and 8K, we had to climb over a mother and toddler. While attempting to store our carry-on luggage, the people behind us shoved us out of the way to get by. Another mother and child came down the aisle, passed us, realized they were going in the wrong direction and turned around. She swung her little boy right into Bryon's new fingers. Bryon winced in pain. Somehow we got into our seats and collapsed. I yelled out, "Please be careful!" No one seemed to hear me.

Of course, we had to sit in the "insane" section of the plane for the next one-and-a-half hours. Kids screamed, crawled over us, and ran up and down the aisles. By this time Bryon was bleeding through the back of his shirt and all over the seat cushion.

We tried to eat some breakfast, but the semolina was sour. I poured the tea, got out the butter and bread, and while peeling a peach the juice ran down my hands and onto my dress. The squirming youngster next to me spilled my coffee and stepped on my white dress.

Getting off the plane, boarding the bus, trudging into the terminal, and going through passport control and baggage claim was the same horrifying ordeal as before. While pushing my cart through customs, a woman behind me drove her cart into my ankle, ripping my pantyhose, and making a deep gash in my skin. I felt my foot begin to bleed.

Thank God, Borus was waiting for us with the clinic van. It took forty-five minutes to get out of the parking lot and another two hours to get to Clinic Cal Deu.

The one reoccurring verse of Scripture that gave me strength throughout this unbelievable day and the next two weeks was 1 Corinthians 11:1 — "Follow me, as I follow Christ" (Scofield). What did Paul mean by that statement? In other words — "Follow my example, as I follow the example of Jesus Christ" or "watch my life and you will see Christ!" What an awesome statement to say to those in our family, people at work, and in our neighborhood. I realized that I was the only "Jesus" that many would ever see. It was a focusing point in controlling my emotions and establishing my priorities.

_____

On August 11, 1986, seventy days since we had departed, we landed in the Pittsburgh International Airport. We were greeted with a flood of hugs and kisses from Leann, Jenell, Brent, and of course, Daddy. Bryon soaked up all the attention and momentary celebration. Yet, Bryon exuded a deeper, quieter joy — for underneath the heavy bandages he wiggled five brand new fingers!

# 18

# I'M READY

The headline for the *Tribune Chronicle* on Wednesday, April 8, 1987 read: "Warren youth's wish comes true, meets Larry Bird." Not only did God bring to pass Bryon's dream for new fingers, but also a secret desire to meet his basketball hero, Boston Celtics' super star Larry Bird.

In September 1986, Bryon was taken to Tod Children's Hospital in Youngstown to clear up a serious staph and strep infection. While he was there, his condition was brought to the attention of a group of businessmen from the Youngstown area who sponsor a program called "Children's Dream." Every year this organization grants the wish of one seriously ill child. Bryon was unanimously selected as a candidate for Children's Dream.

When the group's spokesperson phoned to ask what Bryon's wish would be, two ideas came to my mind. One was a trip to Disney World; the other was to meet his basketball hero, Larry Bird, in person. How could I choose between the two? Normally, only one wish is granted but somehow they pulled the right strings and both wishes came true.

For seven days in February 1987, Bryon mingled with Mickey Mouse, Donald Duck, and the rest of the Disney cartoon creations. The bonus benefit was that our whole family was privileged to go along. "Children's Dreams" paid for our six round-trip tickets on Eastern Airlines, a rental car, accommodations, three day passes to Disney World, Epcot Center, and Sea World, and expense money for one entire week. It was a family memory that will last a lifetime.

Just six weeks later, we found ourselves in the chauffeur' driven limousine on our way to the Cleveland Coliseum to see the Boston Celtics play the Cavaliers. The game tickets and transportation to the April 7 game were provided by Lakeview Limousine Service, with the assistance of Robert Laird of Roberts Funeral Home in Warren, Ohio. Laird was a longtime friend of John Grabowski, a driver with Lakeview.

"It's unbelievable...he's just awesome," Bryon said after he got an autograph from the "Bird." Wearing a Celtics cap and T-shirt, Bryon admitted Larry Bird was his favorite. "Meeting Bird was close to meeting Mickey," Bryon agreed.

What a thrill to drive inside the coliseum and meet the players from both teams as they came from their locker rooms. Coaches Casey Jones and Lenny Wilkins also stopped to talk to Bryon and sign his autograph book. We had the opportunity to shake hands with Robert Parrish, Danny Ainge, Kevin McHale, Fred Roberts, and many others. Even though the Cavs beat out the Celtics, the loss did not dampen the excitement of this momentous occasion. Bryon's picture with Larry Bird on the front page of *The Tribune* was the icing on the cake. It was an evening long to be remembered.

After Bryon spent a week in the Tod Children's Hospital, we made our second trip to Milan, Italy. On October 7, 1986, Dr. Morelli operated on Bryon's left hand and released his other five fingers. Within three weeks new skin formed over his palm and fingers. As the bandages were changed, we observed a miracle of an accelerated healing process. The doctors were amazed at how quickly Bryon was running through the halls and playing soccer ball, while holding his wrapped arm up in the air.

The nicest part of the trip was having three-year-old Brent with us. The Italians fell in love with this spunky blue-eyed blond. The nurses pinched his cheeks so hard that they turned black and blue. They would hug him and say, "Brent...chi' amore'." (Hi, with love.)

Brent quickly caught on and when he saw the ladies coming down the hall to grab him, he would scream, "No Chi'...no chi' amore'!" He would run into our room, hide behind the door, and hold his cheeks, hoping that no one would find him.

Dr. Petrucci, the anesthesiologist, noticed Brent playing "doctor" one day with Bryon's teddy bear — Fudgy. The bear was wrapped in gauze and tape, after Brent had performed "surgery." So the next day, Dr. Petrucci brought Brent all kinds of supplies from the operating room: a mask, gloves, gown, syringes (without the needles), suture removal kits, and thermometers. Brent was delighted. It gave him hours of wonderful playtime diversion.

Brent soon discovered, during his bath time, that when the syringes were filled with water, they made fabulous squirt guns. One morning while Bryon was having his bandages changed, Brent tagged along with me to the operating room. The doctors, nurses, and I were so intent on seeing Bryon's fingers that we neglected to keep an eye on "little brother." All of a sudden, Dr. Manupassa let out an abrupt yelp and whirled around to see who was causing him discomfort. Mischievous Brent was standing behind him with a sheepish grin on his face and an empty syringe in his hand.

"Dr. John, it's only water...how did you like your shot?" Brent inquired.

When the surgical team realized what had happened, they burst into an uproar of laughter. "Punctore, Dr. John...punctore!" Brent had given the doctor some of his own medicine. It was hilarious!

On October 27 we arrived in the States, Bryon waving all ten of his fingers! It was a real miracle. The end of a long journey was coming into focus. God was faithful — Bryon's dream was a reality!

* * *

All of the children have responded uniquely, and sometimes with overwhelming compassion, to their brother's illness. It hasn't always been easy for them. They have learned to give up their mom so that she could take care of Bryon. Unselfishly, they have taken second, third, and at times, fourth place in line, until Mom was free to give them a little attention. The love that they have for Bryon can never be measured.

Following Bryon's second hand operation, he lay in bed, thrashing with pain. Brent walked over to his side and placed his small chubby hand on Bryon's shoulder. "Bryon," he said, "I'm going to pray for you...because Jesus will make you all better. He can do anything...nothing is too hard for Him!"

I watched as my three-year-old (still in diapers) bowed his head and prayed for his big brother, while the tears ran down his rosy cheeks. It was true compassion in living color.

Jenell, also, in her hyperactive, spontaneous way has reached out to show her love. One evening as we sat down for supper, Jenell was nowhere to be found. About ten minutes later, she came bursting through the front door. She ran over to where Bryon was sitting and dumped pockets of change out on the table in front of him.

"What is this for?" asked Bryon.

"This is for you, Bryon," chirped Jenell. "I drew stencil pictures and took them to everyone in our neighborhood. I told them that I was selling these pictures to buy bandages for my brother. Some people didn't know who you were, Bryon, so I said, 'You know Bryon — your paperboy!' "

Then Jenell threw her arms around Bryon's neck and whispered, "I love you so much, Bryon. I want you to get better...so here's a little money to help with your bandages."

Our eyes were moist with emotion at Jenell's display of genuine love for her brother. She has always had a giving heart, but for her to take the time to put her feelings into positive action was unusual. On another occasion she gave away most of the toys in her room to a visiting missionary family and their two little girls. They had never celebrated Christmas and Jenell wanted to share some of her treasures with them.

Of all the children, perhaps Leann has the most intense love for Bryon. One evening, following the Sunday night service, I heard Leann's muffled sobs as she prayed at the altar. I knelt beside her and put my arm around her shoulders. "What's the matter, Honey?" I implored.

"Oh, Mom," she sobbed, "I feel so bad about Bryon and his disease. I wish he could be better. I've prayed so hard for Jesus to heal him...and he still suffers. Sometimes I feel so guilty that I am normal and was born healthy, while Bryon has never known one day without pain. I've told the Lord that if I could exchange places with him — I would be willing."

Perhaps this tenderness in Leann's heart is the reason she feels a definite calling as a medical missionary. Only eternity will reveal the life-changing effect Bryon has had on all of our lives.

Recently, Bryon was hospitalized for severe anemia and extensive dental surgery due to the side effects of Epidermylosis Bullosa. Bryon needed several blood transfusions to bring his hemoglobin up to a safe level for surgery. Four individuals from our church, with the same type, donated blood for Bryon. When the children learned that Bryon needed transfusions, each of them asked, "Can we give blood for Bryon? Do they accept kid's blood?"

Jenell perked up, "Our blood is the best — 'cause we're related, you know!" And then a little more wistfully, "If we give blood for Bryon, does that mean we might die?"

We quickly assured them that the donors don't die because of giving their blood, and "no" they don't accept children's blood, even though we were so moved by their willingness to help Bryon.

Few people remain untouched by Bryon's winning spirit, once they have met him. Even Bryon's football hero, the Browns' quarterback, Bernie Kosar, melted into pieces when his rough hand grasped Bryon's small scarred one. It was an exciting day for Bryon and his dad when they were invited to attend a special football practice for the Cleveland Browns. The team presented Bryon with an official NFL football from their practice, a Browns' cap, and a Browns' official 1989 Yearbook.

* * *

The apostle Paul compares this Christian life to a race that must be run with the finish line in perspective. Hebrews 12:1,2 tells us..."Wherefore, since we have so great a cloud of witnesses surrounding us, let us also lay aside every encumbrance, and the sin which so easily entangles us, and let us run with endurance the race that is set before us, fixing our eyes on Jesus, the author and perfecter of our faith, who for the joy set before Him endured the cross, despising the shame, and has sat down at the right hand of the throne of God."

Paul also tells us to hold fast to "the word of life, so that in the day of Christ we may have cause to glory because we did not run in vain nor toil in vain" (Phil. 2:16).

Our family has always enjoyed sport events, especially the international Olympic Games held every four years. Our favorite category is the field and track events. The track relay is a concentrated effort made by every member of the team. Many a race is won or lost in the passing of the baton. Sloppy hand-offs and a dropping of the baton may cost the race. So it is with all of life.

In her bestseller, *What Is A Family?*, Edith Schaeffer devotes her longest chapter to the idea that a family is a perpetual relay of truth. A place where eternal values are passed from one generation to another. Where strong characters are molded and shaped by the careful examples of moms and dads. Where memories are built into young lives that will last for a lifetime.

Moses had this portrayal of truth in mind when he urged all the dads in his day:

*"...and you shall teach them diligently to your sons and shall talk of them when you sit in your house and when you walk by the way and when you lie down and when you rise up" (Deut. 6:7).*

---

Charles R. Swindoll writes about "relaying the truth" in his book, *Home — Where Life Makes Up Its Mind:*

> *"That's the plan — the inimitable strategy which makes winners out of runners. Relay the truth — diligently, consistently. One final warning, however, if you determine to make this your goal, you'll have to out-distance two relentless foes: slow starts and sloppy hand-offs. Keep in mind, moms and dads, you really don't have forever. Negligence will catch you from behind and beat you in the stretch if you let up. And don't think your kids will let you get away with faking it, either...relays are won or lost at the critical moment when a young hand reaches back and gropes for the baton."*

Shortly after we watched the 1988 Summer Olympic games, I had a realistic, yet startling dream. I knew it had to be a dream — because the entire Sparks family was in the Official Olympics! There we were...all six of us, dressed in our red-white-and-blue jogging suits, warming up on the track for the relay race. When the gun went off, Dad left us in a cloud of dust, as he pounded around the track. Drenched in perspiration and gasping for air, he stumbled across the finish line and placed the baton in my hand.

Somehow I imagined that all this running stuff would be a piece of cake. I took off with all the aspirations of breaking record time. But halfway around the track every muscle in my body begged to quit. I felt like sitting down in the middle of the track and waiting for the paramedics to arrive. Running in the Olympics wasn't as easy as it appeared...and neither is the race of life.

How many times have you felt like giving up? Or quitting? Throwing in the towel? It's just the moment when everything has gone from bad to worse, that "Job's comforters" will whisper to you..."You can't make it! What's the use...who cares anyhow? Why don't you give up? Or run away from it all?"

---

It happens to all of us, especially when we've lost sight of the goal. It was what I saw in my dream that has kept me in the race of life. I visualized four little hands reaching out to me, each one waiting for the baton I held in my hand. The baton represented the "truth" — the truth that Jesus Christ is the reason for living. Someone had taken the time during the formative years of my life to hand to me the baton...and now it was my turn to pass it on.

Their groping hands and a look of yearning in each of their faces still haunts me today. I know it is my awesome responsibility and challenge to place within their grasp the reality of knowing Jesus as a personal Saviour and friend. I have made this my lifetime goal.

So many times when I have been discouraged with the daily rigors of raising a family, living up to the pastor's wife portfolio, and keeping up with the demands of my speaking schedule, it has been Bryon who has encouraged me. One night as I collapsed in my motel room in Lincoln, Nebraska, I found this note tucked into my suitcase:

*Dear Mom,*

*Words cannot describe how much I love you. You will never know how much you mean to me. For you are the greatest mom anybody could have...also the best mom in the world.*

*I pray for you every day. Because you are so special to me. I hope you have a good trip to Nebraska this weekend. I'll be praying for you, Mom, every day and night. God is going to use you in a miraculous way, I know.*

*Pray for me too. I really need prayer. I just have so much pressure on me. Nobody understands how it feels to have EB, an incurable disease, being a fifteen year-old teenager, peer pressure, homework, and everything. Mom, nobody knows how it feels. Just*

*pray for me that God will give me the strength. I
need it!*

*Well, I'm getting real tired, so I'm going to say
good-night. I probably won't see you in the morning, so have a nice trip. See you in a few days.*

*Lots of love,*

*Your son, Bryon*

For almost sixteen years Bryon has helped to keep our pri-
orities in focus. Often he will say to us, "Every day is a gift
from God...I'm so glad to be alive!" Bryon is right — Life is
Precious! No one has a guarantee what tomorrow will bring.
We need to treasure every day as a measured gift of love from
God.

Bryon added a new dimension to my dream of the "Olympic Race" during one of our lengthy conversations. During the
past few months we took numerous trips to the Cleveland
Clinic in hopes of restoring some of Bryon's teeth and in preparation for dental surgery. While on our way home along the
familiar route 422 through Chagrin Falls, Bryon began to talk
about a spiritual finish line.

"Mom, did you know that in youth group Pastor Peter
and his wife, Lilly, have been teaching us about the book of
Revelation?" Bryon inquired.

I nodded no.

"I never knew prophecy and future events could be so
exciting!" he continued. "Did you know how great heaven will
be? Pastor Peter has been explaining the wonderful things the
Christians will experience there...like the Marriage Supper of
the Lamb, the Millennium, the New Jerusalem, the New
Heavens and the New Earth. It will be terrific! Did you know
all that stuff, Mom?"

"Yes, Buddy. I studied Revelation in Bible college quite a
few years ago. It really is the Christian's blessed hope."

"And do you know what else? When we get to heaven we

will never have to go to the Cleveland Clinic again! You will never go to Franklin Pharmacy for bandages and Vaseline gauze...no nurse will ever say to me again — 'Roll over, Honey!' I will never get another injection, or have another surgery, or treatment. For I will be perfectly whole! Won't that be absolutely FANTASTIC!''

Visualizing Bryon totally healed brought tears to my eyes. I responded softly, "Yes, Bryon, that will be a wonderful day!''

"You know, Mom, sometimes kids at school have asked me, 'Bryon, don't you ever get mad at God for not healing you completely? I know He has touched you many times, but yet you still have the symptoms of the disease. Doesn't it make you angry?'

"I really thought about that question for a long time...and you know what Mom? I'm not one little bit mad at God...sure, I would like to be healed...to be normal...but whether God heals me down here (and He has the power to do it!) or whether He heals me when I get to heaven...it's okay with me...because either way I still win!''

The profoundness of his words hit me like a wave of cold water. Here was the body of a boy, barely a teenager, sitting beside me, but inside was the character of a man! His acute accessment of life was astonishing.

Before I could absorb the full meaning of his statement, he continued, "Mom, I want you to know that I appreciate you and Dad. I realize that I am alive today because you guys have hung in there for me. When everyone else gave up on me and said I wouldn't make it...you and Dad believed in God...I know it was your faith that has kept me alive...and I want to thank you. Thanks, Mom, for hanging in there!''

I felt a lump in my throat and effortlessly the tears spilled onto my blouse. I struggled to keep the van on the highway and to see out the window. Bryon's words brought to my mind the letter he had written to us just a few months before and left on our pillows. We discovered his note as we prepared to go to bed.

*Dear Dad,*

*Thank you so much for talking to me earlier today. I learned a lot about what you said of Death. Death will be my very best friend. I just want to be healed so bad, Dad. I've asked God so many times 2 very important questions:*

*1. When will I be healed?*
*2. If God doesn't heal me, when will I die and go to heaven to meet my healer?*

*Lately, I've just felt so lonely for heaven. Dad, I'm just so tired of fighting! I've accomplished a lot down here...you're right. But like you said Dad, "To live is Christ, but to die is gain."*

*When I die I want to die in my sleep...to see the light at the end of a dark long tunnel...and then to see heaven, my home sweet home with Jesus.*

*I promise to get things ready in heaven for you and my family, if I die first. Which I'm ready to go Dad. I AM READY!*

*My trust is in God. May His will be done in my life...so it will be the easiest for me. Whatever happens in the future...just remember ...I love you Dad and Mom!*

*Your son, Bryon*

*P.S. You can share this with Mom.*

Bryon jolted me back to our present surroundings..."and just one more thing, Mom...I want you to know that if there are some days you get a little down or discouraged...or perhaps you don't feel like hanging in there quite so hard...it's okay. Because I'm ready. I'm ready to meet Jesus."

Bryon was right on track...he had the baton firmly in his grasp and was running toward the finish line.

I brushed the tears off my cheeks. Peace, like the warm afternoon sun, bathed my soul. Somehow I knew...heaven will be one place where parents won't cry.

If you would like to correspond with the author you may write to her at:

Lillian Sparks
2924 W. Camino Alto
Springfield, MO 65810
Email: lsparks@ag.org

# BIBLIOGRAPHY

Roy Hession, *The Calvary Road*, Christian Literature Crusade, Fort Washington, PA, 1983.

Charles R. Swindoll, *Home Where Life Makes Up Its Mind*, Multnomah Press, Portland, OR, 1979.

Charles R. Swindoll, *The Quest For Character*, Multnomah Press, Portland, OR, 1987.

For more information about Epidermylosis Bullosa Dystraphica Recessive contact:

D.E.B.R.A.
40 Rector Street
New York, NY  10006
Phone: (212) 513-4090
Fax: (212) 513-4099
Email: debraorg@erols.com